"*Marriage Made in Eden* takes a serious look at our postmodern culture's defense of cohabitation. The book describes the resulting erosion of marriage before lucidly setting forth God's Edenic ideal for marriage. The authors make a cogent case for the transformational and missional nature of marriage, a message increasingly needed in our day."

James R. Beck, professor of counseling,
Denver Seminary

"At last a profoundly biblical book on Christian marriage, which asks and answers the more important question: What does it mean for a husband and wife, who are being reshaped into God's image, to live as a Christian alternative to postmodern self-centeredness? The answer: To live Christianly, and therefore in a missional way, as a basic expression of truly Christian community, where the fruit of the Spirit are at work. Try it, you'll like it."

Gordon Fee, professor emeritus
of New Testament studies, Regent College

"Alice Mathews and Gay Hubbard bring together decades of experience in counseling, higher education, and Christian marriage in this thoughtful, interdisciplinary volume. Readers who are concerned with the present state of marriage in our culture will benefit from their cultural critique and their wise reading of Scripture and tradition."

Mary Stewart Van Leeuwen, professor of psychology
and philosophy, Eastern University

"This book is a refreshing, empowering, interdisciplinary look at Christian marriage and its missional responsibilities to the world as one kind of witness about God and relationships. This is a healing book in the midst of controversy, but clearly understands the mutually and completely shared nature of the marriage relationship, argued with a sound and sensitive biblical basis. It puts to rest the shallow approaches of headship models and argues for equally shared responsibility under Christ as a witness to the world of human dignity and respect."

David M. Scholer, professor of New Testament
and associate dean for the Center for Advanced Theological Studies,
School of Theology, Fuller Theological Seminary

"A must read. This is not your typical 'how to' marriage book. Biblically insightful and practically powerful, *Marriage Made in Eden* grapples with the postmodern relativism that has ravaged the institution of marriage. Chapter 2 on postmodernism's impact on marriage is worth the price of the book alone.

"In a culture where relationships are treated like disposable paper cups, Matthews and Hubbard take us back to what God desired not only for the first couple but for all couples and then tell us how to go about embracing the joy of love everlasting in a marriage."

Rodney L. Cooper, Kenneth and Jean Hansen Professor
of Discipleship and Leadership,
Gordon-Conwell Theological Seminary

"I am tempted to call providential the publication of this book at just this hour in our cultural history when marriage as a till-death-do-us-part union between a man and a woman is being assailed and abandoned. With admirable balance, scholarship, and insight, its evangelically oriented authors discuss the pertinent issues involved in this practice—social, moral, and biblical. All who engage in any aspect of marital counseling or teaching on this crucial subject are advised to read this fog-dispelling study."

Vernon Grounds, chancellor,
Denver Seminary

"Perhaps nowhere is it more evident that the ground is shifting beneath our feet than in societal attitudes toward marriage. Alas, in response, many Christian teachers are simply reiterating a perspective that purports to be biblical but in fact was birthed in the nineteenth century and enjoyed a short reign in the 1950s. Alice Mathews and Gay Hubbard propose a wiser course. They call Christians to recapture the biblical perspective of marriage as missional. In so doing, they have produced a book that is 'must reading' for all Christians concerned with promoting an understanding of marriage that is in accordance with God's intentions. *Marriage Made in Eden* is truly a tract for our time."

Stanley J. Grenz, Pioneer McDonald Professor,
Carey Theological College

"Perfect timing! In the light of the current debate on marriage this book brings a refreshing clarity. Drs. Hubbard and Mathews bring new insight and understanding to the institution of marriage in both historical and biblical contexts. Their clarity and biblical orthodoxy help us to see the need for understanding God's intention for marriage as an essential building block for the whole human community. The authors' insistence on listening to the whole counsel of God provides a clear rationale for a truly comprehensive approach to this critical issue."

Raymond F. Pendleton, professor of pastoral care and counseling,
director of the Clinical Counseling Program,
Gordon-Conwell Theological Seminary

MARRIAGE
MADE *in*
EDEN

Also by Alice Mathews
  A Woman God Can Lead
  Preaching That Speaks to Women

Also by M. Gay Hubbard
  Women: The Misunderstood Majority

MARRIAGE MADE *in* EDEN

A Pre-Modern Perspective for a Post-Christian World

Alice P. Mathews
M. Gay Hubbard

BakerBooks

Grand Rapids, Michigan

Published by Baker Books
a division of Baker Publishing Group
P.O. Box 6287, Grand Rapids, MI 49516-6287
www.bakerpublishinggroup.com

Printed in the United States of America

Library of Congress Cataloging-in-Publication Data
Mathews, Alice, 1930–
    Marriage made in Eden: a pre-modern perspective for a post-Christian world /
    Alice P. Mathews, M. Gay Hubbard.
        p.   cm.
    Includes bibliographical references.
    ISBN 0-8010-6465-1 (pbk.)
    1. Marriage—Religious aspects—Christianity. I. Hubbard, M. Gay, 1931– II. Title.
BV835.M276 2004
261.8′3581—dc22   2004005978

To

Randall Mathews

and

Joe Hubbard

whose steadfast love

and servant hands and hearts

kept us going and encouraged us

all the way to the finish line of this book

Contents

Foreword

My entire adult life has been focused on teaching and training people how to build healthy relationships with God, with themselves, and with others, my major focus being on the marriage relationship. When Gay called and asked me to consider writing a foreword to her and Alice Matthews' book on marriage, I'm not sure what I expected. I knew it would be thoughtful, comprehensive, and biblically and theologically sound. At the same time, I have over one hundred marriage books in my personal library, and I rarely find material that's new or compelling.

When I sat down to read the manuscript, I wasn't prepared for what I found. I didn't expect a book that would grip my heart, challenge my assumptions, renew my hope, expand my understanding, and increase my appreciation for God's mercy and grace. I wasn't prepared to be forced to reevaluate some of my assumptions regarding God's purpose and plan for marriage. I didn't expect something so profound that I would be compelled to reread portions of the manuscript several times.

In 1981 Joe Aldrich wrote what has become a classic in the field of evangelism. When I first read *Lifestyle Evangelism*, one particular quote grabbed my attention and was used of God to redefine my understanding of the potential of the marriage relationship. It's been over twenty years since Aldrich wrote,

The two greatest forces in evangelism are a healthy church and a healthy marriage. The two are interdependent. You can't have one without the other. It is the healthy marriage, however, which is the "front lines weapon." The Christian family in a community is the ultimate evangelistic tool, assuming the home circle is an open one in which the beauty of the gospel is readily available. It's the old story: *When love is seen, the message is heard.*[1]

Marriage Made in Eden is a gold mine, and one of the richest veins is the authors' insight that the purpose of marriage is both to transform us and to witness to God's grace and power in a sinful world. Their discussions on the transformational and missional nature of marriage are profound and will challenge you to embrace the purpose of marriage in the context of sanctification, to take into your heart what I believe with all my heart to be the clear teaching of God's Word: that marriage is designed to be a laboratory in the school of life in which we have the incredible opportunity to become more like Christ, to be shaped into his image, to "become conformed to the image of His Son" (Rom. 8:29 NASB). While God cares for our happiness, in his view, becoming like Christ *is* the greatest happiness, the greatest good, and marriage is an essential part of achieving *that* goal.

Alice and Gay combine a fresh historical, cultural, and sociological perspective with sound exegesis. They are passionate and provocative yet not polemical, academic and yet inspirational, intellectual and yet practical. Their rigorous and relentless commitment to biblical truth as their final authority is refreshing and will challenge you to rethink some of your previously held assumptions. I know the authors well enough to tell you they wouldn't want you to take what they've written at face value. Become a "Berean" and search the Scriptures for yourself. Question their assumptions and dialogue with their conclusions.

If you are like me, you may not agree with everything they have to say. It's a compliment to their intellectual integrity that they would ask an unrepentant complementarian like me to contribute the foreword to their book. Regardless of where you fall on the hierarchical/complementarian/egalitarian continuum, you will benefit from the refreshing reminder that marriage is much more about an expression of God's sense of the importance of sacrificial love than a concern for a demonstration of hierarchical power and subordinate obedience.

In 1 Chronicles 12:32 we read about the sons of Issachar, who understood the times and knew what Israel should do. Gay and Alice are daughters of Issachar who understand the times, understand God's Word, and clearly see that marriage provides us, who are "resident aliens" in a broken world, with a unique opportunity to speak the truths of historic Christianity into our twenty-first-century postmodern culture. In the process we will become more like our Lord Jesus Christ.

I believe the book you are holding is destined to become a classic. I will be using it as a required text for my graduate students at John Brown University and my Doctor of Ministry students at Denver Seminary. I will recommend it at my seminars and workshops. The message of this book is a fresh wind that God will use to help many develop a meaningfully biblical perspective on God's heart for the marriage relationship. I guarantee that this labor of love is something you will read more than once.

It will be impossible for you to read this book and come away not having been challenged, excited, and encouraged by God's love, his mercy, his grace, and his gift—through the potential of your own marriage—to become daily ever more like him. When you finish reading this book you will not only *view* marriage differently, you will also *do* marriage differently. It's that good. Its message is that important.

Gary J. Oliver
John Brown University

Preface

The Hebrew poet was right: "Of making many books there is no end" (Eccles. 12:12 NIV). And certainly on the subject of marriage and family that is true today. The books about husbands and wives or parents and children continue to spin off printing presses at a dizzying rate. So why one more book on a subject on which everything has already been said?

Obviously we the authors do not believe that "everything" *has* already been said or that all that has been said is truly biblical or is necessarily true of real men and women struggling to make their marriages good, strong, and "Christian."

And what can two old women in their seventies bring to this subject? Together we bring three pieces of experience and knowledge, which we believe qualify us to write this book. First, we bring nearly a century of firsthand experience of marriage. Gay and Joe have been married to one another for more than forty years, and Alice and Randall recently celebrated fifty-three years of marriage. Personal, long-term experience counts for something. This is no armchair empiricism, laying out theory without any practical knowledge of the field. Nor is this a wide-eyed idealism untempered by the sometimes brutal awareness of our own human sinfulness in our marital relationships.

Second, we bring to the task the trained observation of two social scientists. Gay, with a Ph.D. in psychology and special education, has worked clinically with women and children for more than three decades, counseling men and women as they have struggled to deal with the pain and confusion in their lives. Alice, with a Ph.D. in religion and social change, has been deeply engaged in ministries to women in church and parachurch organizations for more than three decades. Both have logged hundreds of hours in one-on-one conversations with people struggling in less-than-perfect marriages. Both have taught in the area of gender studies in colleges and seminaries. We've been at this long enough to know that the social sciences do not have all the answers but often can respond to some legitimate questions Christians sometimes fail to ask.

Third, we each bring to this book at least a half century of love for the study of the Scriptures. We take the Bible very seriously and believe that, rightly understood, it can guide us through a potential minefield to God's truth about marriage, the central relationship in most people's lives. While we wear the social science hat in the early part of the book, we lay that hat aside in the second part to take our place under God's Word as our final authority for faith and practice. The bottom-line question, after we've explored the culture's case against marriage, is, What is God's case *for* marriage? That's the point of this book. And that's why we've written it.

Acknowledgments

Ideas enter writers' heads from many sources. That reality makes it difficult to acknowledge our indebtedness to all who over the years have placed seeds in our minds that have germinated in this book. During the past three years in which we have wrestled together with the subject of Christian marriage, we have read widely and talked with one another for many hours. At the least, we have been strongly impacted by the writings of Gordon Fee, Stanley Grenz, Stanley Hauerwas, and William Willimon. Even as we write those names, however, we acknowledge that their ideas may not have taken root in our thinking had many other writers not already cleared away some of the cultural weeds that had cluttered our notions about marriage.

We also want to acknowledge the power and reality of Christian community in the process of writing this book. That community has come in several forms including, for Gay, the members of Bible study groups who had little understanding of the writing process, but who came alongside and prayed the book to completion anyway. It also includes the community-of-two that we (Alice and Gay) discovered more deeply as we worked together. From that community have come thinking and understanding that neither of us could have achieved alone. In addition, we highly value the encouraging community of our editors at Baker—Chad Allen, Mary Suggs, and Paul Brinkerhoff.

And foundational to all has been the community that we, as followers of Jesus Christ, have with the triune God. *Soli Deo Gloria.*

I

Laying a Foundation

If you have bought a new car in recent years, you may have purchased one with GPS, a global positioning system (like OnStar). If you lose your way, it will guide you to your destination, step-by-step. It is an amazing technology that locks into signals from at least three satellites circling the Earth. It pinpoints where you are and shows the route to where you want to go.

This first chapter is a low-tech GPS to orient you to this book. The book is about marriage but not just any marriage. It is about the marriage of Christians, exploring what God had in mind when he designed marriage, and how the purpose of marriage is both to transform us and to witness to God's grace and power in a sinful world. In the following chapters we will orbit our present North American culture "out there" (chapters 2 and 3); then we will investigate changing marriage and family patterns from the Puritans to the present (chapters 4, 5, and 6). In chapters 7 through 10 we will look at Scripture, distilling a biblical theology of Christian marriage that also responds to the alien culture out there (chapter 11). We conclude with some practical warnings in chapter 12. The book is basically in two parts—the culture's case against marriage and God's case for marriage. If you understand this organization of material up front, it will help you find your way.

This chapter also orients you to the ideas you will meet later in the book in a more fully developed form. We include here a brief discussion of marriage as a social institution, and then consider marriage from a Christian perspective (part of God's design). We close this orienting chapter with a definition of culture and a brief discussion of the tension between Christians and culture that shapes our lives and marriages.

What Is Marriage?

"Do you love me?" asked Tevye of his wife, Golda, in *Fiddler on the Roof.*

"I cook your meals; I wash your clothes; I bear your children," a bewildered Golda responded. "What do you mean, do I love you?"

What made a marriage for Tevye and Golda? The current controversy over a definition of the family has engaged everyone from census takers to church officials. Bishops and presidents, sociologists and historians, as well as ordinary people, the man and woman on the street, all have ideas about what a marriage is. Anthropologists know that marriage in some form has been a significant part of human history from the beginning of time.

Christians believe that marriage was a part of creation history (Genesis 1), a history that includes God's basic design for marriage relationships for husbands and wives. They also believe that God's original design for marriage was part of his eternal purpose for his people to be in relationship both with each other and with him.

Throughout human history, people have worked very hard to understand marriage and to describe it carefully, but we should not be surprised by present disagreements over a definition. First, marriage is a complex human institution. Second, marriage occurs in the context of a given culture. It is not generic. It is marriage as it occurred under the watchful eye of Queen Victoria or marriage among the wandering desert tribes when Isaac took Rebekah to be his wife or the marriage of today in the Information Age.

But for Christians, there is another factor to consider. From the beginning, marriage occurred as a part of *God's* relationship to his people. Marriage for Christians is not just a human affair. As Christians today consider "Christian marriage," we struggle with two questions. First, what is marriage as a social institution in this present culture? Second, what does marriage *for God's people* look like in this present time, in this present culture?

Marriage as a Social Institution

Stripped down to its essentials, marriage as a social institution has two broad components. It is a *contract* and it is a *relationship*. In some form, a contract identifies the two people in the marriage and it specifies the provisions under which the union is formed and the conditions under which it is to be maintained. Marriage virtually always entails the distribution of property, wealth, and the continuation of a family line. The contract is part of defining and policing marriage within a given culture for the welfare of all the people.

In our present culture, marriage is licensed by the state. A legal code carefully defines the provisions for distributing wealth and property. The contract governing marriage in our culture is made between the state and the designated couple. In earlier times marriage contracts were for the most part authorized and arranged by the powerful heads of extended families, and they served the political, economic, and safety needs of the clan at large. We see this as Abraham secured an appropriate bride for his son Isaac.

But we need not go back four millennia to see this pattern in action. Shakespeare's play *Romeo and Juliet* makes clear that a Capulet cannot marry a Montague. In Leonard Bernstein's brilliant adaptation of that play (*West Side Story*), a Shark may not form a committed, sexually bonded relationship with a Jet. In this version the biologically based family system represented by the Capulets and the Montagues was changed to a sociologically based group—the gang as family. The definition of *family* had changed. Marriage, once defined as a legal, church-recognized union, had become a relationally based, sexually solemnized connection independent of biological families and the state. Yet the validity of the couple's relationship continued to depend on a contract made according to the rules of the governing power, in this case a fiercely territorial inner-city gang. Throughout history, marriage has never been regarded as a private affair. Whatever the nature of the marriage contract at any given time in history, it has reflected and defined the public nature of marriage.

This is one point of controversy in the present culture wars over marriage. Many people reject out of hand any sense that a relationship between a woman and a man is anything more than a private matter over which neither the state nor the families of origin should have legal or ethical jurisdiction.[1] The same argument has surfaced in current heated debates about same-sex marriages. Christian marriage in the present North American culture conforms to civil regulations in matters of contract, because God's people are called to be subject to existing civil regulations (Rom. 13:1–7). These regulations are currently shifting to reflect changing cultural values. But whatever the specific requirements, marriage entails some form of contract, confirming and regulating the relationship.

Thus *contract* is one component of marriage. *Relationship* is the second broad component. In earlier times the relationship may have been defined economically or politically. In 1 Samuel 18:21 King Saul gave his daughter Michal to David as a wife for political reasons but later removed her from that marriage and gave her to Palti, as palace intrigue deepened (25:44). During his reign, Henry VIII had a succession of six different wives through marriages that were arranged primarily to secure and maintain political alliances. Caught in the treacherous currents of Henry's ambition and the political intrigues of the time, two of the six were divorced by Henry, and two were executed.

Yet in many cases, even in arranged marriages, passionate bonds of personal affection developed. Isaac loved Rebekah. Elkanah tenderly consoled the grieving Hannah, asking, "Am I not more to you than many children?" And from the Puritans, who were decidedly practical about marriage, comes one of the personal love stories we tell and retell. When John Alden came to present Miles Standish's offer of marriage to Priscilla, she responded with an offer of her own: "Speak for yourself, John."

In the present North American culture, the personal relationship between the couple has become the primary factor determining their decision to marry. But bonds of personal affection can be distorted into a romanticized picture that quickly wears thin in the work of daily life; bonds of personal affection can be shattered by adultery and by other life traumas. In large numbers of instances, though, personal affection functions as a powerful positive factor, part of the glue that holds long-term, happy marriages together. One study collected data on 576 couples whose marriages were intact after 50 years or more.[2] When asked which relationship characteristics had helped them stay together, the three most frequently endorsed were trust (82 percent), loving relationship (81 percent), and willingness to compromise (80 percent).

Personal affection does not automatically produce long, satisfying marriages, however. Having examined a number of studies of long-term marriages, Robyn Parker concluded that the distinguishing feature of these relationships was the couple's mutual commitment to the marriage and their mutual willingness to learn and practice those behaviors that kept alive the emotional connection that had brought them together in the first place.[3]

Marriage as Part of God's Story

Marriage is also the relationship of God with his people. While culture shapes both contract and relationship, marriage for God's people is founded not on the culture in which their marriages are lived out but on the relationship with him and with each other that defines their identity as God's people. Four things shape this identity.

First, *God designed his people to be like him.* They were his image-bearers, created by divine intention to be like him, connected to him in an intimate fellowship that flowed out of that part of God's essence that they shared (Gen. 1:26). But they were also created to be like him as male and female, so that they could be intimately linked to each other in their shared humanness and their shared essence as image-bearers. God's design was twofold: Marriage permitted his image-bearers to be intimately linked to each other and to their God. The work of that first pair was dominion over God's other living creatures, and their creative potential included the power to bring other image-bearers (their children) into God's new world.

But the second factor shaping our identity as God's people is that *the image-bearers disrupted and continue to disrupt their relationship with God through their sin.* God's image in them was and is bent and broken. The relationships between the image-bearers themselves were and are bent and broken as well. Marriage as God originally designed it must now be worked out by bent and broken people in a world that also carries the catastrophic consequences of sin.

But that is not the end of the story. The third factor shaping our identity as God's people is hope. *God has promised that he will one day make all well again.* The promise came to the first woman, Eve, that through her seed the serpent would one day be defeated. By clothing Adam and Eve in animal skins before they left the Garden of Eden, God took a visible step down the bitter road to Calvary. But John describes the triumphant end of God's story in which there is a new heaven and a new earth, and all suffering has vanished (Rev. 21:3–4).

But God's restoration of his damaged creation continues to be a process over time. As Adam and Eve set up housekeeping outside Eden, the culture that developed around these broken image-bearers demonstrated with brutal suddenness that the whole creation had fallen with them. The culture that emerged from the fallen creation became actively hostile to God's purposes. *As a result the opposing culture (the "world") forms the fourth factor that together with their personal sinfulness shapes the identity of God's people.*

We are God's broken people in a broken world that actively resists God's effort to reclaim his own.

God's Loving Faithfulness

When they consider the cost, God's people may well stand astonished that God has not given up on his goal of having his people be like him, in fellowship with each other and with him. In order to redeem and restore his broken image-bearers, God willingly acted in a love that lies beyond our human understanding. The apostle Paul wrote, "[God] did not spare his own Son, but gave him up for us all" (Rom. 8:32). Peter reminded the early Christians that God was not willing that any should perish (2 Peter 3:9).

Redemption, however, required that the broken image-bearers accept God's merciful provision for their restoration to fellowship with him. And it required further that they participate with God in establishing a new pattern of life. "Do not conform to the pattern of this world, but be transformed by the renewing of your mind" (Rom. 12:2), Paul urged the Christians at Rome.

This transformation process is a lifelong daily procedure—no instant magic. Eugene Peterson in *The Message* catches the sense of this.

> So here's what I want you to do, God helping you: Take your everyday, ordinary life—your sleeping, eating, going-to-work, and walking-around life [*and your being-married life*]—and place it before God as an offering. . . . Don't become so well-adjusted to your culture that you fit into it without even thinking. Instead, fix your attention on God. You'll be changed from the inside out. Readily recognize what he wants from you, and quickly respond to it. Unlike the culture around you, always dragging you down to its level of immaturity, God brings the best out of you, develops well-formed maturity in you.
>
> Romans 12:1–2

When in the chapters that follow we talk about marriage as *transformational,* we are thinking about marriage as part of the laboratory of daily living through which God shapes his redeemed people to be "conformed to the likeness of his Son, that he might be the firstborn among many brothers and sisters" (Rom. 8:2).

As God's people consider his story, they may well be astonished at more than his steadfast love. They are likely to be astonished also (and in quite a different sense) at the ways in which people have rejected and continue to reject God's offer to redeem and restore his broken image-bearers. As we will see, from Eden on, some have chosen to remain apart from God, content in their brokenness. God often referred sorrowfully to these individuals as "not my people." But God has not given up on those who are "not my people." He seeks them still (see Hosea 2:23).

In the chapters that follow we speak of marriage as *missional* as well as transformational. When we speak of marriage as *missional*, we mean the ways in which marriage as practiced by God's people can be a living demonstration to those who are not his people both of God's love and of the transforming power of the resurrection life. It is in the transformation of our everyday, ordinary life—our sleeping, eating, going-to-work and walking-around life, including our marriages—through which God seeks to reach those who have not yet chosen to be his people.

Yet at each point—marriage as part of our transformation and marriage as mission to the world—God's people soon discover that they have an ongoing struggle with the culture in which they live.

Resident Aliens in a Broken World

God's people live out their lives and their marriages in a given culture. They share broad patterns of thinking and feeling and (at least in part) a system of values with other people around them who make up the given society in which they live. For example, the present North American culture is sometimes called a consumer culture because a large majority of North Americans invest great amounts of energy and resources in acquiring objects or experiences. In a consumer culture, people concentrate on using things, relationships, and experiences to fulfill the needs they think they have. In the present culture, Christians are often participants in the consumer-driven activities of the society in which they live.

When the culture (the activities, thinking and emotional life, and the system of values of the majority) is formed by those whom God calls "not my people," those who are God's people often find themselves seriously out of step. This lack of fit with the surrounding culture is a familiar tension for God's people, who cannot logically expect those who are not his people to construct a world that reflects the values and way of thinking to which God calls his own. Those who are not God's people are not likely to prescribe a way of life that worships and honors the one true God. For this reason Paul cautions the Christians at Rome about the danger of drifting into unthinking conformity with the surrounding culture. And as the following chapters indicate, our present culture is not faith-friendly to Christian marriage, often in ways that God's people are slow to recognize. Heedless cultural drift in relation to Christian marriage is possible and happens more frequently than Christians commonly recognize.

Consequently in this culture as in past cultures, God's people are called to live as resident aliens, as Stanley Hauerwas and William Willimon have described it.[4] In practical terms this means that God's people are *residents*, living in a culture controlled by those who are not his people, but they are at the same time *aliens*—citizens of another country, loyal to another King. Jesus was dealing with this cultural tension when he told his followers that they were to be *in* the world but not *of* it. His instructions have not always been easy to carry out.

History shows that God's people have sometimes shown some rather muddled thinking and have made some bad choices as they have grappled with their surrounding culture.[5] Some have tried to run away from the culture, to organize their lives so that a barrier is erected between them and the culture. Sometimes this barrier has been physical—like that of Simon Stylites, fourth century Syrian hermit, who sat on top of a pole for many years to avoid contamination from the culture. Sometimes the barrier has been social or emotional—Christians limit friends and associates to those in their church or to those who love God. But running away or hiding doesn't fit the gospel mandate at all. Even if it were socially possible, isolation appears incongruent with God's goals for his people. Jesus told his followers to be in the world in ways that would make them visible examples of an alternative way of life. Furthermore, running or hiding denies the reality of human existence. God's people do live in the world and participate to some degree, greater or lesser, in the given culture in which they live.

At times God's people as resident aliens have attempted to reform the culture and eliminate the tension, trying to make the culture fit the pattern God prescribed for his people. This has proven unrealistic and for the most part frustrating for all concerned. It is not logical to expect that those who are "not my people" will want to adopt the lifestyle of God's people.

Sometimes, in an effort to achieve a pattern of peaceful coexistence, God's people attempt to compromise, to cut a deal with the culture, so to speak. They conform to the culture up to a cautious point and, in turn, attempt to persuade the culture to adopt some of the values of God's people. Historically, in most instances, this strategy has shaped Christians into resembling the culture rather than shaping the culture to fit God's mandate for his people.

None of these patterns works very well. Jesus pointed out that his goal for his people was to be in the world in a visible way so that the world would see their good deeds and glorify their Father in heaven (Matt. 5:16). It is at this point that God's plan of transformation and mission come together. By living transformed lives as God's people, we can indeed change the world—not because we have reformed the culture but because we provide a radical alternative to the culture.

The cultural issue is complicated, and Christians disagree about the best approach to the task. It is a challenge to be an active, constructive part of the culture in a way that honors God and yet retains Christian distinctives. Such a balance requires the discipline of self-examination as well as accountability to the family of God if Christians are to avoid cultural compromise.

Constantinian Accommodation

The Greek and Roman cultures challenged the early Christians at numerous points. The Christian idea of the equal value of all persons came up against the cultural practice of slavery. Paul, for example, called on Philemon to receive Onesimus, his runaway slave, as no longer just a slave but as a beloved brother (Philem. 16). The Christian idea of God bodily present in Christ (the incarnation) met head-on the Greek idea of the body as an inferior, repugnant substance that God could not or would not enter. The devaluing of women confronted the Christian call for all people—men and women, slaves and free, Jews and Gentiles—to meet as equals in Christ.

The cultural conflict for those early Christians was intense. Some Christians met the challenge by isolating themselves from the culture. Some escaped to the desert to live out their lives disconnected from the world around them. Others attempted compromise; they were closet Christians who tried to fit into the Roman culture. Paul may have had some of these in mind when he wrote, "Do not be yoked together with unbelievers. For what do righteousness and wickedness have in common? Or what fellowship can light have with darkness?" (2 Cor. 6:14).

Despite severe persecution and struggle, Christians persevered. Then in what must have been an amazing reversal of direction, these early Christians experienced something that resembled a successful conquest of the culture. Constantine, the Roman emperor, became a Christian.[6] Being

Christian was suddenly "in." The culture began to take on the appearance of Christianity because the emperor's action required that his subjects do as he did, think and believe as he believed. If the emperor had become a Christian, then a keen sense of survival as well as an official edict led others to become Christians as well.

This process of the culture becoming "Christian" is sometimes called "Constantinianism" because the first large-scale demonstration of "conversions" occurred when Constantine became a Christian. Constantinianism occurs when people adopt the identity and values of Christianity in conformity to the culture, rather than in personal commitment to the Christian faith. For example, an announcement in the society section of a Sunday newspaper may describe an elaborate wedding, staged in an architecturally beautiful church, the intricate and expensive ceremony carefully orchestrated by a wedding consultant, and officially blessed by licensed clergy. Here is the culturally prescribed "Christian" wedding (a church wedding). In many cases, such weddings do not represent marriage vows taken in response to a personal commitment to live out Christian marriage within the family of God. Such ceremonies are a form of Constantinianism, the commingling of Christianity and the culture. Is it possible for a couple who are not Christians to have a "Christian" wedding? Yes, in precisely the same way that it was possible for a Roman citizen to be officially declared a Christian without an atom of personal belief in Jesus as the risen Son of God.

Constantinianism confronted early Christians with issues of institutional power. Having had more than enough of serving as lunch for the lions, the Christians were understandably relieved when the emperor converted to Christianity. But in the commingled culture it became more and more difficult both to think straight and to live straight the distinctives of the Christian faith. Over time the significance of personal identity as God's people began to fade in importance, and the political and institutional power of the church increased.

The last Roman emperor abdicated in 476. But in 800 when Charlemagne became king and was crowned by Pope Leo III, the pope declared him to be the Roman emperor. Modern historians commonly refer to the large complex of land in central and western Europe ruled by Charlemagne and his successors as the Holy Roman Empire (HRE), although, as Voltaire, the French writer, observed, it was "neither holy, nor Roman, nor an empire." In the tumultuous thousand-year history of the HRE, the political power of the church is remarkable. Few of the kings attained or kept their throne without the endorsement of the ruling pope. But the Reformation made clear that this time cannot be viewed as the glorious spiritual triumph of the church, whatever its political power may have been.

Halting the brutal persecutions of those early centuries was, without question, a gain, but it was not an unqualified gain. When Christians lose politically, they go to the lions. But what happens when they win?

What does Constantinianism look like in North America today? For many people of faith, it is a new idea to consider themselves resident aliens. Contemporary Christians find it strange to think of themselves as having only a secondary allegiance to the culture around them. And it is even more strange to think of marriage as an evangelistic mission to the culture, a witnessing act through which those who are "not my people" may know something of the true and living God.

This book is about marriage, but it is about marriage that takes seriously the biblical mandate to live out a radical alternative in this present culture, which, despite its rhetoric, gives little evidence of loyalty to the true and living God.

Part I

The Culture's Case *against* Marriage

2

Marriage
in the Postmodern Culture

aking a marriage in the current culture is much like grow-ing an English rose garden on a west Texas cattle ranch. It can be done, but the weather rarely cooperates. Growing a marriage—a people-healthy, God-honoring marriage—can, with determination, be done. The couple attempting such a marriage soon discovers, however, that the culture around them provides little in the way of a nurturing environment or encouragement for the project.

From a Christian perspective, marriage is the mutual commitment by faith of two individuals to lifelong sharing of their lives. Weaving two lives together entails an intentional sharing of power and responsibility in the service of the couple's common goals and of the community's common good. Further, it requires, through God's enabling, the will and ability to value another person even when that valuing comes at considerable cost to the self. Christians understand that lifelong marriage is by necessity built on love and respect that transcends physical appearance, shared material goods, and the excitement of sex. Further, Christians understand that lifelong marriage requires a willingness to stay the course that is based on something more than immediate personal gratification.

The apostle Paul noted that Christian marriage is in some respects a mystery (Eph. 5:32). The present culture, however, tends to view Christian marriage more as an antique oddity than a mystery. Christian marriage with its call for lifelong, faithful commitment is increasingly seen as having limited relevance in the contemporary world.

The culture's resistance to marriage, and Christian marriage in particular, has long roots in the past. However, the culture's present case against marriage solidified in the four decades of massive social change that marked the close of the twentieth century. The Berlin Wall; Selma, Alabama; Vietnam; Watergate—all now serve as benchmarks of social change as much as geographical names. *Roe v. Wade*, equal rights, drug testing, Medicare, *in vitro* fertilization, organ transplants, cyberspace, cell phones, videos, and carryout pizza—there was a world before these things, but it is difficult to remember now what that world was like. Changes in law, medicine, social policy, biology, technology, and commerce have permanently reshaped the culture in which marriage and other human relationships are lived out.

This social revolution produced a seismic philosophical shift as well. The way in which truth and reality were defined was altered; the value system of the culture shifted dramatically in response. In the North American culture this social and philosophical change was accompanied by the simultaneous growth of a powerful marketplace approach to life and relationships.

The "wisdom" of the streets expresses the values of the resulting culture in quick sound bites: "Look out for number one!" "If it feels good, do it!" "The one with the most toys wins!" The message of the culture is powerfully expressed through other avenues as well.

The media and the entertainment industry, both influential voices of the culture, discount long-term committed relationships and hold little place for marriage.[1] Unrestrained individualism is advocated in film, plays, novels, advertising, and media accounts of human activities. There is little support for relationships, including marriage, in which others' needs come ahead of one's own. Marketplace thinking, allied with a powerful corporate subculture, encourages addictive consumption at the cost of relationships and the disruption of community. In the present culture *having* possessions is more highly valued than *being* in relationship and living in community.

The academic and professional worlds also support the values of the emerging culture regarding marriage.[2] The rejection of Christian values at prestigious institutions, such as Harvard, Yale, or Amherst, is a matter for continuing concern but is no longer news; it is a fact with which individuals entering these institutions must grapple.[3] Many distinguished academic, professional, and religious leaders have recently identified themselves specifically as advocates of alternative forms of family relationships, affirming marriage as only one of several acceptable options for family life.[4] These influences create a resulting social ecology in which marriages and families can still survive, although, as Jean Bethke Elshtain has pointed out, they do so with serious and increasing difficulty.[5]

Tension between the Christian concept of marriage and the values of the culture at large is not, of course, a new thing. Much that Christians find troublesome in the present culture has a long history. Individualism is an old problem. Historically we Americans have come dangerously close to glorifying the individual at serious risk to the civil good.[6] Materialism is not a new invention either; indeed, from a Christian perspective, it is an old and bitter enemy. In every age Christians (and others) have needed Jesus' reminder that wealth does not consist in the abundance of our possessions (Luke 12:15). Cultural tensions have accompanied major social changes at earlier points in history as well. The Industrial Revolution, for example, produced serious stress in family relationships as well as economic change.[7]

As in the past, materialism, individualism, and the tension that accompanies social change contribute to the present culture's case against marriage. Although these factors appear in new forms in the present, in a fundamental sense they are familiar enemies. What is new, however, and highly problematic is postmodernism.[8]

The power of postmodernism to shape the culture lies not only in the values that accompany this way of thinking but also in the way in which postmodernism interacts with other factors that are intrinsic parts of the current flood of social change. The marketplace mentality that accompanies consumerism, communication marked by the "instant access" of the Information Age, changing relational expectations—none of these factors was spawned by postmodernism. However, postmodernism has interacted powerfully with these and other components of social change to produce a social ecology that is toxic to marriage and family life. Philosophically, in ways that promise further change, postmodern thinking has moved to fill the vacuum left by the decay of modernity, those beliefs of the "old" modern world that have been weighed and found wanting in the Information Age. Increasingly in the post-Christian world, the patterns of thinking and living that characterize the emerging culture carry the stamp of postmodern influence.

"What *is* postmodernism?" bewildered Christians may well ask. It is not an easy question to answer. In the first place, postmodernism is not a single idea that can be defined in a simple sentence. Functionally postmodernism is a set of interrelated ideas that define truth and reality in ways that contrast (sometimes dramatically) with the thinking of the "old" modern world. Additionally, because postmodernism is still developing, it is difficult to describe all that might be properly labeled "postmodern thinking" in the present culture.

A clear view of postmodernism is complicated further by the fact that postmodernism is certainly not the only new player on the current cultural stage. Globalization, for example, is transforming the world in which we live at unimaginable speed. On October 11, 1998, during the recent global economic crisis, Merrill Lynch ran serious full-page ads in major newspapers under the banner: "The World is 10 Years Old."[9] Technology has stamped "Information Age" on the emerging century and functions as the powerful infrastructure through which globalization is reshaping civilization in major ways.[10]

The new world is not a simple one. But whatever the economic and technological factors that influence the developing civilization, the ideas underlying these factors will ultimately shape the values of the new world. For this reason Christians need to give careful attention to postmodern thinking, particularly to the ways in which postmodernism influences the culture's beliefs about people and their relationships. This chapter considers the culture's case against marriage (Christian marriage in particular) in three broad areas:

- postmodernism and the individual
- postmodernism and the community
- postmodernism and the marketplace

Postmodernism and the Individual

Globalization provides frequent visible symbols of its presence. McDonald's familiar golden arches rise over Hong Kong, London, Berlin, Tokyo, and Kansas City, and television provides a wide window on this expanding world. E-mail, instant messaging, and the Internet are concrete evidence of the Information Age and make nearly instant worldwide connections possible. Postmodern thinking also leaves evidence, but in many ways postmodernism is like the proverbial elephant in the living room—it takes large amounts of space but it is rarely recognized for what it is. One way to begin talking about the postmodern elephant in the cultural living room is to think about some of the social changes that marked the transition from the modern to the postmodern world.

The Journey to Postmodernism

"Bye-Bye, Miss American Pie," Don McLean sang as he looked back over the 1960s, "Drove my Chevy to the levee, but the levee was dry."[11] McLean's lyrics remain ambiguous, but as the new millennium opens, there is no doubt that the world to which McLean sang his enigmatic farewell is now gone.[12]

From the vantage point of nostalgia, it is easy to identify what has vanished. It is the world we imagine we remember, the way we never were, to borrow Stephanie Coontz's telling phrase.[13] But other things have also gone away, real things, things that in their going have left a very different world behind.

This different world grew in part as a reaction to the decay of modernity, the system of belief in rationality and experimentation that produced the modern world. Because it grew in response to the deterioration of the modern system of thinking, the label "postmodern" became attached to the new ways of thinking that shaped the new and different world.

The old belief system (modernity) that underlay the modern world viewed humanity as autonomous, rational, and objective. Knowledge (truth) was viewed as certain, fixed for all time, rational, objective, and fully accessible to the human mind through reason. The world was pictured as a machine, with laws and regularity that could be discovered and controlled through human reasoning and mastered for human benefit.[14]

Modern thinking produced many valuable things. No one makes a case for a return to a world without antibiotics or e-mail; few people are willing to take a new drug that has not passed rigorous scientific testing. But the ideas that shaped the modern world contained major flaws that resulted in serious problems. For example, while the ability to think is central to human personhood, the individual is more than a rational mind. Modernity went seriously astray in denying the reality of the emotional, subjective, "irrational" self and the ways in which the self is simultaneously a producer and a product of the social/cultural context in which the individual lives.

Similarly, the claim of the modern world that the "knower" (the scientist) is able to view the world as an unconditioned objective observer is a myth. Knowledge is itself a product of experience. Science, like other human endeavors, is historically and culturally conditioned; all scientists (and all knowers) are subjective participants in the world they seek to see "objectively."

It is ironic that one of the significant mistakes in modern thinking occurred in the field of science. Modern science rested in large part on Newtonian physics with the consequent view of the physical world as a complex machine, the functioning of which was characterized by a predictable mechanical consistency that could be objectively measured. The development of quantum physics demonstrated, however, that, to the contrary, the physical world is not static but consists rather of masses of matter in constant motion, and that, further, the mysterious elements of matter (quarks and leptons, for example) sometimes behave in what appear to be contradictory and unpredictable ways. In the wake of quantum physics, the world of Newtonian physics has been reshaped and in some respects replaced by a scientific worldview in which motion, change, and uncertainty play a central part.

As the society growing out of modernity failed (rather spectacularly) to produce the peace and progress it promised, postmodernism developed as a response and reaction to the limitations and destructive consequences of the modern worldview. It is fair use of McLean's ambiguous lyrics to say that postmodernism was the result of the philosophical levee of the modern world running dry.

This clash of worldviews played out dramatically over the last half of the twentieth century. As the new millennium has opened, Christians are now faced with the challenge of understanding the emerging postmodern culture that surrounds them and learning the language of postmodern thought.

In the postmodern worldview, the individual is assigned a central controlling significance, as was true in the modern age as well. The contrast between the modern and postmodern view does not lie in the significance of the individual so much as in postmodern belief about the nature and function of the individual. The individual in postmodern thinking is distinctively different from the modern individual in the ways in which the individual knows truth, defines self (including gender), and participates in community.

The Individual as Creator of Truth

In the modern world the individual was viewed as an autonomous self, able to see the world as a rational, objective observer, uncontrolled by subjective, emotional responses to culture and personal experience. It was assumed that this rational individual could by logical, systematic means discover truth that existed as timeless, changeless universals external to the individual. The modern individual was thus a *discoverer and knower* of truth. In contrast, the individual in the postmodern world has become the *creator* of truth—the intuitive product of the language and culture of which the individual is a part. The postmodern individual is a *maker of truth* from the experience of the self in interaction with his or her world.

It is difficult to overemphasize the importance of this distinction or to overstate its consequences. People who *discover* truth and people who *create* truth think and behave in quite different ways. Logically, truth *makers* are bound only by their own rules. Since they are the makers of their truth, they and they only can define not only their truth but the way their truth is to be determined. In conversation with a committed postmodernist, a Christian may at times feel like Alice in conversation with Humpty Dumpty.

> "When *I* use a word," Humpty Dumpty said in rather a scornful tone, "it means just what I choose it to mean—neither more nor less."
>
> "The question is," said Alice, "whether you can make words mean different things."
>
> "The question is," said Humpty Dumpty, "which is to be master—that's all."[15]

The postmodern thinker views the individual as the master of truth, hands down. There is no absolute truth "out there." There is only the truth that the individual creates. David E. Daye, in his study of the influence of postmodernism on the family, commented, "In postmodernism, personal preference is the standard of what is right, personal experience is the standard of what is real, and personal desire is the standard of what is best."[16]

In terms of human behavior, this postmodern insistence on the right and ability of individuals to define truth and reality on their own terms produces a "me-first-and-me-only" mind-set. The primary goal becomes the satisfaction of individual needs with little concern about the ultimate cost either to the individual or to others. But it is necessary to go carefully at this point.

On a deeper level, to be an individual in the postmodern sense is to carry an incredible burden of aloneness, a nearly unbearable responsibility for the being of the self. In postmodern thinking the individual alone is responsible for defining and sustaining the essential self. The individual becomes, in effect, the bottom line; the self, the lonely court of last resort. Since the individual serves as the maker and definer of truth, the search for the Holy Grail becomes a driven, endless quest for personal experience and the satiation of personal desire. When the individual is all that there is, then care of the individual becomes legitimately all that is important, and the satisfaction of personal desire is life's overarching goal.

The goal of marriage in postmodern thinking becomes then the satisfaction of the individual's quest for meaning and fulfillment. Marriage is viewed as a personal, private transaction between two individuals. And because people change, and their sense of what is good changes, marriage must remain open to revision—and to termination if or when either of the individuals' needs and desires are no longer satisfied in the relationship.

As the culture at large adopts increasingly this postmodern thinking, the cultural view of marriage challenges the Christian sense of marriage as a lifelong commitment that may legitimately require sacrificial investment of the self in another. In the postmodern view, while this pattern of marriage may be a religiously approved road toward sainthood, Christian marriage holds a frightening risk for injury to the essential self.

The Individual as Creator of the Self

Eden's pattern lies at the core of Christian marriage. Two individuals disengage from their families of origin, commit to each other, then weave their lives together in a lifelong relationship with each other and with God (see Gen. 2:24). Intrinsic to Eden's pattern are people whom God has created as individuals. These individuals are similar (both carry the image of God) and at the same time different (they are male and female).

Christians are quick to acknowledge that nothing (most particularly people) was left unchanged when the first couple chose to disobey God. Nevertheless, in contrast to both the modern and the postmodern view of humanity, Christians view the individual as a God-created person with both a dimension of likeness to others and a dimension of difference. This likeness is twofold: like God (carrying, even after the fall, something of the

imago dei, the image of God) yet different from God (from dust, an earth-
ling); each like other earthlings and yet at the same time each distinctively
different from all other earthlings.

Personhood, from a Christian perspective, has at its core a God-created
gift of being. But at the same time, this God-gifted personhood is not atom-
ized. Christians believe that each individual is created to exist in connection
with God and with other earthlings. Thus, in a sense that initially appears
paradoxical, the individual as a God-created, unique person knows himself
or herself fully only within intimate interaction both with God and with
other earthlings.

The modern idea of the individual as it developed over time was in
marked contrast to the concept of personhood as a gift of God. The modern
self was a self-determining subject who existed outside of and independent
of community or tradition. Stanley Grenz, in dealing with what he has
aptly termed an archaeology of the self, summarized:

> The modern self emerged as the product of a 1,500–year intellectual journey
> that stretched from Augustine to Maslow. This pilgrimage netted a self-assured,
> self-sufficient, centered self that constituted a stable identity in the midst of a
> chaotic world. Yet the reign of the self seems to be short-lived, for the centered
> self of the modern era appears to be one of the casualties of the postmodern
> dethroning of all ruling monarchs.[17]

The modern world created a self that was a small god—independent,
self-assured, self-sufficient, able to know truth through its own rational
activity, and able through its "wisdom" to control the world for the good
of humanity. There were serious flaws in this idea, and postmodern thinkers, in reaction and response to these flaws, set about to develop a quite
different idea of the individual.

The postmodern thinker believes that the individual creates himself
or herself in much the same way that the individual creates truth. But
the postmodern-created self, in contrast to the modern self, is an identity
developed by the individual *in interaction with the culture and its language*.
Because the postmodern sense of personhood is one of an individual that
exists in response to an ever-changing cultural context, the postmodern
self is consequently fluid, unstable, subject to change. In a sense totally
foreign to the modern mind, the postmodern thinker identifies with Alice's
dilemma when in Wonderland she attempted to identify herself to the
caterpillar:

"Who are you?" said the caterpillar.

"I-I scarcely know, sir, just at the present," Alice replied rather shyly. "At least I know who I was when I got up this morning, but I think I must have changed several times since then."[18]

The idea of the modern self, characterized by unity, stability, and constancy through time is rapidly disappearing. It is being replaced by the postmodern self, a "decentered, fleeting self constructed in each moment of existence," as Grenz has described it.[19]

The implications of such a "fleeting self" are far-reaching, particularly in marriage. In postmodern reality, viewed in simple terms, the self that chose a partner in spring may have become by autumn a distinctly different self whose needs and preferences necessitate a different partner. Obviously in such a world the autumn partner may be replaced in turn when winter comes. From the postmodern perspective, reluctance to commit to a relationship becomes logical. Persons making promises can be certain of only one thing—time and experience will bring a new and different self, one to whom the old promise is likely to be, at best, irrelevant or, at worst, destructive to the new emerging self.

In the postmodern sense, gender identity (the socially defined sense of being a woman or a man) and sexuality (the biologically based sense of maleness or femaleness) become intrinsic parts of the fleeting self being constructed out of the given moment. Truth about gender and sexuality, like all other "truth," consists of beliefs the individual creates out of personal experience. Sexual preference is developed out of sexual experience and intuitive understanding of body responses. An individual's sense of truth about gender identity and sexuality is a composite constructed by the individual out of personal experience and affirmed by the community of like-minded individuals with whom she or he affiliates. For the committed postmodernist, sexuality, like other facets of human experience, is subject only to the choice of the individual in response to the search for "what works" in his or her individual life. There is no higher authority that can legitimately define and regulate individual sexual expression or gender identity.

This aspect of postmodern thinking exerts a powerful influence on the present cultural script for relationships between men and women. The power of this postmodern message is intensified further by the way in which it is commingled with debris from the social change that marked the closing decades of the twentieth century. As the modern world fragmented and the influence of postmodern thought increased, the emphasis on individual happiness accelerated. Men and women began to expect increased levels of intimacy and personal happiness from their relationships. They became angry and hurt when these high expectations were not fulfilled. It was in these years that no-fault divorce laws were enacted and divorce rates skyrocketed.

Sexual activity outside the parameters of committed, long-term relationships became more frequent as the pill made contraception more reliable. Legal authorization of abortion separated pregnancy from parenthood. The traditional marital relationship—the "good-provider father" and the "stay-at-home mom"—became only one of the increasing options for marriage. Cohabitation increased in frequency and in social acceptance as a viable alternative to marriage.

Technology altered transportation and communication. Educational opportunities were opened to women and minorities in dramatically new ways. Women entered the labor market in unprecedented numbers. Women and minorities entered professional fields that had been previously closed to them. In the business world, women could establish individual credit accounts and secure bank loans without a male cosigner. In the corporate world, doors previously closed to women and minorities began to open, often under the pressure of coercive legal procedures and social policy. The growing anxiety and anger accompanying such enormous social change became politicized and focused around the issue of *equal rights*. In the intense debates surrounding abortion, no-fault divorce, and child support, the distrust between men and women deepened.

The rise of consumerism fostered marketplace thinking and the pursuit of the "good life" in terms of the acquisition of material goods. Ironically, levels of poverty increased in defiance of antipoverty programs and efforts to establish a so-called social safety net for families and individuals unable to care adequately for themselves in the social and economic chaos around them.

It was an exciting time of firsts—first space station, first successful organ transplants. It was an alarming time of fragmentation, with spiraling divorce rates and unprecedented numbers of single-parent families existing below the poverty line. It was a time of increasing information and decreasing communication.

In the relational world, the majority of women wished and asked for support and encouragement from men as they explored new patterns of life. But men sometimes saw these changes as challenges to their value as men and to their traditional prerogatives or as threats to their control of people and resources.

Similarly, the majority of men wished and asked for support and encouragement from women; they faced the emotionally dangerous work of exploring ways to maintain their value and identity as men in the face of changing values and new patterns of relationships. "Tell me I'm a good guy even if I don't cry at movies," a young man said to his wife. His comment was only half in jest.

Despite good faith efforts on the part of the majority of men and women, communication and development of new patterns of relationship were difficult. For a time, the social alienation between men and women deepened. Issues of change became framed in oppositional terms—men's sense of power and personal well-being versus women's sense of autonomy and right to achieve. Without being labeled as such, issues were increasingly cast in terms of the postmodern emphasis on the rights of the individual and the pursuit of individual happiness for men and women alike.

Marriage was frequently the arena in which conflict over change in roles and expectations was played out. There was a pressed-down, running-over measure of rhetoric from both the "conservative" and the "liberal" fronts that inflamed the antagonisms, distorted the real issues, and failed utterly to identify the postmodern thinking that increasingly controlled the debate. And for the most part, the church, ambivalent and anxious, found itself theologically unprepared to provide biblically grounded guidance or emotional shelter to men and women caught in the storm.

Scientists waded into the fray presumably to provide some factual information about the nature of likenesses and differences between men and women and the impact of new patterns of relationships. But in an unexpected way, much of this research turned out to be a test case of the modern belief in the rational, objective scientist as much as a study of social behaviors. Most scientists held a strong belief in the modern myth of themselves as rational, objective finders of truth. Despite their denial, some of these scientists held strong biases regarding the social issues at stake that influenced their work. In some instances (although, thankfully, not all) the results of such "research" told the reader more about the sponsoring scientist's personal social bias than about established differences between men and women or the impact of new patterns of family life.[20] The subjective, emotionally controlled involvement of both theologians and scientists in the so-called gender wars provided unintentional support to the growing postmodern claim that *all* truth was a matter of subjective, socially conditioned perception. It was an unwitting invitation that welcomed the postmodern elephant to the cultural living room.

Despite the "scientific" infighting, some very fine studies emerged from the last three decades of the century. These studies provided reliable information about established likenesses and differences between men and women. Current research reaffirms these findings.[21] Nevertheless, at the time, good sense, good science, and civil discourse were in short supply. The conflicting findings of poorly designed studies and their exaggerated reports exacerbated the social uncertainty men and women were experiencing. The postmodern idea "Do whatever works for you—there's no absolute out there" found fallow ground in which to grow.

The resulting cultural messages were powerfully antithetical to committed faithful relationships between men and women. The current culture encourages men and women to think:

- I have a right and responsibility to be happy. If I am not happy in this relationship, I may leave the relationship to find someone with whom I can experience happiness. The significance of a relationship is limited to its capacity to fulfill personal gratification.

- I have a right and responsibility to be free. My freedom is of greater importance than the need or desire of a partner (or child) to have me stay. Others' pain is their responsibility, not mine.

- Sexual experience is a means to discover and develop the self. Thus I am free to establish a sexual liaison with any given partner. Pleasure without responsibility and sexual gratification without consequences are consistent with my right to freedom and happiness.

- Sexuality can be separated from relationship; a sexual act can be separated from its context and consequences.[22] Sex is only sex; it is emotional candy; it is a body-based "natural" adrenaline high; it is comfort—it helps me "make it through the night."

- The boundaries of my human sexuality are flexible and changeable. As an individual, I am free and responsible to develop through experience, intuition, and emotion a sexual identity that "works" for me.

- Expression of my human sexuality is a personal, private matter. No social, governmental, or religious regulations can legitimately control my individual sexual expression.

- Sexual expression is biologically justified; whatever my body finds pleasurable and gratifying is morally acceptable.

It is encouraging to note, however, that despite the culture's case against marriage today, many men and women are committed to marriage as a lifelong partnership. They have developed new patterns of relationship that are marked by mutual respect and practical attention to family needs. In these households Dad is not valued less as a man (or Mom less as a woman) if he makes the macaroni and cheese and the grocery bill is paid from his wife's wages. Family needs take precedence over gender egos. With no sense of martyrdom, adults invest vacation days in the care of sick children; a visit to grandparents has higher priority than a week at Club Med. In these households, even when adults and children are tired and the "second shift" is not fun, they help each other—the laundry gets done, the homework gets finished, and the dog gets fed whether these chores "feel good" or not. Immediate personal gratification does *not* control the household routine or relationships. These households, though they exist in the twenty-first century, are *not* postmodern households.

While such families may have successfully resisted the postmodern pressure of individualism, the postmodern concept of community also challenges the building of such marriages in a different but no less significant way.

Postmodernism and the Community

In postmodern thinking the overarching significance of the individual is accompanied by a parallel emphasis on community. Initially this appears paradoxical. However, careful attention to the way postmodernists use the word *community* soon makes clear that the word has undergone a major sea change in its transition from the modern to the postmodern world.

The Postmodern Definition of Community

In the "old" modern world, *community* was viewed as a network of individuals linked by common interests and goals and, in the majority of instances, by a common location and/or a common history. Community responsibility was mutual. Community in the modern understanding of the word was a contractual social order. For example, if a family's barn burned, the community had an unstated, unlegislated responsibility to aid the individuals in difficulty. A barn raising was thus both a social event and a community act of caretaking. In turn, individuals had a parallel, unstated, unlegislated responsibility to the community at large, a responsibility to care for the welfare of others in the community and to contribute to the common good, even when that contribution was costly to the individual.

The stories that Tom Brokaw recorded in *The Greatest Generation* were characterized by this commitment to the common good even at personal cost.[23] The significance of that "greatest" generation did not lie solely in what they did, remarkable as their courage and resilience were. There is no factual evidence that members of the present younger generations have any less capacity for courage and resilience. What is disappearing in the postmodern world is not the capacity for courage but the belief in the common good that made such courage seem to that generation a reasonable response. That vanishing generation believed that there were values of greater significance than the individual's personal welfare or comfort. This belief led them to the beaches of Normandy and the islands of the Pacific and left many of them there. In postmodern thinking, *community* means many things, but for the postmodernist there is no such thing as a network of relationships with a legitimate claim on the individual that merits such sacrificial commitment and service.

The Function of Community in the Postmodern World

Community is nonetheless essential in the postmodern world, where individuals, somewhat paradoxically, require other individuals to fulfill their deepest needs. It is through interaction with others that the individual self and the individual's truth are created. Grenz noted:

> . . . the postmodern self is constituted by social relationships. The socially formed self, however, is highly decentered and fluid, for a person can have as many selves as social groups in which he or she participates.[24]

The postmodern community grows out of this social construction of the self. Postmodern individuals, creating their personal truth and reality out of their individual preferences and experience, link with other individuals with similar preferences and experiences (and thus similar created truths). Postmodern community functions as a network of individuals whose experiences and perception of truth result in a common worldview. Given the entrenched resistance of postmodern thinkers to authority as such, it is ironic that this connection functions both as a source and a validation of the self.

Community in this sense becomes a creator of truth. It is the *individual's* truth, but it is truth (and self) that the individual can create only in the context of the *community* in which the individual participates. In postmodern thinking, whatever the individual accepts as truth and the way the individual envisions truth are both dependent on the community in which that person participates.[25] Community serves, then, both as a source and as a credentialing canon for truth. To Christians whose faith views truth as absolute and grounded outside the individual, this postmodern idea of the "truthing" function of community appears to place the fox in charge of the epistemological henhouse. But even here, the individual is master. When the individual's preferences change and consensus (intellectual or emotional) within the community weakens, the postmodern solution lies in the individual's right, ability, and freedom to move on, to join another community in which to engage a new and more personally satisfying truth-making project.[26]

In the postmodern world, individuals may work together within the community, but they do not do so because the community has value that transcends individual preference and needs. Instead, "communal" groups develop as diverse individuals link together to solve problems directly related to them. While individuals may link together to work toward what appear to be corporate goals, the postmodern individual works on corporate projects only as long as he or she perceives the work as "having something in it for me."

People do indeed need people. Richard Rorty, a major voice in the postmodern world, explains the reason postmodernists believe this is so. "In the end . . . what matters is our loyalty to other human beings clinging together against the dark, not our hope of getting things right."[27] Grenz illustrates Rorty's sense of individuals clinging together against the dark when he describes the Next Generation crew of the Star Trek ship *Enterprise*. Their diversity of skills and differences in being permit them as individuals to function as a "variegated crew . . . [that moves] into a postmodern universe . . . [in which] time is no longer simply linear, appearance is not necessarily reality, and the rational is not always to be trusted."[28]

It is a lonely world for the postmodernist. There is only a loose network of individuals standing together against the dark. And this connection is fragile. There is no legitimate authority with the power to require that the welfare or preference of the individual be subordinated to the needs of the group. As a result, individuals can (and should) exit a community when it no longer meets their individual needs.

Marriage and families are small communities within the wider community at large, and the postmodern idea of community shapes much of the culture's sense of need for easy, uncomplicated divorce. Staying or going, leaving or remaining within the "community" of marriage is, in postmodern thinking, an individual decision in which the welfare of the family (the *common good* in its narrowest sense) should not interfere with the individual's pursuit of personal happiness in a brave new world.

In 1993 Barbara DaFoe Whitehead published an essay in the *Atlantic Monthly* titled "Dan Quayle Was Right,"[29] which evoked a firestorm of response. In it Whitehead confronted head-on the cultural belief in the primary importance of the individual and the consequences of this belief for marriage and family life.

> Increasingly, political principles of individual rights and choice shape our understanding of family commitment and solidarity. Family relationships are viewed not as permanent or binding but as voluntary and easily terminable. . . . [T]he family loses its central importance as an institution in the civil society, accomplishing certain goals such as raising children and caring for its members, and becomes a means to achieving greater individual happiness—a lifestyle choice.[30]

In Whitehead's view, emphasis on individual gratification (often at the cost of the breakup of the family) may benefit some adults in the short term. However, the same cannot be said about children, the weaker, more defenseless members of the family unit.

> Owing to their biological and developmental immaturity, children are needy dependents. . . . Correspondingly, the parental role is antithetical to the spirit of the regime [i.e., individual rights, personal choice, and egalitarian relationships]. Parental investment in children involves a diminished investment in self, a willing deference to the needs and claims of the dependent child.[31]

Children simply cannot function as "equal partners" in the family, Whitehead insists. They are *children*, dependent, with needs they are helpless to negotiate and claims they are unable to mediate. What Whitehead is objecting to, of course, is the postmodern view of community as it works out in the mini-community of the family. As Whitehead points out, this view of community does not obligate the individual to care for others at cost to the individual, even when within the family community those others are children who are relatively unable to care for themselves. In postmodern thinking, the preemptive rights of the individual make the idea of sacrificial service to the mini-community of the family a conceptual Christian dinosaur from a vanishing age. And postmodern thinking has no place at all for the New Testament call for individuals to commit willingly to the well-being of the family of God, even at considerable cost to their personal lives.

Postmodern Community and the Decay of the Modern World

The impact of postmodern thinking on communities is powerful in part because, as with the postmodern concept of individualism, other cultural factors provided fallow ground in which the postmodern concept of community could readily grow. Physical communities were deteriorating, for example. Technology was providing the potential for a "work free, cost free" virtual community that fit well with the "feel good" mentality of postmodern thinking.

During the closing decades of the twentieth century, communities that had developed during the modern age fell on hard times. Communities strongly rooted in location were weakened by the great migrations of the century—people moving from farms and small towns to cities, from city to city, from city to suburb, from home into the labor force, from factory to offices where jobs and working space were technologically defined and working spaces were cubicles circumscribed by separating walls. Physical neighborhoods were broken by the growth of cities in which the architecture of buildings and the structure of streets fostered aloneness and isolation.

Broken communities produced increasing numbers of people with shallow roots in the locations where they lived and worked and minimal connections to the people they knew. Relationships became transient as people moved from apartment to condo, from job to job, from church to church, from New Jersey to Phoenix, from Houston to Atlanta, with a couple of years in Boston in between. The corporate practice of reassigning employees to distant offices contributed to weakened communities and a loss in the sense of the value of community and its function. John Donne was rewritten to read, "Every man is an island and that's just fine—so long as his computer doesn't crash and his cell phone works."

"The job is the thing. You can always find a place to live," a young man said. "One street address is as good as another—of course, you have to find a good neighborhood, but with a decent salary that's not hard to do." For this young man, community was something that salary could buy, and he could leave without regret whenever his individual need or desire made the move advisable. The structure of the upscale condominium complex in which he lived reflected architectural and commercial support of his sense of disposable, leaveable community. "Enjoy your own private home with no responsibilities," the advertising slogan read. "And take your equity with you when you go." Marriage and family survive only with difficulty in a culture that promotes this sense of unessential, disposable community.

The uprooting that accompanied "going where the jobs are" made connection with extended family members increasingly difficult. Consequently the community of relationships and common history that gives family roots also began to fade. "My mother insisted that I attend a family reunion when I went back to see her," a young woman confided. "My husband decided not to go—he wanted to play golf—so it was just the kids and me. I had forgotten a lot of the people—hadn't seen them for ages and didn't ever know most of the people who are part of my cousins' lives. The kids thought the reunion was boring. They wanted to go back to mom's house and watch a video. They'd rather have pizza than Aunt Bessie's potato salad any day. Felt a little that way myself."

Technology and advertising blurred and reinterpreted this loss of community. One greeting card company developed a slogan that read, "When you care enough to send the very best," and the picture onscreen or in print was of a smiling, delighted recipient of the "best" card possible to send. There was no suggestion that the recipient might possibly prefer a personal hug instead. Telephone companies marketed special long-distance rates that allegedly made goodnight stories as possible and as enjoyable when dads were in hotel rooms as when they were at home. Physical separation became allegedly irrelevant in the face of this new technological infrastructure. The corporate message was simple: A story is a story is a story, and it's as good by phone as being there.

In the context of such "progress," community began to slip away—the tapestry of people, places, and traditions, the stories and memories, the common experiences that wove individuals into community frayed and disintegrated. And the consumer culture was largely indifferent to the loss or, when challenged, supported the trend of making people strangers to one another. The argument was consistent with emerging postmodern thinking—the individual is served by this loosing of attachments and commitments to the family and community. The more a person is freed from duties, obligations, and connections, the more free to "go with the flow," the freer the individual becomes to enter into new and exciting possibilities.[32]

The technological subculture supported the postmodern message regarding the disposable nature of community. Its message was: If communities of relationship or location wither away, it is no matter for concern. What technology can and does supply in the place of the vanishing community is exciting, new, and adequate. A two-page, full-color ad in the December 2000 issue of *Fast Company* provides a case in point. A young man stares excitedly at the screen of his laptop computer. The text of the ad reads:

> Now there's a way home for all you road warriors. . . . Find out how the team did (and see the winning goal). Help Kate with her history paper. (The encyclopedia is online.) Say "Happy Birthday" to your nephew. (An online card can even sing it!) Kids, friends, relatives . . . you've got a lot on your mind. Which is why [corporate names of an international chain of hotels and of a computer company] have made those connections easier and 50 times faster for you. All from the comfort of your room. So, no matter where in the world you are, home never seems so far away.[33]

Sounds just fine, but a thoughtful reader will raise some interesting questions. In the road warrior's absence, who will carpool the kids and sponsor the after-game party? Who will attend the parent/teacher conference at Kate's school scheduled for next Tuesday night? Who will keep the community itself functional, its social structure intact, and its streets safe? Who will keep the network of extended family and neighbors unbroken so that there is a place and connected people that enable the nephew's party to occur? The point, omitted in the ad, is that the touted fifty-times-faster connection does very little to build the community on which the meaning of the fast connection depends. Without conscious awareness, the ad reflects the postmodern culture's Little-Red-Hen approach to community—let someone else do it if that's their thing. But whose thing can it be if people are on the road or exhausted from two shifts or spending a seventy-hour week in the executive suite? And what if Dad has a new wife and a new home and Mom is on the road and Grandmother lives in Houston?

The issue is unavoidable. Marriages and families are mini-communities, but their health and well-being depend in part on the health and well-being of the community at large of which they are a part. And to be effective, this community must be a "real" community, one in which, for example, parents, linked together in common purpose, make and police a no-drinking rule for teenage parties. But the technologically sophisticated postmodern world has developed a tempting substitute for "real."

Stanley Grenz describes the postmodern universe as similar to that of the *Star Ship Enterprise* in which appearance was not necessarily reality. "Trekkies" will remember that on a number of occasions, this "virtual reality" provided some interesting challenges for the crew of the *Enterprise*.[34] What the consumer culture provides in place of community as it once was is a community of virtual reality that would, in many ways, make sense to the crew of the *Enterprise*. Television provides what is in effect a virtual community, one that people may enter without effort, commitment, or risk, and leave without being missed or grieved.

A widowed friend in her late sixties lamented the end of the television series *Seinfeld*. "I will miss them," she said, somewhat embarrassed by her response.

"But those screen people were not at all like you," I (Gay) commented. "How is it that you will miss them?"

"You're right. I'm sure not like any of those women," she laughed, then added hesitantly, "It's hard to explain. In some ways that's my neighborhood and I know those people. That George! I'll miss him." She stopped, then after a pause added as if to make everything clear, "You see, I don't really know anyone in this building. Jim and his family are in Houston. He and Helen both have good jobs working in a big hospital. I'm glad for them."

Since 1980 the number of Americans who hold two or more jobs is up 65 percent.[35] Sheer fatigue collaborates with the culture to encourage the television neighborhood. Participation in this virtual neighborhood requires only sitting, watching, and serving as a passive observer. It is entered without effort via the click of the remote control. It can be left without saying good-bye when the news is over and it is time for bed. There is great appeal in this when people no longer have the energy, time, or vision to build real community. The tacit message is simple: *You're tired. You don't have time. Just sit. The community onscreen is all you need.*

This virtual community, of course, produces consumers, and at the same time it reduces the quality of life for its passive television watchers. Despite the protests of the industry to the contrary, long hours spent watching television do not produce either high-quality family life or a high quality of life for those who live alone. Watching Tim the Tool Man does not produce the same results as does repairing bleachers at the Little League field with other volunteers from the neighborhood. The common life of the community erodes, and the human relationships that both evolve from and support the common life erode as well.

The Internet supplements and promotes the virtual community in a parallel way. Through chat rooms and interactive web sites, people do in fact connect. But this connection is by its very nature amorphous, and the "citizens" of this world are voices with uncertain identities. Distorted pictures grow from data coming without context or credentials through cyberspace. It is hard to know where you are on the net, because the virtual neighborhoods of cyberspace, being relatively unpoliced, shift and move without boundaries or roots. The Internet requires firewalls and passwords and carefully designated levels of security but still can be a dangerous place to visit. It is proving to be an utterly destructive place in which to live.

Media and Internet forces alone cannot be held responsible for the present erosion of the common life and the loss of community. But in ways that viewers are slow to see, the media seduce overworked people away from real community. It is true that media in this technologically powerful culture hold a unique and exciting potential for expanding the parameters of human learning. Music from the Met and information from the far corners of the planet can be easily acquired through the media and the World Wide Web. But this information does not automatically produce relationships and active participation in the world in which the watcher/listener lives. Whatever else their value, media and allied technology have not yet proven to be friends to real community, with real people, real places, real problems, and real marriages to support.

Postmodernism and the Marketplace

Postmodernism did not produce the consumer society that characterizes the present culture, but it has certainly fueled it. The hand-in-glove relationship between consumerism and postmodern thinking has made them difficult to separate at some points, but the component parts are easy to identify. Postmodernism teaches individuals that they have a right to whatever makes them happy. Consumerism teaches individuals that what makes them happy is consuming—things, relationships, experiences. The individual is encouraged to conclude: *I have a right to whatever I need and want, whatever makes me happy. So long as my credit card permits me to purchase something that makes me happy, then I have a responsibility to myself to do what is good for me—consume.* One may easily believe that this near perfect match between consumerism and postmodernism was made in another world. The Christian, however, has little doubt that this other world was *not* heaven.

Consumerism as a Way of Life

Rodney Clapp, in a thoughtful analysis of the contemporary family, argues that the common blacklist of social problems presented by Christian family advocates (including pornography, drugs, public schools, and secular humanism) seriously misses the point.[36] These problems certainly challenge marriage and family life, but the deeper problem of our ailing families, in Clapp's opinion, is that capitalism has succeeded all too well.[37] Clapp is no foe of free markets, but the issue Clapp confronts head-on is the rising consumer society in which the business of buying and selling has "decentered the family and faith."[38]

The current culture in our democratic postmodern world affirms (at least in theory) the freedom of each citizen to create his or her own meaning. Increasingly this freedom evidences itself in ever-higher levels of consumption.[39] Shortly after World War II, Victor Lebow, a retailing analyst, wrote: "Our enormously productive economy demands that we make consumption our way of life, that we convert the buying and use of goods into rituals, that we seek our spiritual satisfaction, our ego satisfaction in consumption."[40] What Lebow dreamed and hoped for has become reality. Consumption is now a way of life, and the rules of the marketplace are to an alarming degree becoming the rules by which our lives are conducted.[41] Milton Friedman and his colleagues at the Chicago School of Economics have suggested that marriage, like other exchanges of "goods," can be best explained in economic terms of supply and demand.[42] Observers of current dating and mating rituals may argue that relationships between men and women are more about the supply and demand of things like sexual experience than about securing a spouse. Yet Friedman had a shrewd eye into the mood of the culture; economics is indeed a growing force in relationships between men and women.

The Rutgers National Marriage Project interviewed a group of young, heterosexual, not-yet-married men.[43] Fear of divorce and its financial risks and a desire to own a house before they have a wife were among the reasons these men gave for their reluctance to commit to marriage, although these economic issues were not first on the list. These young men expected the women they date to be economically independent and able to take care of themselves. They said they are turned off by women who evaluate them on the size of their wallets, their possessions, or their earning potential or who are interested in the "big house and car." But their attitudes appear to reflect a pot-calling-the-kettle-black concern. They seemed interested in the big portfolio and sports car, and they structured their relationships with women to protect their ability to increase their consumer potential. While willing participants in casual sex, these men reported that they were afraid of paternity, primarily because of the financial cost of supporting a child were they legally identified as the father. In the event of a partner's unplanned pregnancy, some men were concerned about the unilateral power of the mother to keep them from developing a relationship with the child. Their overriding concern, however, was the potential financial cost a partner's unplanned pregnancy might incur for them.

Greed is not a new problem for the human race, but Christians are slow to recognize that the problem at the core of the present consumer culture is more complex than simple human greed, as destructive as that is. A powerful and impeccable logic is at work that, given the culture's basic presuppositions, justifies—even commends—consumption at ever-higher levels. This logic is the contribution of postmodern thinking. The argument runs like this. If in fact the individual does have an inherent human right to happiness and the right to seek that happiness in whatever way works for that individual, then logically the individual has the right to the *things* that bring happiness as it is intuitively, subjectively defined. Thus the logic of choice in the consumer culture is woven with the postmodern belief in the right to personal gratification. If having things makes me happy, then I have a right to have all the things I need (want) to make me happy, regardless of the cost to me or to others. The question of the capacity of things to bring happiness is lost in the pursuit of more.

A teenage boy pulled a gun and killed another boy who was peaceably supervising younger siblings on a trick-or-treat visit to neighborhood houses. When asked why he had done this, the young man explained that he wanted the football jacket the victim was wearing, and the victim had refused to give it to him when he demanded it. "Why would you *kill* someone for a *jacket*?" a horrified reporter asked. The young man was obviously baffled by the question. After a moment of thought, he answered, "I wanted it." Spoken like a true believer in the consumer culture—I wanted it because I felt that the jacket would make me happy, and I took it by the means available to me (a gun that his peers admired and its use of which they approved). *What is the matter with this reporter?* the young man appeared to ask. *Why does he not understand my behavior?*

No one makes a case for the uninhibited expression of human greed as such. But once the postmodern belief in the unlimited right of the individual to happiness is ceded, the unintended consequence of unlimited human greed is a logical outcome. The dishonesty and greed that marked corporate behavior and that of corporate executives throughout the closing decade of the last century should not be surprising. The financial scandals at Enron and other corporations are not anomalies; they are logical outcomes of a consumer culture buttressed by a postmodern logic.

Ideas do have consequences. The core of the consumer culture is not simply a materialistic belief that the one with the most toys wins. It is the conviction that it is *right* that the one with the most toys wins. It is the way the world *should* run (approved by the Chicago School of Economics, no less).[44] A young mother was having lunch with her son at a fast-food franchise. She said to the four year old, "Don't be greedy." The child, with mouth and both hands full of french fries, asked, "Why not?" Why not indeed.

Advocates of the consumer culture tend to avoid considering the reality of human greed. They point instead to the supposed benefits of unrestrained consumption. It fuels the economy. It provides an enviable standard of living. It is a readily accessible, uncomplicated road to the "good life." And most of all, unrestrained consumption is the inalienable right of the individual because it brings personal gratification and happiness. And while consumer advocates may give lip service to the idea that we cannot buy happiness, their advertising says otherwise. Increasing numbers of people follow the admonition to "shop till you drop." After all, shopping is "good exercise" and great recreation. Consumerism is practical, a comforting faith that can be exercised daily at the mall. Come as you are. Bring your credit card. And, remember, the ATM is available twenty-four hours a day.

In considering the impact of our consumer-obsessed society on families, Jean Bethke Elshtain summarized the relational core of the matter in these words: "We cannot offer the gift of self to one another if we ourselves are consumed by consumption, wholly given over to a relentless fast-paced life in which the more we earn, the more we spend, the more we need to earn—on and on without any apparent oasis in sight."[45] The statistical description of the extent to which our families and our lives have been changed by the emerging consumer culture is astonishing:

The average American worker now spends 163 hours a year more working than he or she did in 1980: that's a whole month stolen from family, friends, church, and community. Fully 71 percent of school-age children have no parent at home full time compared with 43 percent in 1970. Yet only 13 percent of mothers with preschool-age children say they want to work full time. They would rather have more time with their children.[46]

Economist Alan Carlson argues that much of "what we measure as economic growth since 1960 has simply been the transfer of remaining household tasks uncounted in monetary terms—home cooking, child-care, elder care—to external entities such as Burger King, corporate day-care centers, and state-funded nursing homes."[47] At the end of a long day, families derive little comfort from knowing that their dinner at a fast food franchise has added to its corporate profit. It is hard to compute corporate gain at the family's cost of a game of Monopoly or Dad's burgers on the grill as much of a bargain for family or for the marriage. A therapist may recommend increased communication, but realistically what couple can manage that at the end of a twelve-hour day after the children are finally in bed and there is still laundry to do? Elshtain's summary of the dilemma is not encouraging:

> It is, admittedly, difficult to figure out what to do. Many men and women are trying to rearrange their priorities. But many others are in no position to step back from the economic treadmill: they are just barely keeping their heads above water. Besides that, the wider cultural surroundings spread the message of "more" without limit. Having lost an appropriate sense of limits, we have no criteria for determining any longer what counts as "enough." We just believe, and act on that belief, that you can never have "too much." We are trapped in patterns of habituation that preclude glimpsing some better or more decent way.[48]

Historian Stephanie Coontz similarly notes with concern the vulnerability of individuals and families surrounded by the pressure to consume:

> [V]ery few people can sustain values at a personal level when they are continually contradicted at work, at the store, in the government and on television. To call their failure to do so a family crisis is much like calling pneumonia a breathing crisis. Certainly, pneumonia affects people's ability to breathe easily, but telling them to start breathing properly again . . . is not going to cure the disease. The crisis of the family . . . is in many ways a larger crisis of social reproduction: a major upheaval in the way we produce, reproduce and distribute goods, services, power, economic rewards and social roles.[49]

Marriage in the New Millennium

A young couple from two affluent families recently married. An older friend attended the reception. Looking at the mountain of unwrapped packages and the tables filled with expensive wedding gifts on display, she commented privately, "Where's the sign for Toys 'R' Us?" A young friend also attending the ceremony and reception commented more seriously, "I'm actually surprised that they are really getting married. Things were cool until they went in to sign their 'prenups' [consulted an attorney to sign prenuptial agreements], but it's been really rocky since then. They should have left things alone [i.e., continued cohabitation]." After a moment of thought, however, the young woman added matter of factly: "But if you're going to get married, it really is important to have a plan for dividing stuff when you divorce." She had little awareness of the irony of her comment in which "good" marriage planning focused on the preservation of the right to "stuff" when divorce occurred rather than on the preservation of the marriage.

Marriage, by the nature of the relationship, calls two people to attend to the common good, to demonstrate generosity and self-sacrifice, to participate in mutual responsibility. Marriage and the family do not thrive in a culture that promotes goals solely or primarily concerned with possessing and enjoying, *having* rather than *being*. The fact that marriage entails a commitment that transcends and countermands the cultural call to consumption is not entirely lost on the emerging generations. A vague awareness of this is reflected in their talk about postponing marriage in economic terms. When they say, "I will marry after I have acquired," they give an implicit acknowledgment that the uncontrolled drive to acquire and the requirements of marriage are essentially incompatible.

The culture's case against marriage is complex and powerful. It speaks through the marketplace, the academy, the media, and the entertainment industry. It speaks through its neglect of institutions and structures that provide the social ecology in which marriage and family can flourish. The message it gives is clear: Marriage was probably once a good thing; however, there is a much smaller place for it in the brave new world of the new millennium. And what the culture offers as an alternative is a pattern in which couples choose each other and live together but do so without choosing marriage.

3

The Culture's Alternatives to Marriage

The culture's case against marriage has already won a large number of adherents. Official census figures report that the number of individuals who are choosing alternative forms of family is growing rapidly. It is clear that many North Americans no longer regard marriage as an unquestioned social good.

Although the status of marriage in the culture is far from positive, the news is not all bad. Many reports, like Mark Twain's mistakenly printed obituary, record a death that "has been greatly exaggerated." Announcements of fiftieth anniversary celebrations are common, and sixtieth anniversary celebrations are not unknown. In 2002 a large national study of changes in teen attitudes toward marriage noted that *increasing* numbers of teens say that marriage and family life are "extremely important" to them.[1] Most want their marriages to be lifelong.

However, while marriage is still very much alive, it is not an exaggeration to report that marriage as a social institution has fallen on hard times. Love and marriage no longer "go together like a horse and carriage" (if they ever did in real life). The Rutgers National Marriage Project indicates that Americans are becoming less likely to marry, and fewer of those who do marry report having marriages they consider to be "very happy."[2] To the majority of people, this fact does not qualify as news. They know that the streets where they live are not completely filled with happily married couples who warmly endorse marriage as a way of life. But this fact can be a bit slippery. Unhappy people generally have unhappy marriages. The relationship between these two factors is not always clear. Does the unhappy person make the marriage unhappy or does the unhappy marriage produce the unhappy person? Marriage is a complex relationship, and many factors affect its well-being.

There are some surprising statistics that indicate that marriage as an institution is in serious trouble. In testimony before the House of Representatives in May 2001, David Popenoe, codirector of the Rutgers National Marriage Project, summarized the current situation:

> As the recent results of the year 2000 confirm, marriage as the basis of family life continues to decline in America. Since 1970 the rate of marriage has dropped by about one-third, the out-of-wedlock birth ratio has climbed from 11 percent to 33 percent of all births, the divorce rate has doubled, and *the number of people living together outside of marriage has grown by over 1,000 percent.*[3]

Pause and consider that last fact—a *thousand-plus percent increase in cohabiting couples* over a thirty-year time span! Such a massive shift over a relatively short time is enough to raise the eyebrows as well as the concern of both Christians and non-Christians. What is happening here? Why is there such a dramatic increase in the number of people saying "I don't" to marriage while saying "I do" to each other?

Even though Christians may not like what they see, the statistical evidence cannot be ignored. In the present culture a significant and steadily rising number of adults (including a share of young Christians) have in their own minds made a convincing case *against* marriage. In choosing cohabitation, they declare their objection to marriage as they believe it to be yet choose what they report to be a committed relationship as their preferred alternative. The majority of those choosing cohabitation believe their case against marriage rests on solid reason and that cohabitation is a morally acceptable alternative to marriage.

The Alternatives to Marriage Project (AtMP) was initiated in response to the Rutgers National Marriage Project, and it already has a growing and influential support base. The AtMP position paper, "Affirmation of Family Diversity," has been signed by nearly a thousand experts (professors of sociology, psychology, marriage and family studies; mental health professionals; therapists; public health professionals; religious leaders) as well as supporting citizens. The position paper does not call for the abandonment of marriage but for the acceptance and support of alternate structures for family:

> We agree with the newly formed "Marriage Movement" that marriages should be supported. What worries us is the mistaken notion that marriage is the only acceptable relationship or family structure. . . . The picture that is painted by these opponents [of nontraditional family forms] is bleak. In reality, however, there are millions of happy, healthy unmarried families. The challenge is to find effective approaches to supporting these successful families, as well as the ones who are having difficult times.[4]

Are there in fact millions of happy, healthy unmarried families, as the AtMP insists? There is little trustworthy research investigating the relationships of cohabiting couples, but there is ample evidence of the increasing number of couples who are choosing cohabitation. The U.S. Census Bureau indicates that the number of unmarried couples living together increased 72 percent between 1990 and 2000. There are now 9.7 million Americans living unmarried with a different-sex partner, and 1.2 million Americans living with a same-sex partner. Marriage is not the only game in town.

Christians are rightly concerned about the rejection of marriage that is reflected in these rising rates of cohabitation. However, despite disagreement with their choices, thoughtful Christians must acknowledge that those who question the value of marriage have some valid points. Given their underlying assumptions and life experience, their choice of cohabitation has a logic and validity that Christians, even while disagreeing, would do well to consider. In examining this opposing point of view carefully, Christians have the opportunity to rethink the distinctive nature and value of Christian marriage. And one additional thing is certain. If Christians want the current cohabitation-oriented culture to consider marriage as a viable option, Christians must understand the reasons cohabitation seems to be an attractive alternative.

Cohabitation is a social choice in process, and much of the current dialogue about marriage and cohabitation takes place in the immediacy of the Internet, its web sites, and chat rooms. One search engine produced literally thousands of entries in response to the simple prompt *cohabitation*. Sources ranged, for example, from online information posted by the Alternative to Marriage Project, reprints from the Vatican archives and Vatican-approved articles, the Rutgers Marriage Project studies, papers from the Jewish Forum, dialogue from chat rooms, Christian pro-marriage articles, papers and abstracts of papers from various academic faculties, serious op-ed pieces from major newspapers (pro and con), tables and summary reports from the U.S. Census Bureau, and literally hundreds of additional, widely differing sources. The reader may even choose between French, Spanish, and English. All are readily available.

This mountain of material makes clear that couples who cohabit (like couples who marry) differ widely, and the goals of their relationships are different. For some, cohabitation is a temporary arrangement in anticipation of a planned marriage. For others, it is the context of a committed, long-term relationship that includes a mutual agreement that they will never marry. Older cohabiting couples are frequently committed to each other but mutually agree that, for economic and family reasons, they will never marry. Some couples cohabit casually, expecting the relationship to dissolve as soon as one or both decide that the relationship no longer contributes enough to their individual pleasure and happiness.

The present culture encourages this wide diversity in relationships. When a couple decides to "be together—unmarried," it is a highly personal decision, but it is a decision that is influenced by the current climate of social change. The sexual revolution, the consumer culture, aspects of government social policy, the women's movement, for example—all these factors have influenced the rising frequency of cohabitation as well as the diversity in goals. Even more, people's choices about cohabitation continue to be influenced by postmodern thinking, which values individualism and materialism in ways that make marriage appear to be an undesirable option.

Evangelical Christians tend, at least initially, to think about cohabitation in stereotypic ways, assuming that people who "just move in" are different from them economically, ethnically, and most of all religiously. But a visit to cohabiting couples on the residential streets and in the apartment complexes of ordinary neighborhoods uncovers a different reality. Specific examples of cohabitation may include a couple who moved in together while in college or a couple from work whose cohabitation began when they decided that it made economic sense to move in together. It may be a couple who are "good, decent kids," obviously in love with each other (and may have a child together), but who reject the option of marriage. Some are couples who maintain separate apartments but who "sleep over" regularly and monogamously at each other's apartment, buy groceries together, and on religious holidays may go to church together. They regularly join each other's extended family for birthday celebrations and special dinners. They are a couple with a personal commitment and a shared life, but they are not married and state openly that they have no intention of becoming so. Some of these couples grew up as members of the family of faith; some are quasi-regular communicants in the church of their adult choice.

In a recent magazine article a mother reported with concern the decision of her son and the young woman he had been dating to move in together. The article ended with a lengthy sidebar of suggestions to parents for how to maintain a positive relationship with adult children who choose cohabitation despite parental disapproval. The magazine in which this article appeared was not just "any" magazine. It appeared in a recent issue of *Today's Christian Woman*.[5] While the author's name was concealed in a pseudonym, both sets of parents of the cohabiting couple were long-time, active members of their local church. The cohabiting pair were professing Christians who had grown up within the faith community and as young adults had maintained at least episodic attendance at their local church. Evidently the editors of the magazine, aimed at a religiously conservative audience, viewed the problem of cohabiting Christians as sufficiently widespread that advice to parents for dealing with cohabiting adult children merited a substantial use of space.

The young man gave two reasons for the choice the couple made. First, they were postponing marriage until they achieved financial stability. Second, they wanted to explore the level of their compatibility to ensure permanence in marriage when (if) they ultimately married. At the time the article was written, the couple had been living together seven months, despite the distress of both sets of parents and the disapproval of their local church. Apparently marriage had little appeal for this young couple and no place in their immediate future.

The culture's case for cohabitation as an alternative to marriage is rarely presented formally as such. More frequently it appears as an appeal for tolerance, as in the AtMP paper cited above. But while the case for cohabitation is wrapped in an appeal for diversity and tolerance, marriage continues to be cast as the core of the problem. If marriage were not so problematic, cohabitation would not be such an appealing (or necessary) alternative. But when asked why marriage is not the preferred alternative, the conversation becomes interesting indeed. Whether presented formally as a position paper or argued in a kitchen table discussion, the case for cohabitation as an acceptable alternative to marriage pivots around the following issues:

- The divorce rate proves that for the majority of people marriage simply does not work. Furthermore, the process of leaving marriage when it fails (divorce) is so destructive that this risk should be avoided at all costs.
- Marriage is restrictive. It limits individual freedom prohibitively.
- Marriage is rigid and inflexible. It does not provide sufficient space for individual growth and change, particularly for women.
- Marriage raises unreasonable and often negative expectations. People expect more and differing things from each other as husband and wife than they do if they are living together unmarried.
- Marriage is not the only vehicle through which commitment can be expressed and family established.
- Marriage is not the only way to establish and maintain a morally responsible relationship.
- Marriage permits religion and government to regulate and to interfere in private and personal decisions. The slogan "Keep your laws off my body" is being augmented by an additional one: "Keep your laws off my relationship."

When thinking about these cultural objections to marriage, Christians may initially be tempted to respond flatly, "You're wrong!" But if Christians are intent on Christian marriage as mission in an alien culture, it is necessary to proceed with caution at this point. Examining these objections more closely provides further insight into the thinking of the postmodern world.

Cohabitation and the Divorce Culture

Cohabiting couples range in age from those in early adulthood to couples in their sixties or older, but most are in their twenties and thirties, with a fairly large number in their early forties. Reviewing the marital history of their parents and grandparents (and uncles and aunts), along with their family history of divorce, this generation has concluded that in practical, everyday life, marriage simply does not work. When pushed to be candid, they will say frankly that in their opinion marriage has been deceptively advertised and grossly oversold.

These successors to the aging Boomer generation are not being unfair. They acknowledge that a small minority of couples has made marriage work well. But for the most part, they view these marriages as irrelevant evidence. When the post-Boomers look at the history of divorce in their families and the continuing high percentage of failed marriages around them, they conclude that the odds against a successful marriage are too high to risk. But at the same time, large numbers say paradoxically that they may attempt marriage themselves—some day. That possibility remains remote—something that may happen *some* day, some *long* day in the future. Even more interesting, these people are often willing to say that they wish marriage (the old-fashioned, one-person-for-life model) *did* work. That's the kind they dream about when they think about a someday marriage for themselves. But when they consider marriage as an option in their immediate plans, they say emphatically, "Nope. It's not for me. Not now. Maybe someday. Maybe never."[6]

Many young people who choose cohabitation rather than marriage are annoyed when their rejection of marriage is attributed simply to immaturity and indignant when their choice of cohabitation is characterized as immoral. They feel misjudged and misunderstood by Christians and by large segments of the Boomer generation as well. They point to the Boomer generation's denial of their own immaturity and the moral consequences of the divorce culture they generated. In this light the majority of current cohabiting couples see the Boomer charge of immorality as a classic case of the pot calling the kettle black. Although they do not frame the issue this way, the case cohabiting couples seek to make is more accurately a case against divorce than a case against marriage. And they have reason for their point of view, however phrased.

In the 2001 report of the National Marriage Project, Barbara Dafoe Whitehead and David Popenoe provide a brief description of the period of social disruption that has in major ways shaped the view of marriage held by these young people now choosing cohabitation:

Although the long-term trend in divorce has been upward since colonial times, the divorce rate was level for about two decades after World War II during the period of high fertility known as the baby boom. By the middle of the 1960s, however, the incidence of divorce started to increase and it *more than doubled over the next fifteen years* to reach an historical high point in the early 1980s. Since then the divorce rate has modestly declined, a trend described by many experts as "leveling off at a high level.". . . Although a majority of divorced persons eventually remarry, the growth of divorce has led to a steep increase in the percentage of all adults who are currently divorced. . . . *This percentage, which was only 1.8 percent for males and 2.6 percent for females in 1960, quadrupled by the year 2000.* The percentage of divorced is higher for females than for males primarily because divorced men are more likely to remarry than divorced women. Also, among those who do remarry, men generally do so sooner than women. Overall, the chances remain very high—between 40 and 45 percent—that a marriage started today will end in divorce.[7]

It is difficult to translate this statistical description of the marital firestorm into human terms, but consider the following passionate letter from a young woman, mother of a baby fathered by the man with whom she is cohabiting:

As the unmarried mother of a new baby, I am the object of much indignant scrutiny among the older generations, who seem to have conveniently forgotten the last thirty years, in which almost everyone I know has been emotionally pummeled in some way by divorce.

As my boyfriend asked at a recent family gathering, while playing a board game in which you have to prompt the other players to supply a particular word, "What must you do before you get married?" The answer, of course: "get divorced." My father and his wife thought this was hilarious. And yet aging Boomers seem shocked and befuddled that someone would choose to avoid the whole swampy mess of broken vows and failed traditions that they've left in their wake.

People over forty flinched with disdain when I first announced my pregnancy. "Oh," they would exclaim, barely masking their disapproval. "And . . . what do your parents think?" They struggled to understand my lack of panic. "Are you going to keep it?" they asked, wide-eyed.

As if the '60s, '70s, and '80s never happened. As if at least one-third of marriages don't fail. As if everyone in my family and my boyfriend's family, grandparents included, hadn't broken their marriage vows. At least once. . . .

But the fact that my parents divorced well—and they really did—doesn't grant them immunity from their actions. The fact that my uncles and aunts and grandparents and family friends felt they had absolutely no choice other than to divorce doesn't change the outcome. They still got divorced, all of them. They still showed my generation, by example and by forcing us to go along with their example, that marriage was something easily and amicably exited from.

Marriage, they said, was not that big of a deal. Premarital sex is fine. (Or at least that's what they implied when they presented their boyfriends and girlfriends at the breakfast table—before we were even out of high school.) Families, they said, do not need to stay together if things become too boring. . . .

I am not whining about or regretting the events of the last three decades. When my parents divorced in the late '70s, we children went along with it like troupers. When they started bringing home boyfriends and girlfriends in the '80s, we ultimately accepted these new people into our family. Sometimes, the new people went away. And we dealt with the divorces and separations all over again. And accepted the new people all over again. Fine. Exhausting, but fine.

It's a wonder we 18- to 35-year-olds even have the energy to date. . . . But for myself, the scattered, patchwork concept of family I grew up with has only increased my quest for commitment. I've seen firsthand the pain and futility of divorce culture and I don't intend to relive it, or to drag my children through the nightmare of watching their parents flirt with strangers. . . .

My generation would just as soon steer clear of the fatuous feel-good mess of getting divorced and remarried. The tradition that was passed down to us—in which divorce is a logical and expected conclusion to a marriage—is one we would just as soon pass by. . . . Of course marriage is on the decline. But don't blame us.[8]

This young woman is painfully representative of many in this generation, and it is not only young women who feel this way. The 2002 report of the National Marriage Project explored the attitudes of young, not-yet-married men on the timing of marriage. These men are reluctant to commit to marriage in their early adult years for a number of reasons, among them their desire to avoid divorce.[9] However skewed the underlying assumptions may be, their reasoning is clear. How do you avoid divorce? Simple—do not get married.

While Christians may assume that they are immune to the fallout from the divorce culture, this is not so. In the story of the cohabiting young Christian couple reported earlier, the young man cited fear of divorce as one reason for cohabiting, even though both he and his companion came from families with intact, stable marriages. Many of their friends did not, however. These two young Christians experienced the impact of the divorce culture outside the faith community through relationships with friends, and, equally powerfully, through the world they observed in movies, television, and novels.

Further, Christians have been reluctant to acknowledge the degree to which divorce among Christians has impacted families within the church. It is a rare family for whom holiday gatherings do not include tangible evidence of the fallout from the divorce culture in some form—single parents, "new" spouses, cohabiting partners, step-grandchildren. There is a sense of unacknowledged loss. Despite the anger and pain that characterized former relationships and the conflict that may have marked their departure, those who have gone are not forgotten. Life goes on after divorce, but often to people's surprise, so does the persistence of attachment to those who were once part of the family.

After years of clinical experience, the distinguished family therapist Carl Whitaker described these continuing connections in these words:

> The craziest thing about marriage is that one cannot get divorced. We just do not seem to make it out of intimate relationships. It is obviously possible to divide up property and to decide not to live together any more, but it is impossible to go back to being single. Marriage is like a stew that has irreversible and irrevocable characteristics that the parts cannot be rid of. Divorce is leaving part of the self behind, like the rabbit who escapes the trap by gnawing one leg off.[10]

For children, as for the divorcing parents, the effects of divorce are painful and injurious, and these effects do not automatically vanish with time. Many children develop the resilience and ability to deal with the injury in positive, productive ways, but the scars that result from the disruption remain.

In the early 1970s the underlying assumption of the divorce culture was an optimistic denial both of injury and its long-term effects. Divorce was regarded as a brief, intense crisis from which men, women, and children could and would recover relatively quickly and get on with their new lives.[11] Everybody will be better, the mantra ran, when the unhappy marriage is dissolved. But divorce does not make everything better for everybody, despite the culture's wishful thinking, and the biggest losers, hands down, are the children.[12] Divorce has lasting negative effects on children that extend into adulthood.[13] Divorce doesn't go away.

Certainly no two families come to the crisis of divorce with the same strength or resiliency or with the same financial, emotional, or spiritual resources. Many complex variables affect both the ways in which children deal with divorce and their ability to recover from it as adults. Despite the resiliency and resources that enable many children to manage their parents' divorce without overt evidence of incapacitating trauma, none survive the experience untouched. John's story, recounted by Judith Wallerstein, demonstrates the struggle of the resilient child.

> When six-year-old John came to our center shortly after his parents' divorce, he would only mumble, "I don't know." He would not answer questions; he played games instead. First John hunted all over the playroom for the baby dolls. When he found a good number of them, he stood the baby dolls firmly on their feet and placed the miniature tables, chairs, beds, and eventually

all the playhouse furniture on their heads. John looked at me, satisfied. The babies were supporting a great deal on their heads. Then, wordlessly, he placed all the mother dolls and father dolls in precarious positions on the steep roof of the dollhouse. As a father doll slid off the roof, John caught him and, looking up at me, said, "He might die." Soon all the mother and father dolls began sliding off the roof. John caught them gently, one by one, saving each from falling to the ground.

"Are the babies the strongest?" I asked.

"Yes," John shouted excitedly. "The babies are holding up the world."[14]

And for some children with less strength and resilience than John (and with less adult resources to help), the problems associated with their parents' divorce can be serious. E. Mavis Heatherington, together with writer John Kelly, report that 20–25 percent of children of divorce suffer serious adaptive difficulties compared to just 10 percent from intact families.[15] Divorce does have negative effects on children, and for some children (although not all) it appears to increase significantly their risk of serious, lifelong problems. Further, life after divorce is not simple, as Heatherington and Kelly report. After six years, a quarter of the children of divorce see their noncustodial father once a year or less. Most stepfathers give up the struggle to connect with resisting stepchildren after two years.

People who as children of divorce experienced serious adaptive difficulties, as cited by Heatherington, are not the only ones who are defenders of cohabitation. Often children whose strength and resilience enabled them to avoid overt social and emotional trauma take refuge in cohabitation when they become adults.

Larissa Phillips, whose letter to the editor in the web-based journal *Salon* was quoted earlier, appears to be one of those resilient children. Now as a young adult she is a partner in a committed relationship, and the mother of a welcome new baby. She has a good job and has, with her partner, qualified for a mortgage. She is relationally connected to her birth family and, in adult retrospect, considers both of her parents to have "divorced well." By conventional measures she would *not* be considered part of the group who suffer serious adaptive problems. But listen again to the passion that reflects her old pain:

I am not whining about or regretting the events of the last three decades. When my parents divorced in the late '70s, we children went along with it like troupers. When they started bringing home boyfriends and girlfriends in the '80s, we ultimately accepted these new people into our family. Sometimes, the new people went away. And we dealt with the divorces and separations

all over again. And accepted the new people all over again. Fine. Exhausting, but fine.

It's a wonder we 18- to 35-year-olds even have the energy to date. (And
maybe some of us don't.) But for myself, the scattered, patchwork concept
of family I grew up with has only increased my quest for commitment. I've
seen firsthand the pain and futility of divorce culture and I don't intend to
relive it, or to drag my children through the nightmare of watching their
parents flirt with strangers. . . . My generation would just as soon steer clear
of the fatuous, feel-good mess of getting divorced and remarried. The tradition that was passed down to us—in which divorce is a logical and expected
conclusion to marriage—is one we would just as soon pass by.[16]

This is from a young woman who would qualify as a successful survivor
of divorce in a family in which parents "divorced well." Many, like Larissa,
survived, but their memories of their family's divorce make marriage seem
too great a risk to take.[17] At some basic points, couples who choose cohabitation have a more realistic idea about the true nature of marriage than
do many of their friends who blithely assume that a state-issued license,
"love" (however they define it), and an official clergy prayer will carry
them through. It won't. These couples are right. Marriage can (and often
does) fail. And they are right about the results of failure. When marriages
fail, the consequences are destructive, lifelong, and intergenerational.

Cohabitation and the Loss of Personal Freedom

In addition to the high risk of failure, arguments against marriage also
pivot around the issue of personal freedom. Many singles reject marriage
as a life option because of the ways they see marriage interfering with
personal freedom. One study of couples living together asked the couples
to speculate how their lives together would be different if they married.
On other items in the study, couples thought life would stay about the
same, but on this item they saw marriage interfering significantly with
"the freedom to do what you want."[18]

Again at some basic level this generation is dead right. Marriage does
constrict personal freedom, and the restraints marriage imposes are not
trivial. These restraints result in true loss of personal freedom at levels that
impact personhood. They limit significant options for life choices. Furthermore, this loss of freedom is an enduring loss, continuing throughout the
life of the marriage. Christians know that there are rich gains—emotional,

spiritual, sexual—which more than compensate these freely chosen limitations, but that does not negate the reality of the loss.

His Constricted Freedom

Marriage is often described as a ball and chain. A wedding is the time when a couple ties the knot. (Who can run free when "tied" to another? A local cynic described marriage as a three-legged race with your worst enemy.) Marriage is commonly pictured as the last move in a sneaky contest between the man's effort to retain his freedom and the woman's scheme to acquire a mate. In this script, sex is the none-too-subtle bait the woman offers to reward the man for losing the contest.[19] "She let him chase her until she caught him," the old joke runs. Hunting motifs still run through descriptions of the courtship process. She "caught" him, she "hooked" him, or she "landed a man" as though a mate were a fish to be pulled to shore on some matrimonial beach. "He's a good catch," mothers once said; "he'll be a good provider."[20]

Bachelors' dinners were often bawdy celebrations of the groom's last night of "freedom." His ring on her finger signified his loss of freedom to relate openly to other women sexually and to come and go as he chose without accountability to anyone. "Have to be home? Have to call and let her know where you are?" jokes the footloose crowd with a barb. And perhaps worse, his freedom to spend money solely at his discretion becomes limited.

"Listen," the man complains to the marriage therapist, "she takes my check and all I get is an allowance. I just got tired of it—that's all. I work hard. I deserve the boat (bike? fishing gear? car?) I bought. She just doesn't understand."

"And where," the woman counters, "is the money to pay the orthodontist's bill and make the house payment? And when do I get to go shopping? My paycheck went for the grocery bill and to fill up the car."

Although these stereotypes present a distorted picture, the underlying issue is real. Marriage does constrict personal freedom, sexually, economically, and in the daily activities of life.

Her Constricted Freedom

Stereotypically the loss of freedom in marriage is presented primarily as the experience of the man—his loss of sexual, economic, and emotional freedom. This picture is not accurate; women's loss of freedom is no less real. It is, however, less recognized in part because it has traditionally been believed that freedom is less important to women (after all, they are dependent and need a man to take care of them). Furthermore, the bargain struck in marriage has traditionally been viewed as an advantage for a woman. Her loss of personal freedom was viewed as balanced by the economic security that marriage brought her and her children. Women's loss of freedom was also overlooked because until recent decades alternatives to marriage for women were limited and socially unattractive. If a woman did not marry, what could she do?

Young women in the present post-Boomer generations struggle with the "opportunity costs" of marriage in ways that did not impact their grandmothers. The corporate culture intensifies the competing claims of work and family in ways particularly difficult for women. Recently a young woman who has chosen to marry remarked realistically (though a bit wistfully), "No, I won't make partnership in my [law] firm. That requires sixty hours a week—sometimes more if you're the junior person in the firm and the partner is in court. We cannot build a decent family life if I'm keeping hours like that. Family has a high priority for me. The cost of partnership is too high if it requires injury to my family." Options now available to women have multiplied, but with the increase in opportunity has come growing tension between work responsibilities and the accompanying augmented cost to marriage and family. As a result, personal freedom is becoming an issue for women as it has been for men.

Also in significant ways, when women marry, they lose control over their own body. In past decades, a married woman's physical safety was subject to her husband's concern for her well-being. Through marriage the woman's body was commonly assumed to have become the man's possession so that legally the kind and frequency of sexual intercourse was determined by the man's choice and physical strength. Until recently in the majority of courts, the concept of marital rape was thought to be a self-contradicting term. How could a man rape a woman who was his wife? And whose business was it anyway if she had a bruised face or a broken rib? She was his wife, and how he behaved physically with his wife was his own affair. Fortunately, most men marry women whom they love and they are concerned for their wife's well-being and safety.

The church, particularly its evangelical arm, continues to demonstrate a shameful disregard for women's safety in marriage.[21] The scandal of domestic violence in the church, with its dark sexual shadow, has been the terrible secret of far greater numbers of Christian marriages than even now the church is willing to acknowledge. There is some improvement in safety for women within marriage, but it is painfully slow in coming. Today the law is more willing to intervene in instances where the woman's physical safety is at risk, but that intervention is often delayed and ineffective. Despite small steps toward change, present practice as well as that of the recent past provide a basis for the concern of young women who explore alternatives to marriage. Marriage continues to be a risky proposition in more than one way for women.

It is important to note, however, that cohabitation as such does not solve the problem of violence between men and women. Violence occurs within cohabiting relationships as well as within marriage. Efforts to establish a reliable comparison between the frequency of violence between cohabiting couples and married couples have proven to be difficult. Christians sometimes point to those studies that indicate higher levels of violence in cohabiting relationships than in marriage as an argument for marriage.[22] Caution is needed at this point, however. Serious researchers have been reluctant to trust these results completely because in complex ways a woman's need to ensure her safety can unwittingly confuse cause and effect in these studies. Thinking through a hypothetical woman's dilemma makes this problem clear. Suppose that the woman finds herself cohabiting with a man who demonstrates a tendency toward violence. The man may be willing (perhaps eager) to marry, but at this point the woman may choose cohabitation over marriage, reasoning that, by staying in a cohabiting relationship rather than marrying, she can more easily (and safely) leave if this becomes necessary. In this scenario, cohabitation is the *result* of the violence, *not* the *cause;* the woman chooses cohabitation over marriage because of the violence. Women appear, sensibly, more likely to marry men they believe to be safe. As a result more cohabiting men than married men may be identified as violent, but these numbers may be the result of women's choice limiting marriage to safe men rather than proof that the cohabiting relationship itself produces violence.[23] But the overriding point remains. Neither cohabitation nor marriage as a social institution prevents or causes domestic violence. Violence is an issue of the human heart.

Their Constricted Freedom

A couple's ability to control their fertility obviously has the potential to compromise the freedom of both men and women. The risk, however, is uneven. Pregnancy and child care impact women's lives in ways that are dramatically different from the impact of these concerns on men. Contrary to more radical feminist literature, however, men and women have understood the unevenness of the risk and together have sought to control their fertility for the mutual benefit of both.[24] Technology has increased the degree to which fertility control is now possible, and new laws have made contraceptive information and products readily available.[25] However, control of pregnancy continues to remain an uncertain process. And pregnancy, whether by mutual choice or as the result of contraceptive failure (or carelessness), has differing implications for the woman and the man.

While pregnancy entails greater potential loss of freedom for the woman than for the man, the significant issue in cohabitation does not involve the freedom of either the man or the woman; it is the well-being of the child. There are no currently available studies that describe conclusively the impact of cohabitation on children. It appears probable, however, that those instances of cohabitation in which adults shift partners from time to time will produce children much like the children of the divorce culture; they will survive with courage and resilience, but the impact of parental choices will have lifelong consequences. At the present time there are only sketchy, poorly defined legal precedents to govern adult responsibility for children born into cohabiting partnerships. As in the divorce culture, it appears that in the cohabitation culture, while the structure may seem to benefit some adults in the short run, in the long run the children appear to be the losers, hands down.

Loss of Civil Rights

In the past, a major argument supporting cohabitation was the loss of civil rights that marriage imposed on women. At twenty-six years of age, Gloria Steinem rejected the value of men (and, by direct implication, marriage). However, at age sixty-six she chose to marry, to the consternation of a number of colleagues in the women's movement. When a reporter chided her for abandoning her feminist principles in favor of marriage, Steinem pointed out that among the things that had changed over the years was the degree to which women are now able to retain their civil rights within marriage: "If I had got married when I was supposed to have in my twenties, I would have lost almost all my civil rights. I wouldn't have had my own name, my own legal residence, my own credit rating. I would have had to get a husband to sign off on a bank loan, or starting a business [sic]. It's changed profoundly."[26] As Steinem pointed out, while changes in civil rights are very recent, they have occurred. For the most part, the advantage of cohabitation over marriage in terms of preserving women's civil rights continues to shrink.

The Cost of Personal Freedom

Concern about the possible loss of personal freedom in relationships has presented the post-Boomer generations with a somewhat paradoxical dilemma. Standing as they do on the rubble of the divorce culture, they have an intuitive understanding that marriage entails a special commitment. Their scorn of the divorce culture reflects their unacknowledged belief in the permanence of marriage and their disrespect for those who do not keep that commitment. But while commitment in this context makes sense, at the same time it threatens an unbearable compromise of personal freedom. They distrust the demands of marriage; it sets the bar too high; they fear that perhaps they too will fail to keep the commitment it requires. They distrust the "rules" of marriage, suspecting that marriage by definition is a destroyer of personal freedom. Cohabitation looks like a logical accommodation, allowing them pragmatic allegiance to both of these conflicting values—commitment and its call for permanence, and personal freedom as the highest form of individual good. But this attempted accommodation has its own emotional cost.

The music of the past encodes this struggle.[27] Aging Boomers remember Glen Campbell's performance of "Gentle on My Mind"—Campbell, sitting alone on the empty stage, his voice wedding the telling lyrics with the driven complex rhythms of his lonely guitar.

> It's knowing that your door is always open
>   And your path is free to walk
> That makes me tend to leave my sleeping bag
> Rolled up and stashed behind your couch
>   And it's knowing I'm not shackled
>   By forgotten words and bonds
> And the ink stains that have dried upon some line
>   That keeps you in the back roads
>   By the rivers of my mem'ry
> That keeps you ever gentle on my mind.[28]

In the ballad, the roots of the relationship were deep. The singer describes his wandering—the back roads, the railroad tracks, the junkyards, and the wheat fields, his relationships with other women, and yet, always, as he travels, her haunting presence "by the rivers of my mem'ry . . . ever gentle on my mind." Despite the loneliness, the ballad insists that the journey is necessary. Freedom trumps commitment, whatever the pain of relational loss.

John Denver's "Leavin' on a Jet Plane" similarly echoed the relational dilemma:

> All my bags are packed, I'm ready to go,
> I'm standing here, outside your door
> I hate to wake you up to say goodbye.
> But the dawn is breakin', it's early morn',
> The taxi's waitin', he's blowin' his horn,
> Already I'm so lonesome I could die.

In Denver's lyrics there is acknowledgment of the fundamental unresolved conflict:

> There's so many times I've let you down
> So many times, I've played around,
> I tell you now, they don't mean a thing.
> Ev'ry place I go, I think of you;
> Ev'ry song I sing, I sing for you.
> When I come back, I'll bring your wedding ring.
>
> So kiss me and smile for me,
> Tell me that you'll wait for me,
> Hold me like you'll never let me go.
> 'Cos I'm leavin' on a jet plane,
> Don't know when I'll be back again,
> Oh, babe, I hate to go.[29]

Again, in Denver's lyrics, freedom to go trumps the relational pain of parting. Freedom to go carries the cost of going if for no other reason than to demonstrate that the ties that connect are not the ties that bind.

For the majority of the present successors to the Boomer generation, cohabitation permits an uncertain staying, while it ensures presumably an open door if/when it comes time to leave. Post-Boomers may not know Denver's lyrics, but they understand the message that he sang.

Cohabitation and the Moral Issues of Commitment

Those who choose to cohabit, remaining unmarried but together, object to others calling their choice immoral. They believe that cohabitation can be a morally legitimate alternative to marriage. Christians will disagree, but it is only fair to do so thoughtfully, not out of hand.

Postmodern Morality

To understand current thinking about cohabitation, Christians need to remember that the majority of cohabiting couples define morality in a postmodern context. The postmodern position does not grant any outside authority the right to overrule an individual's choices. Consequently in postmodern thinking, to be moral requires only that an individual faithfully do that which personally seems right to him or her. Moral behavior, by definition, is that which is congruent with an individual's subjective sense of what is right and wrong for that specific individual. Reflecting these basic premises of postmodern thinking, most cohabiting couples believe that if they feel or think that their choice is moral *for them*, then it *is* moral *for them*.

In postmodern thinking, Christians, like everyone else, have moral authority only in their own lives; they have no legitimate basis for questioning the standards of others. To do so is hypocritical—that is, Christians themselves are acting immorally (they "judge" others) at the same time they are charging others with immoral behavior (cohabitation). Since morality in the postmodern world requires tolerance of another's definition of *right*, Christians sometimes find to their surprise that their rejection of cohabitation has earned them the reputation of the person willing to pull a splinter from his neighbor's eye while neglecting the plank in his own.

Many cohabiting couples approach the moral issue pragmatically, comparing the behaviors of people who are married with those who cohabit. Their argument focuses on the fact that marriage does not necessarily produce moral behavior in those who choose to marry. Unfortunately, this is so. Marriage licenses are not moral magic, and marriage does not automatically bring into being a faithful, permanent relationship. It does not prevent neglect or abuse, nor does it cure selfishness. A marriage license does not necessarily produce moral people who are loving, responsible, committed, and skillful in resolving the inevitable conflicts that occur in the context of intimate daily living. When unprincipled, irresponsible people marry, they have an unprincipled, irresponsible marriage. Cohabiting couples arguing from a pragmatic basis are right. A couple's moral strength must be rooted in something other than a license issued by the clerk of a civil court.

If carried further, the argument grows philosophically somewhat complicated at this point. If marrying cannot make people moral, can cohabitation make them immoral? If a cohabiting couple demonstrates commitment to each other, if they are just, honest, and kind in their interaction with each other, are they not moral? And in comparison to some of the worst-case scenarios in marriage, are not some instances of cohabitation arguably more moral than some marriages? Many cohabiting couples argue on this pragmatic basis that cohabitation does not inevitably contribute to the erosion of civil society any more than marriage inevitably contributes to the common good.

Christians are well advised to enter the dialogue cautiously. A specific marriage may not in fact contribute to the common good; this does not mean that marriage as a social institution does not do so. A specific instance of cohabitation may not in fact erode society; this does not mean that cohabitation in lieu of marriage as a social institution does not do so. And it is fair to argue that, while the commitment that by definition is presumed to accompany marriage cannot automatically produce moral people, such commitment does strengthen the moral choices of those who in good faith choose marriage as a lifelong faithful partnership.

The postmodern culture and the Christian come closer to consensus at this point. While disagreeing about the value of marriage as an institution, Christians, with no reservations, can agree with the postmodernist about one central point. Morality is truly a matter of the individual heart. No known social institution—marriage or cohabitation—can prevent human sinfulness in king or commoner. Christians believe that only God can transform the human heart. Congruent with postmodern values, Christians believe that the good news of the gospel *is* an individual matter, and any person who becomes relationally connected to Christ receives the power to behave morally in radically new ways that will astonish a cynical age. In the context of that power, permanent faithful partnership is possible.

Legal issues surrounding cohabitation are presently in flux. In most states cohabitation is legal between same-sex partners, and the recent Supreme Court decision in *Lawrence v. State of Texas* found a constitutional right to homosexual cohabitation for the petitioners (John Geddes Lawrence and Tyron Garner). For the most part, couples are not legally required to have a license to live together. It can no longer be argued simplistically that cohabitation is immoral because it is illegal, something similar to hunting without a license.

However, all societies set some limitations on the practice of the sex act, sometimes in the forms of social taboos and customs, sometimes as civil laws.[30] The present debate about cohabitation and marriage entails a change in the present culture's regulation of sexual behavior and the privileges and obligations that go with this powerful expression of human emotion. In our current culture the balance of freedom and responsibility for the sake of social well-being is one of the pressing challenges of the day.[31] It is far from resolved.

The Christian's Dilemma

Out of the biblical principle that God ordained civil government for the common good (Rom. 13:1–2), Christians support society's right, need, and obligation to regulate the behavior of its citizens for the well-being of the whole. This, of course, includes the legitimate authority of the state to regulate marriage. Christians retain one essential caveat, however. The state may regulate for the common good *as long as such regulation does not require the Christian to act in a manner proscribed by Scripture.*

In the context of culturally changing values, however, this is not the pressing issue. The state may choose (as indeed it has chosen in *Lawrence v. Texas*) to approve cohabitation, although Christians disagree with this ruling on scriptural grounds. Thankfully, this decision does not require Christians to approve cohabitation or to abandon marriage themselves in favor of cohabitation. Nevertheless, the decision, along with others, does pose a different kind of dilemma for Christians. As citizens in a democracy and an increasingly pluralist society, to what degree should Christians lobby for marriage to be required of all couples, including those who are not confessing Christians? What biblical principles should inform the answer to this and similar questions?

For the Christian, the moral imperative of marriage does not rest principally on a civil regulation. It rests rather on a scriptural foundation. Christians are called to marriage as the people of God. Marriage is the God-established structure that provides for faithful, lifelong partnership between a man and a woman and the establishment of an individual family within the larger family of God. Also marriage demonstrates God's relationship with his people. In the present culture, love and marriage may no longer go together like a horse and carriage, but they still do for Christians, who marry in response to God's direction for his people in all cultures everywhere for all time. And Christians marry under state license because *in this culture at this time this is how marriage is legally defined*, and, as Christians, they are biblically obligated to concur with state regulations, unless such regulations call for scripturally proscribed behaviors.

Walking a biblically faithful line in a pluralist culture is not easy. In such a culture, not everyone is Christian or interested in Christian marriage. It is neither wise nor logical to expect a non-Christian to behave like a Christian. "Thinkest because thou art virtuous there shall be no more cakes and ale?" asked the wily old Falstaff. It was a clever question then and a thought-provoking question today as Christians face the issue of cohabitation in a post-Christian world.

Cohabitation and the Issue of Roles and Expectations

The post-Boomer generation objects to marriage because of the damage to the personal relationship they believe the roles and expectations of marriage bring. Again, although Christians may disagree, they are wise to deal forthrightly and realistically with the issues at stake.

Without question, marital roles and expectations can be a source of serious trouble. When a couple marries, each individual brings to the relationship a set of expectations, a blueprint, so to speak, specifying how the marriage is to be constructed, the tasks each partner is to perform, the contributions each is to make, and the satisfactions each is to receive. People commonly enter marriage with a blissful ignorance of their partner's blueprint (or their own for that matter). In spite of all those courtship hours "just talking," couples rarely know each other or themselves as well as they think they do. As life together proceeds, these expectations collide with reality and result inevitably in some surprises, including some unromantic and decidedly uncomfortable moments. "Getting to know you, getting to know all about you" is not limited to courtship; it is a lifelong process.

In the process of learning to know one another, couples discover that if love is not blind, it at least bends things to an odd angle. Differences that seemed insignificant in courtship can become major barriers in marriage. Behaviors that were "charming idiosyncrasies" before marriage become peace-destroying irritants in the daily routines of married life.

It is not wise for Christians to enter the argument for marriage by attempting to market marriage as being less difficult than it is. Marriage requires that individuals learn, day in and day out, how to walk together side by side. Couples discover, usually to their astonishment, that this is much more difficult than they anticipated, despite the love they share. Walking side by side in peaceful cooperation inevitably requires changes in the expectations each individual brought to the marriage and a willingness to make practical accommodation to the reality of life together. Pepper Schwartz quotes a husband who had been married sixteen years:

> I started out pretty traditional. But over the years it made sense to change. We both work, and so we had to help each other with the kids. . . . And we worked together at church, and we both went whole hog into the peace program. So that got shared. I don't know. You can't design these things. You play fair, and you do what needs doing, and pretty soon you find the old ways don't work and the new ways do.[32]

But not all couples negotiate these changes with fairness, consideration, and common sense. Resistance to change is not unusual. In extreme instances, changing expectations and roles can seem to one or both partners morally wrong and emotionally dangerous, however sensible the alternatives may appear. The struggle to work out patterns of responsibility and power in marriage can be and often is the rock on which the relationship founders.

Observing this, cohabiting couples vote against marriage because they believe that marriage by definition results in a husband-wife blueprint that is unlikely to succeed and difficult to change. And they do not want to deal with the pain of divorce. They argue, "Divorce is destructive. Avoid it. Don't get married." And in a parallel way they argue, "Expectations and roles prescribed by marriage are destructive. Avoid them. Don't get married."

While Christians disagree with cohabitation as the solution, it is important to understand the way in which the ordinary problems of marital adjustment, significant in themselves, are being increased by current patterns of social change. In any time of change it is hard to be clear about essentials—what must be left behind and what is necessary to pack up and take along despite the inconvenience or difficulty.[33] Many cohabiters (including those over sixty) say that marriage itself is a legitimate "leave behind," arguing that *marriage as an institution shapes destructively the negotiation of a workable blueprint for the relationship between men and women.*[34] The argument runs this way: It is not enough for a married couple to figure out a blueprint that works for them as a *man* and as a *woman;* as a married couple they must work out a blueprint for the relationship as *man/husband* and *woman/wife.* This generation argues that there is baggage attached to the husband/wife roles that interferes with a good man/woman relationship. They advise: Don't run the risk of ruining the relationship by marrying. Make the relationship work on the basis of the negotiated relationship itself rather than the straitjacket prescription dictated by old roles from an irrelevant past.

In their view, marriage brings relational risk even after a couple has lived together successfully: "It seems that once the marriage contract was official, we began to expect each other to perform the roles of husband and wife rather than two people just wanting to love and live with each other. We didn't think that would happen to us."[35]

Do people imagine this alleged bad effect that marriage roles have on couple relationships? How valid is this charge in the case against marriage? This is an impossible question to answer scientifically.[36] There are some studies, however, that point to a negative influence of the husband/wife roles. The effect of such roles can be seen, for example, in studies examining household work in two-career families.

In instances where the blueprint (pattern for the marriage) permits a dominant partner to control the subject partner's choices, the effect of marital roles can result in severe loss of autonomy and a resulting sense of helplessness for the subject member of the partnership. The marital rules under these conditions permit any decision by the subject partner to be overturned at will by the dominant partner who holds a role-vested right to rule. Such a prescription for marital roles is frequently coded in theological language. However proper such religiously sanctioned roles may appear to those who sanction them, their psychological impact is hurtful to the marital bond. And the intensity with which such patterns have been defended by portions of the church has increased the distrust of the cohabiting generation who conclude that marriage is not safe, particularly marriage where religion is involved.[37] "I will never marry," said an attractive young woman who was cohabiting with a young man she had known throughout her college years. "I want to have a child, but I will never marry, at least not in the church. The church is no friend to modern women."

The world of work further complicates the issue of marital roles. Women now compose well over half of the labor force. Sociologist Arlie Hochschild wondered what really went on at the end of the workday in thousands of families where both the husband and wife work outside the home.[38] She found that, overwhelmingly, it is the working wife/mother who takes on the "second shift," the additional six to eight hours of household labor and child care necessary for a family to survive. In Hochschild's study husbands shared housework equally with wives in only 20 percent of the families where both husband and wife worked. To keep marital peace many women accept this inequity without protest.

Prescribed roles can "legalize" selfishness, a selfishness legitimated by the privileges of the role ("It's not my job"). A young husband said, "In our marriage we believe that God gave the wife responsibility for the children. I know she's tired, but I'm praying for her that she'll have strength for her responsibilities." The wife's role in this case included sole responsibility for the night care of colicky twins. It is important to understand that Hochschild's study *did not prove that marital roles cause the unfair distribution of family work*. Her study did show the influence of marital roles in the inequitable distribution of household labor and child care and in the conflict couples experienced in their effort to negotiate fair solutions to problems.[39]

Theoretically the assignment of household work should be a mutually negotiated allocation by adults to adults of the necessary work to be done. Realistically it turned out to be a role-sensitive allocation negotiated on the basis of what was appropriate to *husbands* and *wives*. Hochschild found that the cost of inequitable distribution was high in forfeited health and happiness of *both* partners and often put at risk the survival of the marriage itself.

While Christians may not be pleased to face the fact, Hochschild's study can support the objection to marital roles as they are traditionally defined. In a later study Hochschild found that working parents were *not* taking advantage of "family friendly policies," such as flextime or paternity leave. Instead, parents were fleeing homes for the workplace where, despite the tensions of work, they felt more appreciated and more competent and where the emotional gratification of relationships with friends was greater than the "rewards" of home.[40] She states flatly that in the competition between work and family, work has won. The reversal in which work is "home" and home is "work" raises a couple-focused question: Does the stress at home that drives this reversal include inequitable home-labor assignments that are complicated by marital roles? Hochschild's work underscores the serious implications of the role issue in the case against marriage. Cohabiting couples ask, "If marital roles increase the difficulty of the already Herculean task of sustaining family and couple relationships against the encroaching inroads of the corporate business world, who needs marriage?"[41] It is the growing conclusion of many in the emerging generation that the impact of marital roles is negative.

There are enough academic studies of marriage to fill a very large library, basement to attic. Many of these studies are well planned and give helpful information. Some are carelessly done. A few are dangerously misleading because of distorted reporting that presents the opinions of the researcher as scientific findings. But the good studies come to a cautious conclusion that, in most cases, marriage is good for people. But most people do not base their beliefs about marriage on the conclusions of these academic studies. They consult each other. They learn from the films, theater, and music of the culture. And in ways that fuel the growing rates of cohabitation, they reason something like this: *To be together with someone is good. But who wants to be a husband or a wife? Who needs the baggage that goes with that?*[42] What we do *not* need, couples say, is one more set of nonnegotiable roles for living and relationship.[43]

Cohabitation and Marketplace Tensions

The year 1980 marked the "tipping point" when more married women were employed outside the home than within it. Whatever the unintended consequences of this massive migration of women into paid employment, it has reached a proportion that, as Jessie Bernard has noted, is not likely to be reversed.[44] In 1997, according to the United States Census report, about 60 percent of women over the age of fifteen were employed. Sixty-two percent of these employed women were mothers of preschoolers.[45] This means that in most instances, when men and women choose to marry, they must work out their marriage and family in the context of the competing reality of the impact of the workplace on both partners in the relationship. For most women this means accepting primary responsibility for the "second shift," as Arlie Hochschild has termed it, often with only erratic help from their partner. As a result of this "second shift," most working women tend to be chronically tired, chronically behind, and usually chronically frustrated because they are tired and behind. Marriage under such conditions is not a walk in the park for men or women.

When both partners in the marriage work outside the home, they must find and pay for adequate child care, especially day care that will provide for a sick child. Most corporate work environments are not yet functionally or politically "child friendly" and do not view employee absence for care of a sick child with much sympathy.[46] Inevitably the tension of managing children spills over into the marriage relationship, despite the best efforts of the marriage partners to avoid it.

Women in the workplace also come face-to-face with issues of economic injustice and workplace exploitation. In 1995 Jerry Jacobs reviewed a wide range of studies examining job discrimination.[47] He concluded that women at all levels of employment still have a long way to go before they attain true parity in the workplace. Women managers, for example, continue to trail their male counterparts in both earnings and authority.

For women in the workplace, sexual harassment is a frequent reality. Discrimination in performance evaluation is common, subtle, and difficult to document. It is even more difficult to counteract.[48] For the most part, the corporate workplace is not a worker-friendly environment for women (or for men, in the viewpoint of many). Sexual harassment, job discrimination, and the daily pressure to perform in the context of stereotyped expectations combine with the demands of the work itself to make the workplace an emotionally and physically challenging environment in unique ways for women.

But the corporate subculture is equally demanding for men. The average workweek for Americans has lengthened substantially in recent years. Joan Williams, codirector of the Gender, Work, and Family Project at the American University Law School, noted, "Factory workers in 1994 put in the highest levels of overtime ever registered. Nearly one-fourth of office workers now work forty-nine hours or more a week."[49] The increased hours are an increased expectation that an ideal worker with a half-hour commute to a "good job" will be away from home from 8 A.M. to 7 P.M. Neither marriage nor children can thrive under such conditions.

In the majority of contemporary marriages, the residue from work—the anger, anxiety, disappointment, and fatigue, along with the excitement and personal satisfaction in achievement—all spill over into the home environment and into the marriage relationship. A young attorney on the fast track to partnership in her firm put it this way: "Well, if we just live together, it's easier. When I'm flat out at the office and I come home, I just crash. Jim understands that I'm not his wife and he can't expect me to do wife things, and I don't expect it of myself either." She paused, then added, "His work is just as bad and his hours during tax season are worse. Maybe we can make it together, but I don't think we can do husband and wife."

Cohabitation and the Conflict of Shifting Roles

As women joined the labor market in unprecedented numbers, educational doors opened to women in new and exciting ways. As a result, women

could move into professional positions for which they are technically qualified but for which they have not been socialized. For example, when she
receives her degree, a woman engineer is likely to carry in her mind both a
template of instructions for being a woman and a template instructing her
how to be an engineer. Where these two templates give conflicting instructions (and there are many such points), how is she to choose what to do?
Suppose, further, that she is married and the template of instructions for
being a wife conflicts with the template for engineer and with her sense of
herself as a woman (her giftedness, for example). In such a case, work and
marriage both carry tensions not easily described or resolved, which affect
both men and women in working out roles and relationships.

As doors have opened into new experiences and possibilities, women
have received conflicting messages. At one level women heard, "Go for it,
girl!" But at a darker, more subtle level women heard, "Bad girl! You are
aggressive and unfeminine! No one will love you." And for women who
were married, the shaming message often included a warning: "You will
lose your marriage. You cannot have both a career and a marriage."

These shifts in roles and conflicting messages impact daily life for both
husbands and wives. The wife of a young friend was passed over unfairly
for promotion. "What am I supposed to do?" her frustrated husband asked.
"Am I supposed to invite her to cry on my shoulder or advise her to suck
it up and get on with things? Is she my wife or one of the crew? Am I
supposed to act like a husband or a friend? And who can figure out how
to do both at the same time?"

The confusion experienced by both men and women is illustrated in the
somewhat ridiculous conflict over opening doors: "Do I open the door for
her or not? If so, when?" men ask. "She makes as much money as I do,"
one man said. "Let her open her own doors." "I open doors for women,"
another man said belligerently. "I'm a gentleman, and I'll open the door
for her whether she wants me to or not!"

"Do I let him open the door for me or not? When do I do it for myself?" women ask. "This is idiotic," one woman said,"I'm in charge of 150
employees and I can't open the door myself?" "I may be in charge of a
budget," another woman said, "but I'm still a woman and I like to have a
man open the door for me. I'll stand and wait until he does."

The issue is not the door, of course, but the new and conflicting templates for men and women at home and at work. It is not an easy time
to figure out how to be men and women together. The emerging generation reasons there are hard things at work and at home, and by avoiding

marriage they at least avoid the additional complex business of being a husband and wife.

A Practical Alternative

The present culture argues that cohabitation is a practical alternative to marriage. Cohabitation avoids the risks and trauma of divorce. It protects personal freedom. It sidesteps the tangle and restrictions of traditional marital roles. It prevents civil interference with personal decisions. And it permits a moral, committed relationship into which children can be welcomed. Cohabitation isn't the problem, the cultural argument goes. Marriage is the problem, and cohabitation is the answer, perhaps not for all, but certainly for many. And census bureau figures indicate that increasing numbers of couples agree.

Marriage has indeed fallen on hard times. But historically, marriage as an institution has been in trouble before and has survived. What may appear to be unique in our day is not as new as we may suppose.

4

The Myth
of the Victorian Ideal

*Y*es, marriage has fallen on hard times in our culture. Because this is true, it is easy for us as people of faith to wring our hands about the godless dominant culture in our nation at the beginning of the twenty-first century. The culture *is* godless, and it does *permeate* our lives from the national media to the local mall. We worry particularly about the culture's inroads into our homes, marriages, and family life. Divorce statistics for Christians are nearly the same as for the wider population. Domestic abuse statistics are alarmingly high even for churchgoing husbands and wives. We are easily convinced that the status of marriage and family life today is as bad as it gets, worse than ever before. But what we think is unique to our times is not new.

To help us put our situation into historical perspective, step back 150 years into what we know as the Victorian age (1867–1901) in North America.[1] Many people of faith today have an idealized view of the middle-class Victorian family, drawing on everything from Currier and Ives Christmas cards and Alcott's *Little Women* to more substantive knowledge of that era's child-centered family life. While many Christians today repudiate Victorian "prudery," they applaud that era's clarity about male and female marital and parental roles and have attempted to shape their concept of the Christian family by it. Yet, despite the warm glow surrounding our idealized vision of nineteenth-century family life, the reality is that many Christian Victorian men and women experienced severe strain within its confines. Great numbers rebelled against the societal pressures to conform to the prescription that historians call the Doctrine of Separate Spheres. This doctrine supported the idea that men and women possess fundamentally different natures and thus must have completely separate spheres of activity. Men have the skills and temperament for public life, whereas women are designed to be exclusively in the home.[2]

As thousands of men chose to escape the confines of nineteenth-century life for the expanding western frontiers, tens of thousands of women refused the roles middle-class society tried to force on them. Even though it was a time when spinsterhood was despised and women had few resources to support themselves, large numbers of American women chose not to marry rather than to enmesh themselves in the constraints of Victorian marriage patterns. Historian Carl Degler observed:

> The highest proportion of women who never married for any period between 1835 and the present [1980] were those born between 1860 and 1880. . . . Although some women may have felt excluded, or deeply unhappy because they could not marry, for others remaining single was a conscious choice and one that promised a richness of experience that marriage did not. For a woman to have a life of her own outside of marriage could be not only unusual but liberating. . . . For many such women marriage appeared to be a straitjacket, rather than an opportunity or an improvement in life and status as it may well have seemed in earlier and different times. Nowhere did this conflict between women's aspirations and marriage surface more obviously than among those women who were graduating from the new women's colleges and coeducational universities during the last half of the [nineteenth] century.[3]

Not only were Victorian women refusing to marry. In the United States married women were seeking divorces in unprecedented numbers, causing the divorce rate to soar in the final decades of the Victorian era. The ratio of divorces to marriages had been climbing since the 1840s, but a quarter of a century later, the number of divorces reported throughout the country in 1867 was still under ten thousand. Degler reports:

> The increase was sufficiently noticeable by the 1880s to provoke the first serious study of divorce by an agency of the United States government . . . [revealing] that between 1870 and 1880 the number of divorces had

grown one and a half times as fast as the population [at a time when immigration was very high] and that in 1886 the annual number of divorces was over 25,000. A second government report calculated that during the 1890s the number of divorces was climbing at a rate almost three times that of the increase in the population. Not surprisingly, therefore, by the opening of the 20th century, the country entered upon a full-scale debate on the meaning of the rising divorce rate.[4]

We must ask what was going on to produce so many divorces in the final decades of the Victorian era, a divorce rate exceeding that of the first sixty years of the twentieth century. In some way, the Victorian home and the Doctrine of Separate Spheres were implicated in men's ambivalence about the strictures of marriage and women's ambivalence about motherhood and vocational homemaking. In 1867 women filed two-thirds of all divorce petitions, and that figure continued to rise to nearly three-quarters of all divorces. The Christian periodical *Watchman* in 1880 puzzled over the fact that "the sex which is most interested in the security of the home and maintenance of social purity has taken the lead in the war upon both through our perverted legal machinery."[5] In those cases in which husbands filed for divorce, 80 percent of the grounds cited concerned wives' failure to live up to the ideal of the Cult of True Womanhood (in which she was to be characterized by piety, purity, submissiveness, and domesticity). Something was going on in the Victorian home that caused both men and women increasingly to turn their backs on marriage and file for divorce.

This widespread exodus from marriage set off alarm bells throughout the Christian press. In 1886 T. DeWitt Talmage, editor of *Christian Herald and Signs of Our Times*, expressed his concern in these words: "Yonder comes . . . a ship having all the evidence of tempestuous passage: salt watermark reaching to the top of the smoke-stack; . . . bulwarks knocked in; . . . main shaft broken; all the pumps working to keep from sinking. That ship is the institution of Christian marriage."[6]

John Milton Williams, writing in *Bibliotheca Sacra* in 1893, insisted:

Woman has no call to the ballot-box, but she has a sphere of her own, of amazing responsibility and importance. She is the divinely appointed guardian of the home. . . . She should more fully realize that her position . . . is the holiest, most responsible and queenlike assigned to mortals; and dismiss all ambition for anything higher, as there is nothing else here so high for mortals.[7]

Every one of the turn-of-the-century Christian periodicals carried editorials, articles, or sermons on the topic, decrying divorce as "the deadliest foe of the home" and "a monster of iniquity" that "threatens to destroy the American home." More than eight decades later, in 1987, the Danvers Statement, a document setting forth the rationale, purposes, and affirmations of the Council on Biblical Manhood and Womanhood, expressed a similar grave concern about women who forsook "vocational homemaking." This 1987 statement is a rerun of the nineteenth-century female disaffection with the domestic role.

The Victorian marriage model was no walk in the park for either men or women. This chapter examines primarily the strains created by the Doctrine of Separate Spheres for women in the nineteenth century; chapter 5 examines those strains for nineteenth-century men.

Victorian Women at College and at Work

Before 1860 few if any careers were accessible to middle-class women, except as writers or school teachers. But in spite of that reality, increasing numbers of women made the conscious choice to remain single. In 1867 Louisa Mae Alcott,[8] author of family-friendly novels, like *Little Women*, *Little Men*, and *Jo's Boys*, gave as her rationale for refusing to marry: "Liberty makes the best husband." This was particularly characteristic of those women who seized the opportunity to attend one of the new women's colleges.[9] From the 1870s through the 1910s, between 40 and 60 percent of women college graduates chose not to marry at a time when only 10 percent of all American women did not marry.[10]

Education for women was widely attacked in the popular Christian press between 1880 and 1900. Some writers argued that women's education should be limited to training for their tasks of child rearing and housekeeping. Others were concerned that a college education would alienate women from all that was "properly feminine." Even women's athletics was criticized:

[I]t is high time to . . . revolutionize or abolish college athletics for girls. That some of our women aspire to . . . mannishness is painfully evident, but we can hardly afford to facilitate this tragic transition. . . . An unsexed man, or woman, is a solecism worthy of withering contempt. Evermore may we pray to be delivered from the masculine woman and the feminine man.[11]

Some Christian writers were certain that education for women threatened the Christian faith. According to an article in *Truth, or Testimony for Christ* (1888–1889), education rendered women "a ready prey to the wiles of the devil." The *Western Recorder* concluded that the education of women was an offense before God. By the end of World War I, the concern was deep and widespread. An editorial in *King's Business* cried out, "WANTED—MORE MOTHERS. We are short on homes, *real* homes. We are short on mothers, *real* mothers. . . . God designed woman as the *homemaker*, but somehow she seems to have gotten side-tracked."[12]

What was going on? While the college-educated woman captured Christian media attention, growing numbers of other women in blue-collar, clerical, and service occupations entered the workforce. By 1890, 19 percent of women in the United States over age sixteen were in the labor force, with that number steadily rising over the next three decades. Earlier, most working women were from new immigrant populations or from working-class families that needed the second income to survive. But by the 1890s middle-class married women began moving into the labor force in large numbers.

The Doctrine of Separate Spheres had turned women into consumers, instead of producers of income, and it took more income to satisfy the growing consumer appetite. Furthermore, the consumer role, without the self-esteem gained from being part of income production, was unsatisfying for many women. At the same time, the professions were opening up for educated women so that the nature of work available to them changed from clerical and domestic service to more varied options. Growing numbers of professional women with graduate degrees entered the labor market. This too was viewed with alarm by the Christian press.

How could this widespread revolt against marriage have taken place in an idyllic period like the Victorian era? Its Doctrine of Separate Spheres remains for many Christians today the biblical model for domestic marital bliss, and most find it inconceivable that the era could have been characterized by the kind of profound gender-based antagonisms that would lead so many people out of marriage.

Ideas Have Consequences

To understand the roots of this animosity, step back a hundred years before the Victorian era. In the eighteenth century, before the American colonies became the United States, at least six new ideas were taking root in people's minds and were altering perceptions of what it meant to be male or female.

Independence of the Individual

The first new idea was a change in the way both men and women thought about themselves in relation to the group. While the colonies in the seventeenth century had aimed to create societies based on economic and personal *inter*dependence, Americans throughout the colonies in the eighteenth century were talking about John Locke's "natural rights" philosophy and the focus on the individual, rather than on the common good of the community. Some of Locke's ideas eventually made their way into the American Declaration of Independence—ideas like the inalienable rights of man to life, liberty, and the pursuit of happiness, or the notion that all men were created equal. The focus on *inter*dependence shifted to a focus on *in*dependence. This shift in how men and women thought about themselves in relation to the group is with us today, as documented in chapters 2 and 3.

Changing Role Relationships

A second new idea altering men's and women's perception of what it meant to be male or female came from changing role relationships in the emerging Industrial Revolution. Earlier, wives throughout the seventeenth century usually had a good knowledge of their husband's business and often took over running the business or assuming an appointed office when their husband died. For example, in 1710 Ariante Dow was appointed to succeed her husband as sanitation commissioner of New York. Colonial papers abounded with notices that the widow of a particular shopkeeper or craftsman would continue to operate the business as usual.

Women in colonial America had important roles as "deputy husbands," which meant that a woman could shoulder male duties—anything from planting corn to managing the external affairs of the family. A deputy was a surrogate not merely a helper. The range of occupations open to women was much wider in the seventeenth century than in later centuries. Historians find records of women serving as blacksmiths, butchers, barbers, hunters, attorneys, physicians, sextons, undertakers, loggers, shipwrights, gunsmiths, pewterers, jailers, retailers, and typesetters. Women in the colonies kept taverns, ran ferries, painted houses, and operated sawmills, gristmills, and printing presses. They ground eyeglasses and managed livery stables. Every kind of work done by men was done, at least occasionally, by women.[13]

For the most part the settlers coming from Europe to the New World lived very sparsely. Imagine a large room (fifteen by twenty feet) dominated by a huge fireplace on one wall. Along the other walls are a bed or two, a table, perhaps a chair or a bench, and several chests. In the earliest years houses consisted entirely of this single room with few furnishings. Over time, the loft, reached by ladder, became a sleeping space as well as a storage space, or a second large room was built onto the first, with a fireplace sharing the original chimney. Out back one might find a lean-to shed, providing more storage, and smaller buildings for washing, storing milk, keeping hens, or brewing cider and beer. But the main room was the center of household activity.[14]

As the eighteenth century approached, this hardscrabble life of most colonial families gradually changed. Economically the colonies were very successful in trade with Europe, and as second- and third-generation colonists had more permanent lifestyles, homes grew in size and household inventories came to include the marks of gentility—tablecloths and napkins, forks, chairs, and mirrors.[15] As the economy flourished in the eighteenth century, "the pretty gentlewoman" emerged, marking a strong difference between well-to-do city women, focused on the upkeep of their home and family, and the rural women, whose lives had changed very little from seventeenth-century modes of living. The eighteenth-century gentlewoman was much less likely to know about or help in the management of her husband's business.[16] Gradually women's work and space were separated from men's work and space, and a new construct of ideal roles began to emerge.

Revitalization of Religious Faith

The third major new idea affecting people's sense of what it meant to be male or female came out of the First Great Awakening that swept through the colonies as a revitalization of religious faith.[17] The message preached by George Whitefield, Jonathan Edwards, William and Gilbert Tennent, and others was the orthodox Calvinist message that sinful men and women were totally dependent for salvation on the mercy of a pure, all-powerful God. But there was more. Fiery revival sermons also called on people to "forsake their 'unconverted' ministers and receive assurance that they were God's children through the experience of the New Birth."

This assurance of salvation was new. Battles raged within churches and entire denominations over the challenge to clergy authority and over the evangelical approach to conversion from "the heart" rather than from "the head." Thus the First Great Awakening polarized colonists sharply along religious lines. But it did more. It encouraged women's participation, along with that of African Americans, in revival and congregational activities. On occasion, women spoke and exhorted in meetings. They voted in congregational decisions, they organized their own prayer groups, and they even initiated revivals. The First Great Awakening gave many women a first taste of active participation in some form of ministry.[18]

Politicization

A fourth new idea changed perceptions of what it meant to be male or female. Along with the men, women were politicized. As the Industrial Revolution began to take root in America and mill towns sprang up in the mid–eighteenth century, great numbers of people moved from small villages and farms to the mill towns and cities and became the new waged labor. In addition, as the frontier expanded, many people moved west. In all of the crosscurrents of Locke's "natural rights" philosophy, religious conversions that opposed former ministers and churches, and the economic eddies of the Industrial Revolution, men and women alike were caught up in revolutionary ferment. All of these changes challenged new restrictions on female behavior that had begun to predominate in the eighteenth century.

In the consumer boycotts of British goods in the 1760s and 1770s, women signed public pledges not to drink tea (a political act that shocked some observers).[19] This brought women to a new level of self-understanding as political participants. With patriot men away at war, fighting the British Loyalists, women of all classes and races ran farms and businesses, struggling together to provide for their families in the face of wartime scarcity and extreme inflation.[20] In the process, "patriot women experienced growing pride and self-respect as they learned to manage financial decisions and to act autonomously while their husbands fought the enemy."[21]

Nature and Role of Women

A fifth new idea that impacted how men and women thought about themselves came directly from the American Revolution. It raised questions about women's nature and changing roles. When the Declaration of Independence declared, "all men are created equal," the founding fathers used the word *men* literally. Their vision of the "citizen" did not include slaves, women, or propertyless men. Every statement of republican principles implicitly assumed that women were excluded.[22] Though they could not vote and lacked other civil rights, women now saw themselves as citizens of the new nation. But what did that mean for women? The solution to the problem of female citizenship was to give domesticity a political meaning by creating the idea of *republican motherhood*. Women now had a political role, that of teaching and training virtuous young citizens for the new republic. This was a civic role and an identity distinct from men's, yet a role essential to the welfare of the new nation. It directed women's new political consciousness back into the home and it spawned the sentimentalizing of domestic duties.[23] But more important, it spurred a debate about women's education and resulted in the founding of female "seminaries."[24]

As late as 1750 half of all Euro-American women in the colonies were illiterate, unable even to sign their name.[25] Schooling had been reserved primarily for sons who received it from their father. But now those fathers, because of the Industrial Revolution, worked from dawn until dusk away from home in businesses or in factories. If sons were to be prepared for further formal education, mothers had to acquire the basic skills to teach their children to read, write, and do arithmetic. Historically there had been a hostility to female learning based on the assumption that women had an inferior nature and capacity, but in the second half of the eighteenth century, Judith Sargent Murray and others argued that women should be educated, not to make them like men but to enable them to fulfill their calling as republican mothers. Historian Sara Evans notes:

> Founded and run by women, the seminaries offered curricula paralleling the studies offered by schools for boys with the omission of classical languages. They produced a new generation of literate women with a very different sense of their own capabilities. That sense of self represented an amalgam of the inward-looking individuality fostered when written culture replaces oral culture and a strong sense of identity with other women. . . . [I]t increased women's awareness of themselves as a group. Within these schools women not only discovered themselves as intelligent but they also experienced an intense community of women suffused with the ideas of women's difference and special mission.[26]

Thus the first steps were taken to provide some formal education for women.

The Industrial Revolution

The sixth new idea bringing major change to beliefs about gender roles in marriage was the Industrial Revolution. This revolution changed the way the world produced its goods—no longer primarily by craftsmen working in a shop attached to their home but now in factories away from home. It also changed society from being primarily agricultural to one in which manufacturing and industry dominated, which expanded with each new technology (such as the invention of the steam-driven machine).[27] Already the self-sufficient household of the early colonies had given way to a cash economy. Women as well as men found jobs in the new factories.[28] By 1816, for example, while the cotton textile industry employed ten thousand men and twenty-four thousand boys, it employed sixty-six thousand women. Families moving to mill towns from farms and villages often lived in company-owned housing located near the mills. They shopped at company stores and attended company-sponsored schools and churches. Although families may have improved their standard of living when they moved from farm to factory, they gave up self-sufficiency for a credit-based economy centered on the company store. Child care often became a problem. Who was at home to care for the littlest ones who were not working in the mill?

More than 90 percent of all Americans were of necessity in dual-income or multiple-income families. In fact the abuse of laborers in the factories was so monstrous in the early decades of the nineteenth century that state after state enacted child labor laws to protect young children. (Children as young as five or six earned less than a dollar a week while working fourteen-hour shifts at looms or other machines in unhealthy mills and factories.)[29]

The full-time homemaker with a husband who earned enough to cover all of the needs of the family became the mark of entry into the tiny but growing American middle class. In reality at no time in the eighteenth or nineteenth centuries did the middle class comprise more than 10 percent of the American population. While many women clung to the dream of being a full-time homemaker, a "pretty gentlewoman," for the great majority of families throughout the eighteenth and nineteenth centuries that dream remained a fantasy not a reality. The relatively few families who attained the middle class found that their hold on that status was tenuous. In the economic roller coaster of the nineteenth century, many fortunes were made and lost rapidly, and few could count on remaining in the middle class for life. This brought great strains to marriages and families living on the economic edge.

The Doctrine of Separate Spheres

"Slowly and inexorably the growth of commerce and industry was separating 'work' from home. For middle-class women this meant that marriage was no longer understood as an economic partnership."[30] It is impossible to overstate the disruption to the family caused by the Industrial Revolution. While life in the colonies on small farms or in small home-based businesses was far from easy, families worked together for the common good, and child care was never an issue. Wives and children worked alongside husbands and fathers in the fields or in the family business—blacksmithing, candle making, keeping an inn, or running a ferry. Farm families, if they owned a handloom, shared the work of spinning and weaving throughout the winter. Children were taught at a very early age to card the wool, flax, or cotton while the mother spun it into thread and the father wove it into cloth for family clothing or blankets. With the advent of the Industrial Revolution, however, the siren call of cash wages in factories drew many families to the mill towns and cities. But the price paid by those families was dear. Fathers, mothers, and children were often separated from one another, working in different places. Sons no longer saw fathers exercising their considerable skills on the farm or in the family small business. When the farms were left behind, there was little for sons to inherit. And because boys could earn their own wages in the towns and cities, the fathers lost much of their control over their sons. Thus the Industrial Revolution began the fragmentation of the family, which accelerated throughout the nineteenth century.

Out of this constellation of ideals and events emerged four major changes to the family, as documented by historian Carl Degler:

1. Marriage came to be based on affection and mutual respect between the partners. Coming out of the American Revolution, love as the basis for marriage was the purest form of individualism. It subordinated all social and group considerations to personal preference. It was the liberty to pursue happiness guaranteed by the new Constitution and Bill of Rights.[31]
2. The Doctrine of Separate Spheres made income production exclusively the husband's task and homemaking exclusively the wife's

task.[32] Evans noted: "Maleness and femaleness came to symbolize a series of oppositions characterizing these spheres. Work, as defined by men, meant the competitive, changing world of waged labor and entrepreneurship. Women's efforts in the home, though physically arduous, were no longer 'work' both because women were unpaid and because of their increasing invisibility from the perspective of men."[33]

3. Parents increasingly focused attention, energy, and resources on rearing their children. (It was in the nineteenth century that families first began celebrating birthdays.)[34]

4. Husbands and wives worked to limit the number of children they brought into the world. On the farm or in the small family business, more children provided more hands to do the work, but in a waged economy, more children meant more mouths to feed and backs to clothe with no reciprocal benefit until they became adults. Throughout the last half of the nineteenth century, the voluntary motherhood movement worked to help women limit their conceptions.[35]

Each of these changes in family life during the nineteenth century related directly to the impact of the Industrial Revolution on marriages and families. When work moved out of the home to factories, mills, or offices, a chain of consequences was set in motion that is with us today. Wives and husbands no longer worked side by side in producing what was needed for a family's survival. Sons no longer saw father at work, demonstrating skills to be passed on to them. The Doctrine of Separate Spheres was created to deal with this new state of affairs.

As early as 1792, Mary Wollstonecraft observed middle-class wives who were now merely "kept women," no longer integral in providing for their families. Instead, women were, in Wollstonecraft's words, "confined in cages like the feathered race, they have nothing to do but plume themselves, and stalk with mock majesty from perch to perch."[36] Wollstonecraft saw what many others could not see—that a new and growing middle-class economy was creating a generation of women without purpose and without choices, birds in a cage, with nothing to do but preen themselves, stalking from perch to perch. It was an apt picture of middle-class female life at that time, and it is not surprising that women came to be characterized as witless, frivolous creatures, caring only about themselves.[37]

By 1830 the Doctrine of Separate Spheres for men and women had been firmly cemented into the social structure through sermons and the plethora of women's magazines, gift annuals, and religious literature. Women's activities were increasingly confined to the care and nurture of the children and husband and the physical maintenance of the home. In that role women became the moral guardians of the family, responsible for the ethical and spiritual character of the family as well as the comfort and tranquility of the home. Men, immersed in the new capitalism, needed a sanctuary, an oasis from the competition, conflicts, and insecurities of an expanding capitalist democracy.

Historian Barbara Welter described the nineteenth-century society as an economic roller-coaster ride. Fortunes were made and lost overnight.[38] Social and economic mobility caused so much to be unstable in society that it was vital that there be a still point in a churning world. That still point was the True Woman. Her world was her home where she exhibited four cardinal virtues. She was pure, she was pious, she was domestic, and she was submissive. Without these, it did not matter what she achieved in fame or wealth. But with them, a True Woman had happiness and power. From her home such a woman performed her great task of bringing erring men back to God.[39] Home was supposed to be a cheerful place so that brothers, husbands, and sons would not go elsewhere in search of a good time.

In the home, women were not only the highest ornament of civilization, but they were to keep busy at morally uplifting tasks. A woman was expected to master every kind of needlework and have a special affinity for flowers. She could write letters or practice singing or playing a musical instrument. She could read, but she must be very careful about what she read. The nineteenth century knew that a book could ruin a girl.[40] If girls proved difficult, marriage and a family were seen as the cure.

In a sermon the Reverend Samuel Miller said of woman: She is

> counselor and friend of the husband; who makes it her daily study to lighten his cares, to soothe his sorrows, and to augment his joys; who, like a guardian angel, watches over his interests, warns him of dangers, comforts him under trials; and by her pious, assiduous and attractive deportment, constantly endeavors to render him more virtuous, more useful, more honorable, more happy. . . . She should consider nothing as trivial which could win a smile of approbation from him.[41]

The conclusion was inescapable. "Noble and sublime is the task of the American mother." But even while the women's magazines and sermons encouraged this ideal of the perfect woman, forces were at work in the nineteenth century that drove women to change and play a more creative role in society. Welter noted:

> The very "perfection" of True Womanhood . . . carried within it the seeds of its own destruction. For if woman was so very little less than the angels, she should surely take a more active part in running the world, especially since men were making a hash of things. [At the same time] real women often felt that they did not live up to the ideal of True Womanhood: some of them blamed themselves, some challenged the standard, and some tried to keep the virtues while broadening the scope of womanhood.[42]

Thus we come to the end of the nineteenth century with the highest proportion of women opting out of marriage (either by refusing to marry or by divorcing spouses) in any period between 1835 and 1980. To many women, marriage impeded or stifled the realization of their personal potential and aspirations.

Despite our idealization of the Victorian model of the family, there was severe role strain for both men and women. Ideal and reality did not mesh. Men as well as women found the shift to the Victorian model difficult. Some of the best scholarship on the development of the concept of masculinity deals with the negative impact of the Industrial Revolution on men's identity. What happened to men when they lost their central position in the family as teacher-father? What happened to their relationship to sons, daughters, and wife when their work was divorced from the home and the family could no longer see the competencies and knowledge that men brought to their work? What happened to men's self-esteem when sons no longer followed in their footsteps but chose other vocational directions? What happened to their sense of manhood when their masculinity, formerly attached to their physical strength and bravery, was challenged at a machine or a desk demanding no show of strength or bravery?

When the traditional (pre–Industrial Revolution) family structure had given way to the nineteenth-century Victorian model, husbands and fathers faced enormous crises of identity. This kinder, gentler family model left men as baffled and as uncomfortable as it left women. Some men tried to recapture what they had lost by being authoritarian in the home, but the real power base had shifted and intuitively they knew that. Some tried to recapture feelings of manhood by bringing the tactics and vocabulary of warfare into corporate life where they could fight battles and crush opponents. Competitive team sports where men could publicly display or admire physical strength and skill became important substitutes for a life they no longer lived.

A Constantinian Accommodation to the Culture

People in every age must have a stance vis-à-vis their culture. Some stand against the culture and others accommodate themselves to the culture. If we step back to colonial America, we may ask in what ways the Puritans stood against the culture or accommodated themselves to the culture. Moving into the nineteenth century, we ask in what ways the Victorians stood against the culture or accommodated themselves to the culture.

The Puritans immigrating to the New World between 1620 and 1640 purposed to create a godly society characterized by order, love for God, and love for neighbor. In the Puritan communities *order* meant hierarchical arrangements from the governor down. But ministerial tracts on family life describe a balance between subordination and mutuality in which a husband was not to demean his wife by "overstepping the bounds of his authority."[43] When Thomas Shepard decided to marry, he noted in his journal: "I had bin praying 2 yeare before that the Lord would carry me to such a place where I might have a meet yoke fellow."[44] The "meet yoke fellow" captures the meaning of Genesis 2:18—an appropriate woman who would walk side by side with him as they were yoked together.

Historian Barbara Epstein notes that women in colonial New England had more power, both legal and informal, than elsewhere, and also more power than they would hold in New England itself in the early nineteenth century.[45] Puritan society was based on *inter*dependence, with a strong sense of community accountability.

The Genesis 1:28 marriage markers of shared parenting and shared provisioning were clearly evident in the legal standing of women as "deputy husbands" as well as in structures of work within families for the common good. The Puritan venture into the New World began as a counterpoise to the culture left behind in Europe. Even the Puritan shift in the understanding of marriage as *contract* instead of *sacrament* was an effort to overturn an Old World cultural misunderstanding of biblical marriage. Historian Edmund Morgan notes: "although marriage retained a solemn religious significance, all ecclesiastical ceremonies connected with it were abandoned; and the minister was replaced by a civil magistrate, who was forbidden to join any couple unless they were 'published' according to the law."[46]

The Constantinian accommodation to the surrounding culture set in within two generations, however. As the seventeenth century gave way to the eighteenth century, one of the most striking shifts was the rapidity with which the commercial success of the colonies marginalized the churches. The nascent middle class in the growing cities produced "the pretty gentlewoman," the antithesis of the "meet yoke fellow" of an earlier day. She was not part of the production of income for the family but emerged as a consumer of the income her husband produced. Gradually men and women developed separate work in separated spaces, and the pretty gentlewoman was, in many cases, little more than a "bird, pluming itself, stalking from perch to perch."

When many women insisted on substantive roles in the new republic, the cultural response was *republican motherhood*—the producing and training of stalwart sons and daughters. With republican motherhood, the moral training of children shifted from father to mother, along with formal academic training. The shared parenting extending back to Genesis 1 and characteristic of families for millennia was replaced by the emerging Doctrine of Separate Spheres. Increasingly throughout the nineteenth century, this doctrine received strong support from clergy sermons and writings as well as in gift annuals and women's magazines. The evangelical periodical *Western Recorder* stated: "the student of nature places men in the public world of work, education and politics, and leaves the domestic realm for the woman whose frailty and spirituality make her unfit for the world of men."[47] In 1886 the popular evangelical preacher T. DeWitt Talmage stated that the spheres of men and women were so well defined and discrete that they were like "the boundary line between Italy and Switzerland. One can no more compare them than you can oxygen and hydrogen, water and gas, trees and stars."[48]

The Industrial Revolution had taken work out of the home into offices and factories, so that in middle-class families fathers spent most waking hours away from home and mothers took on the family responsibilities, which had been shared in earlier times. Rather than calling into question the economic structures that caused the splitting of the family, the church baptized the emerging Doctrine of Separate Spheres into the Christian faith in a Constantinian accommodation to the culture. The laissez-faire industrial expansion subverting the family was disturbing to a great many men. The clergy response was to allow men free rein to exercise aggressive tactics in the marketplace while emphasizing the passive virtues that women possessed. In the process they sentimentalized the Christian faith to accommodate the culture. Historian Ann Douglas observes:

> Many nineteenth century Americans in the Northeast acted every day as if they believed that economic expansion, urbanization and industrialization represented the greatest good. It is to their credit that they indirectly acknowledged that the pursuit of these "masculine" goals meant damaging, perhaps losing, another good, one they increasingly included under the "feminine" ideal. . . . The minister and the lady were appointed by their society as the champions of sensibility. They were in the position of contestants in a fixed fight: they had agreed to put on a convincing show and to lose. The fakery involved was finally crippling for all concerned.[49]

The capitulation to the culture was complete. Christian religion at the end of the nineteenth century had removed itself some distance from the Calvinism of the early colonists. Douglas notes:

> By 1875, American Protestants were more likely to define their faith in terms of family morals, civic responsibility, and above all, in terms of the social function of churchgoing. Their actual creed was usually a liberal, even a sentimental one for which [Jonathan] Edwards and his contemporaries would have felt scorn and horror. In an analogous way, Protestant churches over the same period shifted their emphasis from a primary concern with the doctrinal beliefs of their members to a preoccupation with numbers. . . . Nothing could better show the late nineteenth century Protestant Church's altered identity as an eager participant in the emerging consumer society than its obsession with popularity and its increasing disregard of intellectual issues.[50]

The biblical vision of shared parenting, shared provision, and shared accountability had been subverted by Constantinianism. Many of us have grown up believing that the Doctrine of Separate Spheres comes straight from the Bible and, if properly applied, will guarantee happiness to husbands and wives. But the historical record forces us to ask if this is true. Chapter 5 will take a second look at this model embraced by many Christians today.

5

Accommodation to the Culture

A subject often discussed in Christian circles is the dichotomy between masculinity and femininity. Scores of books, seminars, workshops, tapes, web sites, and weekend retreats offer various descriptions of maleness and femaleness. But it is possible that putting the focus on such a distinction is seriously unbiblical. At the same time, we are not the first to entertain such questions. As early as the second century C.E., the church father Origen set the terms *masculine* and *feminine* in opposition to one another, and in varying degrees men and women have been preoccupied by the issue ever since. If we as Christians in North America fail to examine our assumptions about masculinity and femininity, we may lapse into very unchristian thinking about gender and sexuality.

The classic secular study of gender perceptions by Inge Broverman[1] produced two lists in which men are characterized, in part, as "aggressive, unemotional, logical, rough, blunt, direct, ambitious, active, independent, and sloppy"; women are characterized as "unaggressive, emotional, illogical, gentle, tactful, sneaky, unambitious, passive, dependent, and neat."[2] Why would mental health professionals conclude that descriptions of a mature healthy adult man and a mature healthy adult woman were polar opposites? This study, conducted in 1970, merely reflected the persistent Doctrine of Separate Spheres that had dominated Victorian homes in the nineteenth century. The doctrine was a direct descendant of the Industrial Revolution, which had created a crisis not only for women but also for men.

Signposts of Manliness

In the last chapter we identified certain characteristics that gave men their masculine identity from ancient times. Historian Betty DeBerg summarizes three factors that helped men confirm their manliness prior to the Industrial Revolution:

1. Manliness had been identified with work, particularly work requiring great skill, physical strength, or serious risk to life and limb. Because the family was an economic unit working together for their subsistence, men daily demonstrated that skill, strength, and courage in full view of wives and children.
2. Traditional manhood also rested on bloody aggression—the hunter or warrior. Whether on the hunt or at war, men knew the camaraderie, terror, pain, and joy of battle from which women were excluded except as spoils.
3. The patriarchal family structure also supported a traditional masculine identity. A man's main role in the family was as father not as husband. The emphasis in patriarchy was on controlling sons through promised economic security passed on by the father.[3]

Chapter 4 noted that when men's work was separated from home so that wives and children could no longer witness the skill with which husbands and fathers worked, men lost what for them had been a major signpost of masculinity.[4] As work moved into offices and factories, the tasks at a desk or a machine did not require the actual skills of a hunter or warrior, nor did they provide in any meaningful way "the camaraderie, terror, pain, and joy of battle." As men moved into waged labor away from the farms or village small businesses, sons had little or nothing to inherit, and thus fathers had less control over them. The old cultural signposts had been destroyed by the Industrial Revolution.

When we turn to the nineteenth century and to the Victorian family, we find men in search of new cultural signposts to masculinity. Historian Barbara Berg noted that men in the early nineteenth century reached out for inner direction and self-awareness, which they ultimately realized through the creation of complicated theories about women. Confused and unsure of themselves, men found a foil for their own ambiguous identities through the specific and stagnant qualities they ascribed to women. . . . Women in the antebellum era formed the negative imprint of the desirable male self-portrait. Men may not have known who they were or what characteristics they had, but by insisting that woman possessed all the weak and inferior traits, they at least knew what they were not.[5]

Signposts of Gender Difference

In the nineteenth century womanhood was defined as the opposite of manhood. It was possible for someone to use any similarity between men and women to show that women should have the same privileges and opportunities that men enjoyed. Out of this need to define manhood *via negativa* came an elaborate philosophy of womanhood, encapsulated in the Doctrine of Separate Spheres.

The pre–Industrial Revolution colonial culture had acknowledged differences between men and women but also acknowledged enough similarities so that men and women had worked together in the home and in business in complementary ways. But in the new economy, men needed new measures of what it was to be a man. The Doctrine of Separate Spheres, supporting the idea that men and women possessed totally different natures, provided the way to keep women from jeopardizing this new masculine identity. The press and the clergy together reasoned that gender difference is God-ordained. But the rationale went further. Gender difference is God-ordained *and* we must do everything we can to support a strict separation of women's spheres from men's spheres.

In the nineteenth century it was widely believed that only men were equipped with the right stuff to be in the public square, because only men possessed the necessary aggressiveness and ruthless competitiveness that business required. Throughout the century, numerous printed sermons, pamphlets, and newspaper articles underscored the danger women courted if they entered the men's world of commerce or if they tried in other ways to use their brain. Charles Butler, writing in *The American Lady* in 1836, explained that women's "gay vivacity, and the quickness of imagination . . . have a tendency to lead to unsteadiness of mind . . . to trifling employment . . . [and] to repugnance to grave studies."[6] Physicians of that day reminded women that any female who spent time trying to use her mind would irreparably damage her reproductive organs, causing them to shrivel up and become useless. Even poets joined their voices to the chorus. The English poet laureate Alfred, Lord Tennyson put it this way:

> Man for the field, the woman for the heart:
> Man for the sword, and for the needle she:
> Man with the head, and woman with the heart:
> Man to command, and woman to obey;
> All else confusion.[7]

No, a woman's place at all times is by her fireside as "the angel" of the home "where she is enthroned in more glory than all beside, where she is to adorn the doctrines of God her savior in the bearing, bringing forth, training, uplifting those who are committed to her keeping."[8] Four qualities characterized the virtuous woman: She was pious, pure, domestic, and submissive. As historian Barbara Welter put it:

> If anyone, male or female, dared to tamper with the complex of virtues which made up True Womanhood, he was damned immediately as an enemy of God, of civilization and of the Republic. It was a fearful obligation, a solemn responsibility, the nineteenth-century American woman had—to uphold the pillars of the temple [of True Womanhood] with her frail white hand.[9]

Nineteenth-century rhetoric made an icon of the home as the haven from the rough world of commerce, a man's castle and a woman's domain. No longer the *locus* of work, it was now *a place of retreat from* work. And in the Doctrine of Separate Spheres the wife was crowned queen of the home. The nineteenth-century family values were clear, and the four walls of the home her husband provided circumscribed the woman's world. If she stayed in her place and remained pious, pure, domestic, and submissive, all would go well.

In the man's world, he was a captain of industry or commerce. With astuteness and diligence he could support his wife and children on a single income. Even more, he could provide plenty of domestic help for the "angel of the home." Immigrants coming to America provided a ready supply of cheap labor, and in the nineteenth-century middle-class home, servants were paid to cook, do the laundry, keep house, and tend the children. But what today's woman might think an idyllic life (lots of servants and very little to do) actually worked against the success of marriages and led directly to the sharp increase in divorces and women's refusal to marry by the end of the nineteenth century (as documented in chapter 4).

Shifting Signposts from the Puritans to the Victorians

Note what has happened over a period of two hundred years. Studies of earlier family life in colonial America support a concept of the family as one of companionship, mutuality, and a certain equality of the sexes.[10] Pre–nineteenth-century American family life is best described as an economic partnership in which the wife and children worked alongside the husband, in some cases on the same tasks; in other cases, with a division of labor by gender. The colonial home was the central locus of production for the entire society.[11]

At the same time, the fact that family members worked together for their common good does not mean that the weight of authority was evenly distributed among its members. The husband was the moral arbiter and the ultimate decision maker in the home. The marital relationship was far from egalitarian. A wife was considered, under English common law, a *feme* [sic] *covert*, i.e., she was "covered" by her husband and had no independent legal standing.[12] Yet, when her husband died, a widow had great freedom in the Dutch and Plymouth colonies to continue the family business, administer estates, make contracts, dispose of her own property, serve as guardian to a minor child, and even participate in community meetings of property owners. A single woman could sue and be sued. In colonial America the Plymouth Colony courts were explicit about the impact of women's productive role on their legal rights.[13]

In the nineteenth century, as the "ideal" for the relationship of husbands and wives shifted from an economic partnership, in which both contributed equally to the production of the necessities for family survival, to a middle-class family, in which the husband produced all of the income and the wife processed it as a consumer, there developed in many families a mutual animosity between husband and wife. A persistent theme in diaries, letters, and other historical documents is that men resented being expected to provide lifelong for a wife and their children; women resented having their lives limited to the domestic realm. Historian Barbara Epstein describes the conflict:

> Nineteenth-century men married because they wanted families, because the pressures of their lives created a need for the emotional support that marriage promised, and because, without wives, men would have had to cook their own meals, mend their own clothes, and perform countless other vital tasks for which they were ill prepared and which they would have regarded as demeaning. But although nineteenth-century men had many reasons to

marry, over the course of the century they began to show their resentment of women. Young men dreamed of going west and escaping the constraints of what they regarded as an effeminate civilization; once married, divorce was virtually impossible, but it was commonplace for men to leave their families for extended periods of "travel.". . . Domesticity contributed to male hostility toward women but was a much more important factor in female hostility toward men.[14]

These sources of animosity were obvious to see or experience. A man daily going off to work for twelve or fourteen hours, six days a week, *felt* the pressures of being the sole provider and he *felt* his growing resentment of a wife who was able to stay home every day. A woman confined within the four walls of her home daily *felt* her frustration and growing resentment of her continued confinement. Berg reports the words of one woman expressing in 1858 the sense of stagnation and misery that scarred the lives of many nineteenth-century American women:

> The greatest trial . . . is that I have nothing to do. Here I am with abundant leisure, and capable, I believe, of accomplishing some good, and yet with no object on which to expend my energies. . . . I cannot be happy without being employed. Alone as I am, my mind seems to prey upon itself until I am weary of life.[15]

A further source of animosity between men and women was less easy to see, but it eroded marital relationships significantly throughout the century. It had to do with the repudiation of the values of the other sex, values on which each one was dependent. To understand this, step back to the earlier signposts of traditional masculinity (physical strength, skill, and risk taking in his work, roles as hunter or warrior, and a patriarchal role as father and teacher in the home). With the Doctrine of Separate Spheres, men needed a new set of cultural signposts to compensate for their losses and insecurities. Historian Betty DeBerg notes:

> Men in business, who no longer knew how to demonstrate masculinity when their jobs took them to offices rather than to fields and mines, developed a new measure of manliness. These businessmen, according to Stearns, developed the idea of "business as battle, the business world as the jungle." Businessmen and captains of industry waged campaigns, fought battles, achieved victories, and risked defeat in competition with other businessmen. The world of the breadwinner was depicted as an unsavory and strenuous world in which ruthlessness and aggression were prized. Men sought to eliminate

the competition and to exploit workers in order to maximize profits, and hence, to win.[16]

The warrior motif had been transferred to the marketplace virtually intact. But its dominant ethic was diametrically opposed to the ethics inculcated into wives—ethics of care and love. Wives were dependent on husbands who had to behave in the workplace daily in ways that were counter to all that women had been taught to value. Husbands were dependent on wives for the care of the home and children, and they too experienced conflict over the clash between their provider role and the values of the home. For both men and women, this caused cognitive dissonance, a disconnect between their values and their dependencies. Historian Barbara Epstein describes the conflict this caused for both men and women:

> As long as women were required to be domestic and men to compete with one another in the outside world, no real resolution of this conflict was possible, for while male and female roles required one another, each was built on the repudiation of the other's values. Domesticity, or "femininity," required that a woman have a husband who brought home the rewards of competitive labor, and also that she reject the values such work entailed. The reverse was true for men: "masculinity" required having a "feminine" wife while rejecting "feminine" values.[17]

The Doctrine of Separate Spheres pitted men against women and women against men throughout the nineteenth century, with growing animosities. But there is more. DeBerg observed that "the stability of the economic warrior (or breadwinner) symbol depended on keeping women out of the male sphere of business, labor, politics, and government."[18] As the nineteenth century ended, women began working in far greater numbers both in factories and in new white-collar jobs. Between 1880 and 1910 the proportion of employed women increased from 14.7 percent to 24.8 percent. In the ten years between 1900 and 1910, the percentage of married women working outside the home more than doubled (from 5 to 11 percent). And there was a marked difference in the kinds of employment women sought and held. In 1870 almost 60 percent of all employed women were in domestic service, but by 1920 less than 20 percent were. The greatest increases in the number of working women took place in business and the professions—the middle-class male empire. Between 1870 and 1920 the number of women clerks and secretaries increased "a thousand times to one million." The number of women teachers went up 8 times to 645,000, and nurses and midwives rose 20 times, up to 280,000.

New technology made physical tasks in factories and shops lighter and thus more accessible to women. The number of women employed as shop assistants during that period increased 60 times to 534,000. What did this do to a masculine identity centered on keeping women out of the workplace? The first nineteenth-century signpost of masculinity (strictly maintained separate spheres for men and women) was becoming irrelevant as tens of thousands of women surged into the workforce.[19]

Sexuality for Victorian Men and Women

According to DeBerg, an important signpost of masculinity in the nineteenth century centered on male sexuality. Traditional Christian culture from the earliest centuries has portrayed woman as the sexual temptress, the one who had little control over her primal sexual urges and power. Men were warned to avoid women so they would not be seduced and brought down by them. Borrowing from Aristotle, the church fathers considered men to be creatures of the intellect and spirit and women to be creatures of the body and earth.[20]

Now in the nineteenth century this was turned upside down. Women were transformed from being sensual temptresses into "passive partners with little sexual appetite," and men became those who had unbridled and dangerous lust. Remember the four characteristics of a True Woman? She was pious, pure, domestic, and submissive. Purity became the hallmark of womanhood, and maintaining that purity was eased by the fact that it was widely believed that women did not have natural sex drives. Dr. William Acton, author of *The Functions and Disorders of the Reproductive Organs,* one of the most widely quoted books on sexuality in the English-speaking world during the mid–nineteenth century, wrote:

> The majority of women (happily for them) are not very much troubled with sexual feelings of any kind. What men are habitually, women are only exceptionally. . . . The best mothers, wives and managers of households know little or nothing of sexual indulgence. Love of home, children and domestic duties are the only passions they feel.[21]

Men in the nineteenth century were quite sure that no True Woman could have sexual desires. At the same time, norms for manliness dictated a certain sexual prowess and level of activity. But because a man could not be manly and still preach sexual restraint, women had been assigned a new task as the guardians of decency. If a man worried about controlling his sexual drive, he could place the burden on women and feel safer from the sin lurking within him. Women were taught to *repress* their sexuality while men were given freedom to *express* their sexuality.[22]

The double standard, which allowed men a wide range of freedom in their sexual conduct, also markedly increased the demand for prostitutes in the cities, and from 1780 onward there was an increase in illegitimate births. To deal with this, one of the many moral reform societies that women started in the Victorian era was the Social Purity movement, organized to influence the morals of home and society. Historian Carl Degler observes: "behind the movement lies the assumption that men's sexuality was as manipulable as women's—that is, it was as susceptible to control and regulation."[23] While today Christians may view much of the literature of this movement as repressing sexuality, the movement basically called for a single standard of sexual behavior for both sexes. This flew in the face of the male sexuality signpost used to define masculinity.

Women as Custodians of Morality

A third way in which men affirmed their sense of masculinity was by giving Christian morality to women for safekeeping. This was another reversal in Christian history. Tertullian, one of the early church fathers, had written this about women (between 196 and 212 C.E.):

> In pains and in anxiety doest thou bear, woman; and toward thine husband [is] thine inclination, and he lords it over thee. . . . And do you not know that you are [each] an Eve? The sentence of God on this sex of yours lives in this age: the guilt must of necessity live too. *You* are the devil's gateway; *you* are the unsealer of that [forbidden] tree; *you* are the first deserter of the divine law; *you* are she who persuaded him whom the devil was not valiant enough to attack. *You* destroyed so easily God's image, man. On account of *your* dessert [i.e., punishment], that is, death—even the Son of God had to die.[24]

A thousand years later, Thomas Aquinas wrote about women in derogatory terms:

> woman is something defective and accidental; she is a male gone awry; probably she is the result of some weakness in the father's generative power; or of

some external factor, like a damp south wind. . . . The woman is subject to the man, on account of the weakness of her nature, both of mind and body.[25]

John Knox, writing in 1668 in "The First Blast against the Monstrous Regiment of Women," described women as "weake, fraile, impatient, feeble and foolish . . . unconstant, variable, cruell and lacking the spirit of counsel and regiment. . . .woman in her greatest perfection was made to serve and obey man."[26]

How was it, then, that by 1835 woman had become synonymous with virtue and was the custodian of morality? A part of the answer moves us back again into the seventeenth century. When the Puritans settled the Massachusetts Bay Colony, the goal was the creation of a God-fearing and God-honoring "city on a hill." But while men outnumbered women in the first immigration from England and Holland by ratios of 3 to 2, sometimes 3 to 1, within one generation (by 1650) the Puritan clergymen were already commenting on the lack of men in church pews on the Lord's Day. The New World offered new opportunities to people who were willing to work hard, and already the second generation of colonial men had become less religious and more attentive to economic opportunity. By the end of the seventeenth century, "women outnumbered male church members by a ratio of 3 to 2. This loss of male piety also meant a loss of power for the male clergy."[27]

Women became a majority of churchgoers at the same time that churches moved from the center of community life to the margins. The goal of religion—to create a godly society—often conflicted with the goals of business, and business often won. As the eighteenth century dawned, the Puritan vision of creating the city set on a hill was being changed into a vision of a city built on making money—lots of it.

In addition, during the revolutionary eighteenth century, virtually everyone was reading Thomas Paine's tract *Common Sense*, which among other things called Americans to protect the freedom of conscience for religious dissenters. The religious ferment churned up by the Great Awakening before the American Revolution had profound implications for American politics. It became a short step, after the revolt against British rule was successfully concluded, to disestablish the churches.[28] Historian Ann Douglas tells us that "in the mid-eighteenth century, America had a smaller number of church members in proportion to overall population than any other Christian nation. In 1800 only one [out] of fifteen Americans belonged to a religious society."[29] Furthermore, most of those church members were women. (It is ironic that many Christians today appeal to the religiosity of the founding fathers of the American republic, when in fact Americans were the least religious among people in the Western Christian nations.)

Disestablishment of state churches meant that individual churches and ministers could no longer rely on state support to keep them afloat. They would have to compete with other churches to survive. To do this, throughout the nineteenth century the clergy "rehabilitated" the image of womanhood from the pulpit. In the process, Calvinism lost some of its influence and Methodism triumphed not only on the frontier but also in the newly emerging urban middle class.[30]

As the nineteenth century progressed, under women's influence in the church, hymns became softer and more sentimental, infants were baptized earlier, and the idea of infant damnation was discarded. Jesus was interpreted in a more "feminine" light, stressing his meekness and his sacrifice. The wife and mother in the home became the religious agent of the family. Religion was assigned to women, and thus religious expression became less relevant to the male definition of masculinity. All of this contributed to what historian Peter Stearns called "a polarization between male and female virtues."[31] Not only were women now the moral superiors of men, but religion had become women's special realm, a lean-to built onto the Victorian home for women to oversee and in which to find volunteer work to occupy their leisure time. DeBerg notes:

> although Victorian gender ideology placed many complex limitations on women and their sphere of activity, it also elevated women to a status they had never enjoyed previously. Because men could not in good conscience entirely brush aside the domestic and religious realms, because they wanted legitimate heirs who would be raised to value and respect patriarchal authority, and because they sensed that they must make domesticity look sweet in order to keep women within its confines, they produced a sentimental, gushing exaltation of home, woman, and motherhood. Never before had women been praised so highly, nor had their day-to-day lives been described as being so worthy and vital. Women were given an important social role that only they could fill.[32]

But that role was marginalized just as the church had been marginalized. "The skyscraper replaced the steeple as a symbol of the American dream," in historian Barbara Welter's words.[33] Women and the clergy worked from the margins of society to draw men back into the church, but the church had been "feminized" in theology and in practice, and it held little attraction for many men.

The nineteenth century gave way to the twentieth century, and the Victorian home was unraveling as women tried to escape it and men attempted to deal with an ambiguous masculine identity. Men were antagonistic toward women because women had challenged the new signposts of masculinity—by entering the workplace in great numbers and by insisting on a single rule of sexual conduct. Women resented men for assigning to them all of the "negative" qualities in the rigidly separate definitions of a man and a woman.

Muscular Christianity

In 1892 Albert Lawson asked the question on many people's minds: "Where are the men? Why are there not more men in our churches?"[34] This widespread concern led to efforts to diminish women's influence and power in the church and also to replace a "feminized" Christianity with "muscular" Christianity. Historian Leonard Sweet noted "an overwhelming fear of effeminacy and an exaggerated attention to masculinity" in the decades between 1880 and 1920.[35] Preachers chose to depict the era as "effeminate":

> America needs iron in her blood. Her age is effeminate. . . . Men don't have the nerve to execute the laws, and the women and the clergy, by overworking the cult of mercy, are making it impossible for men to do so, if they should feel themselves strong enough.[36]

> Only a man can preach the Gospel. . . . It takes courage . . . to preach the infallible Bible and the vicarious atonement. . . . It takes no courage to go to pink teas and present to the world social service platitudes. There isn't anything effeminate about the gospel nor . . . about a real . . . preacher of the Gospel. . . . The pulpit offers a greater opportunity for real men, who possess real manhood, than any other position in the world.[37]

DeBerg called evangelist Billy Sunday "the prime example of exaggerated masculine demeanor," citing his sermon "The Fighting Saint," which he regularly preached at his revivals:

> Jesus Christ intended his church to be militant as well as persuasive. It must fight as well as pray. . . . The prophets all carried the Big Stick. . . . Strong men resist, weaklings compromise. . . . Lord, save us from off-handed, flabby-cheeked, brittle-boned, weak-kneed, thin-skinned, pliable, plastic, spineless, effeminate, sissified, three-caret Christianity.[38]

Historian Douglas Frank, studying Billy Sunday's obsession with "manhood," concluded that Billy "spoke intuitively to the deepest confusion of his age and to the realities most troubling his evangelical audiences."[39] Some would say, with good reason.

The True Woman's Metamorphosis

Meanwhile, as the twentieth century opened, the True Woman was evolving into the New Woman, a woman who was often single and nearly always highly educated and economically autonomous.[40] Such women turned their backs on marriage, or if married, they avoided motherhood. It is impossible to understand the New Woman apart from her most salient characteristic, a college education.[41] The college degree became a passport to freedom from Victorian familial strictures. Despite the fact that most Victorian parents saw a college education as merely an interlude in a daughter's march toward conventional marriage, college women discovered knowledge and skills that would enable them to function as autonomous professional women. They shifted irrevocably out of their mothers' and grandmothers' domestic mindset.

At the turn of the century, popular Christian magazines were filled with the separate-spheres ideology, most likely triggered by profound cultural changes, including drastic changes in gender ideology and behavior between 1880 and 1920. It is impossible to overstate the severity of this dislocation of traditional gender values in that period. Choosing singleness as they earned bachelor's, master's, even doctoral degrees, women moved into the white-collar workforce or engaged in organizing social and political reform. Many indulged in sex before marriage, and those who were married sought divorces at a rate that alarmed observers. For some in the church, the answer was to develop and promulgate precise, rigid gender roles to stabilize a society running amok. Yet the strength of the Victorian gender ideology created special problems for the women who had taken it most seriously. Historian Barbara Welter concluded:

> Real women often felt that they did not live up to the ideal of True Womanhood; some of them blamed themselves, some challenged the standard; some tried to keep the virtues and enlarge the scope of womanhood. Somehow through this mixture of challenge and acceptance, of change and continuity, the True Woman evolved into the New Woman—a transformation as startling in its way as the abolition of slavery or the coming of the machine age. And

yet, the stereotype, the "mystique" if you will, of what woman was and ought to be persisted, bringing guilt and confusion in the midst of opportunity.[42]

The turn-of-the-century emergence of the New Woman—educated, independent, and self-aware—appeared to her critics to epitomize all that was wrong with American society. Even worse, as the second generation of New Women overturned the last vestiges of the Victorian gender ideology in the 1910s and 1920s, the *flapper* became the symbol of evil incarnate in a female body.[43] These second-generation New Women had not struggled as their mothers and grandmothers had—for the vote, for legal standing, for access to equal education, for access to birth control, and a host of other issues. The second-generation New Woman took these rights for granted. World War I had ended, and these young women wanted to enjoy life. "Young, hedonistic, sexual, the flapper soon became a symbol of the age with her bobbed hair, powdered nose, rouged cheeks, and shorter skirts. Lively and energetic, she wanted experience for its own sake. . . . She danced, smoked, and flaunted her sexuality to the horror of her elders."[44]

Two radically different sets of cultural expectations were now on a collision course—conservative Christians had just made the defense of Christian civilization a major goal,[45] and the flapper had just emerged, flouting every value of Christian civilization. Women began appearing in public places like dance halls, amusement parks, and theaters along with men. The media no longer referred to single workingwomen as *spinsters*, but now called them *bachelor girls*.

DeBerg notes that the greatest proliferation of articles written against women's immodest dress came between 1920 and 1925—against the short tight skirts, dresses with backs that plunged to the waist, and fabrics that clung or slithered provocatively around the female form. The flapper—sinuous, sensual, and overtly sexual—was also seen as "mannish" because she bobbed her hair, smoked cigarettes, and adopted male privilege by openly defying sexual mores for women.

Throughout the first four decades of the twentieth century, Christians focused on their growing fear of the androgyne and the need for a sharp distinction between male and female in dress, attitudes, and behavior. The reaction to societal excesses became as extreme as the excesses themselves, because it was believed that the threat to Christian civilization had to be met with equally extreme measures to control women's appearance and behavior. To counteract the female behaviors they deplored, preachers and theologians wrote hundreds of articles and books that powerfully impacted

Christian women, calling them back to True Womanhood. Out of this came some harsh rhetoric about women.

One such book was *Bobbed Hair, Bossy Wives, and Women Preachers* by John R. Rice, a prominent evangelist, radio preacher, Bible school teacher, and founder of the weekly paper *The Sword of the Lord*. In this widely read book, Rice is clear about what it means to be male or female:

> A man is not like a woman. A woman is not like a man. It is a sin for a woman to try to appear like a man, and it is likewise a sin for a man to try to appear like a woman. . . . It is a sin for women to appear masculine. It is equally a sin for men to appear effeminate. . . . [A]mong the adulterers and fornicators and drunkards and thieves and covetous and extortioners (1 Cor. 6:9–10) God put the effeminate. To be effeminate is a horrible sin in God's sight. Man is made in the image of God. God is a masculine God. The masculine pronoun is used of God everywhere in the Bible. . . . God is not effeminate. God is not feminine, but masculine. And man is made in the image of God. On the other hand, a woman is not made so much in the image of God, but in the image and as a mate to man. . . . Blessed is the woman who remembers this: her glory is in being a help to a man, and in submission to her husband or her father.[46]

At no point does Rice attempt to mitigate the prescription for women. His is a one-sided version of the Doctrine of Separate Spheres. His language is devoid of any softening or mollifying elements. He is clear that a wife must *submit* to her husband under all circumstances, be *subject* to him, *fear* him, and *reverence* him.

The importance of Rice's book lies not only in the historical interest of his prescription for female behavior in marriage. Much more significant is the wide readership the book garnered during the 1940s and 1950s. This book became the bible on Christian women's roles among conservative Christians for nearly two decades. It was quoted from pulpits, read to youth groups, and discussed in Christian college dormitories. It is still read in some circles today, not as an item of curiosity but as a source of truth.

Rice wrote before the start of World War II, a crisis that sobered Americans to the point that the "fear of the flapper" was dissipated. The war was followed by the "peace and prosperity" of the Eisenhower era and the advent of television. In the 1950s Americans tuned their new black-and-white television sets to watch idyllic family sitcoms like *Leave It to Beaver* with the flawless True Woman, June Cleaver, in the home. Female images on the screen showed smiling contentment in caretaker roles, living out the domesticity of the Doctrine of Separate Spheres.

In 1958 a second major effort to articulate the Doctrine came from the pen of theologian Charles C. Ryrie in *The Place of Women in the Church*. In this new bible on women's roles in church life, Ryrie included a chapter examining the domestic status of wives. He concluded:

> In domestic relations, then, God has appointed an order which includes the husband as the head and the wife in a place of honor though a place of subordination. . . . Whatever else may be considered an "interim ethic" or for "the present distress," this teaching of subordination cannot be so considered, for it is based on the headship of Christ over His church which is an everlasting relationship. As long as the race continues and men are men and women women, then women are to be subject to their husbands as unto the head. This teaching is based on unalterable facts. . . . The early church clearly considered the subordination of the wife in domestic relations the normal and fixed status.[47]

Note the shift in tone from Rice's polemic. In Ryrie, while the wife is still subordinate, her place has become "a place of honor." This revives the Victorian effort to elevate the wife honorifically in the home. The hierarchical relationship has not changed, but putting women down is now absent.

The Eisenhower years gave way to the 1960s, which brought Vietnam, the women's movement, and the civil rights movement. The war in Vietnam forever changed the way Americans viewed government, and the women's movement altered the debate about the family. The top-down language that was natural to Rice and Ryrie was replaced with a different vocabulary of hierarchy. In 1981 James B. Hurley, writing in the context of cultural expectations that were not present in Rice's or Ryrie's worlds, published *Man and Woman in Biblical Perspective*. This book was the most thorough treatment of the question of role relationships in Christian marriage at the time, and it was widely acclaimed as the definitive word on the subject as it presented a kinder, gentler hierarchy within marriage:

> Jesus taught his disciples that the rulers of the Gentiles saw authority as a way to set themselves over others. Using his own willingness to wash their feet as an illustration, he taught them that, among his followers, authority was for the purpose of service: the greatest should be like the least and the one who rules like the one who serves (Luke 22:24–27). . . . Paul calls husbands to imitate the Lord, not by setting aside authority, but by serving the needs of their wives. . . . Husbands must learn that form of sacrificial leadership which fosters the growth of others. Wives must learn that form of active obedience which is not self-demeaning but joyfully upbuilding.[48]

For the first time in a major, conservative Christian book teaching gender-based hierarchy, the author made room for the self-sacrificing nature of male headship, which appeared to open the possibility of mutuality in the marital relationship. Both Rice and Ryrie had been intent on instilling the necessity of female submission with little or no effort to define or restrict the parameters of male dominance or leadership.

Hurley took husbands to task who "wish to hold all the reins" and for whom "any initiative on the part of others threatens their relatively fragile sense of control." He was clear that such an exercise of headship crippled a marriage. The Doctrine of Separate Spheres in his hands had been downsized: Tasks may be interchangeable in marriage. He asserted that we must not assume those tasks to be biblical that have their roots in custom or tradition. This was a major step away from the twin notions of God-ordained roles and traits. No longer was the wife restricted to her fireside because of her innate emotional frailty and delicate nature, nor was the husband restricted to the public square to test his virility and attest his manhood. According to Hurley, "the circumstances of a family may cause reassignment of tasks."

At the same time, Hurley held the same asymmetrical relationship in place. He was culturally sensitive as he wrote, but in the end he found a way to affirm male headship and female subordination despite his efforts to mitigate for women the effects of hierarchy.

The social upheaval in the United States during the 1960s created an almost identical backlash among conservative Christians as had the flapper scare in the 1920s. While few could deny that discrimination based on sex persisted in virtually every sector of American life, and most would have agreed that fairness demanded such things as equal pay for equal work, the more radical feminist voices overpowered the reasonableness of many moderate feminist demands, and they terrified conservative citizens across the land. Antifeminism emerged and, in the hands of a gifted organizer like Phyllis Schlafly, it aroused deeply held fears in both men and women, including the fear of androgyny with its undifferentiated gender roles. Feminists were dangerous. The *Phyllis Schlafly Report* characterized feminists as "the unkempt, the lesbians, the radicals, the socialists," women who had rejected womanhood with its God-given roles of wife and mother. They were women-who-wanted-to-be-men.[49]

Several books appeared in the early– and mid–1980s promoting what was called "evangelical feminism" or "biblical feminism." Among these were Mary Evans's *Woman in the Bible* (1983), Aida Besancon Spencer's *Beyond the Curse* (1985), and Gilbert Bilezikian's *Beyond Sex Roles* (1985). As more biblical scholars published books and articles supporting equality in marriage, an edited volume was prepared to counteract their influence. That book was John Piper and Wayne Grudem's *Recovering Biblical Manhood and Womanhood*, published in 1991, exactly fifty years after the appearance of John R. Rice's *Bobbed Hair, Bossy Wives, and Women Preachers*.

Anyone who has read the books by Rice or Ryrie is impressed with the tone of the Piper and Grudem book. The editors explicitly changed terminology, replacing *hierarchy* with *complementarity*, because "it suggests both equality and beneficial differences between men and women." But despite the kinder, gentler rhetoric focused on complementarity, the prescription for separate spheres or discrete roles had not changed. The man leads, and the woman "affirms, receives and nurtures" the strength and leadership provided for her by the man. The authors defined manhood first and then stated that womanhood is a response to manhood: "At the heart of mature masculinity is a sense of benevolent responsibility to lead, provide for and protect women in ways appropriate to a man's differing relationships. At the heart of mature femininity is a freeing disposition to affirm, receive and nurture strength and leadership from worthy men in ways appropriate to a woman's differing relationships."[50]

Although Piper and Grudem do not list "the positive masculine traits" of the right kind of man, they do include a list of "positive feminine traits" borrowed from Rhonda Chervin's book *Feminine, Free and Faithful:*

> [A woman should be] responsive, compassionate, empathetic, enduring, gentle, warm, tender, hospitable, receptive, diplomatic, considerate, polite, supportive, intuitive, wise, perceptive, sensitive, spiritual, sincere, vulnerable (in the sense of emotionally open), obedient, trusting, graceful, sweet, expressive, charming, delicate, quiet, sensually receptive (vs. prudish), faithful, pure.[51]

A moment's consideration of this list makes it clear that the prescription remains essentially the same as the nineteenth-century qualities of a True Woman within the Doctrine of Separate Spheres.

Note what has happened. The paradigm of asymmetrical gender relationships has not changed fundamentally. The husband is still the leader in the home, and the wife is still expected to submit. Why? Because they have complementary roles to fill. In the end, it is a proclamation of equality within hierarchy. The line from John R. Rice's unilateral female subordination in 1941 to John Piper and Wayne Grudem's Edenic vision of gender hierarchy as *complementarity* in 1991 can be traced not only in books but also in the pressures of the culture, raising consciousness and insisting on modification of the Doctrine of Separate Spheres. By 1991 the guardians of complementarity found a way to retain the doctrine within a rhetorical device designed to remove its sting for women. The broader culture forced the issue to the point that the Doctrine of Separate Spheres has been completely reformulated over the last fifty years, but the broader culture has not succeeded in overturning the core belief in male dominance and female subordination.

Standing against the Culture

How are we to think about the changes in the last one hundred years? On the question of the Doctrine of Separate Spheres, in general the culture has shifted 180 degrees. Equal opportunity, fair labor practices, and antidiscrimination laws, in the main, have struck down overt sexism and continue to open doors to women in most sectors of the workplace. Women can vote, open their own bank accounts and credit card accounts, get mortgages, and run businesses. Television sitcoms no longer feature True Women like June Cleaver but are peopled by women as well as men in every sector of public and professional life. The world has changed for women, because the various feminist movements in the last half century have raised consciousness in ways that have benefited them.

At the same time, women's growing self-awareness has triggered a drive for increased self-awareness for men, leading to the formation of numerous men's movements.[52] Among these is the 1990s Promise Keepers movement, which gathered tens of thousands of Christian men for two-day rallies in sports arenas where speakers focused on the seven promises of a Promise Keeper.[53] The Promise Keepers movement has retained some of the distinctions between men and women found in the Broverman study cited at the beginning of this chapter. "Men are headliners, women are fine-print people," according to Promise Keeper speaker Ed Cole.[54] Men are logical, rational, the big-picture thinkers; they are the initiators. Women, on the other hand, are responders, nurturing and relational, who crave stability rather than challenges. Cole encourages men to cultivate the same manly traits exhibited by Jesus Christ: "Jesus was a fearless leader, defeating Satan, casting out demons, commanding nature, rebuking hypocrites. . . . Since to be like Jesus—Christlike—requires a certain ruthlessness, manhood does also."[55] This is a replay of the muscular Christianity of a hundred years earlier. At the same time, Promise Keepers promoted the image of the "sensitive new age guy," teaching men the practical biblical virtues of encouragement, forgiveness, mutual confession, and mutual aid.

Leon Podles believes that the feminization of Christianity in the nineteenth century "set the ideology of masculinity free from the faith,"[56] stating that the old idea of masculinity as stoic manliness has been replaced in American culture by a fascination with the passions of youth expressed in sexuality and in the world of sports. "For modern men, team sports are more transforming than religion because they provide a greater escape from the self."[57] He then writes, "Men do not go to church. They regard involvement in religion as unmasculine, and almost more than anything they want to be masculine. . . . Is there a way that Christianity can reach men in a long-lasting and effective manner?"[58]

How the church responds to that question speaks directly to the issue of how Christians see their gendered selves. And it answers the question, Is the church for or against the culture? The answer must be that any obsession with definitions of masculinity or femininity is an idolatry that breaks the second of the Ten Commandments. Mennonite clergyperson Lois Barrett pulls us up short with these words: "The pervasiveness of individualism in North America's dominant culture reaches into the Church as well. Church becomes defined apart from community, in terms of individual choice, individual morality, individual self-actualization, and individual decisions about where to obtain the best spiritual goods and services."[59]

The church's message for men and women must not cater to what makes them feel "masculine" or "feminine." That focus on individualism within the church strengthens a consumer mentality. The church is the gathered people of God, in communion or community. It is the body of Christ gathered. Despite some gendered rhetoric to the contrary, the Promise Keepers were on the right track in their emphasis on corporate worship, faithful support of the church, efforts toward racial reconciliation, and commitment to the Great Commandment and the Great Commission. But these commitments are not merely "masculine." They are for the whole family of God. And they call us away from the tendency to gendered individualism, asking, "What's in it for me? Who or what will make me feel most like a man or a woman?" Churches and parachurch organizations that reinforce such individualist tendencies in any way are not standing against the culture. They have accommodated themselves to the culture. They are Constantinian.

God created humanity in his image as male and female. The creation mandate given to the first man and woman called them both to two tasks. They were to procreate ("be fruitful and multiply and fill the earth") and they were to exercise responsible dominion over every living thing on the earth. Both the man and the woman were to engage in the tasks of parenting. Both the man and the woman were to engage in responsible dominion (Gen. 1:28). The focus of Scripture is not on masculinity and femininity. It is on the interdependence of a man and a woman who leave father and mother, cleave to one another, and become one flesh. Whenever we get tangled up in defining the tasks, feelings, or characteristics of what it means to be masculine or feminine, we have shifted from the Bible to the culture for our norms. We have become Constantinian.

Many things have changed in the last one hundred years. Does the Doctrine of Separate Spheres work better in Christian marriages today? Or does it still produce some of the strains that overturned it at the end of the nineteenth century? Chapter 6 will explore the effects of the Doctrine of Separate Spheres among Christians today.

6

New Wineskins for New Wine

I n *All the King's Men* Robert Penn Warren speaks of the problem of living in a house with great big promise. It is dangerous to stake one's life on a promise that will not, even cannot, be kept. For many women of faith, hierarchically structured marriage poses the problem of living in such a house. The promise is that in exchange for a one-sided surrender implicit in asymmetrical roles, a wife will enjoy a gratifying relationship with a caring, dependable husband. Popular Christian proponents of hierarchy[1] in marriage stress a substantive return for such self-surrender.[2] Judith Miles expressed that substantive return in these words:

> What does the woman gain by submission to her own husband? Only the infinite security of yielding to the duly constituted chain of authority in the universe; only the deep joy of living with a real man who grows stronger every day; only the fulfillment of fully participating in a genuine love relationship; only the completing of what is partial in her human nature; only the opening of her yielded being to the influence of God's Spirit, who comes where humble and yielded spirits are seeking Him.[3]

Yet such self-surrender for women does not always lead to such promised fulfillment. The question addressed in this chapter is whether men and women formulating their marriages according to the Doctrine of Separate Spheres today find that promise fulfilled.

In a typical wedding ceremony, the bride and groom are expected to make promises to one another. In some ceremonies, some officiants merely ask the couple to pledge to love and respect one another; others add wifely obedience to the woman's vows. The word *obedience* is less frequently used in current parlance, *submission* being the more acceptable term. But in either case, the relationship is unmistakably hierarchical. Theologian Wayne Grudem defines this hierarchical relationship as meaning "that a wife will willingly submit to her husband's authority and leadership in the marriage."[4] Authority rests with men, and a woman's role is to obey or to submit to male authority.[5] Most proponents of hierarchical marriage ground it in the biblical injunction of Ephesians 5:22–23: "Wives, submit yourselves to your own husbands as you do to the Lord. For the husband is the head of the wife as Christ is the head of the church, his body, of which he is the Savior." This submission is interpreted to mean a woman's nonreciprocal "total dedication" to her husband.[6] Such dedication is possible because it is mandated by God for the woman's benefit.

The Promise

Various Christian writers supporting hierarchy in marriage stress a substantive return for a woman's self-surrender. If she submits, she will experience her husband's protection,[7] his provision,[8] and harmony in the home.[9] These three themes of protection, provision, and harmony weave throughout much of the literature on hierarchical marriage. When a woman lives in proper submission to her husband and she experiences these benefits, she is fulfilling the "Biblical vision of complementarity" which, in turn, fulfills her "femininity."[10] John Piper describes the ideal hierarchical marriage in these words:

> In the home when a husband leads like Christ and a wife responds like the bride of Christ, there is a harmony and mutuality that is more beautiful and more satisfying than any pattern of marriage created by man. *Biblical headship* is to take primary responsibility for Christ-like, servant-leadership, protection and provision in the home. *Biblical submission* for the wife is the divine calling to honor and affirm her husband's leadership and help carry it through according to her gifts. This is the way of joy.[11]

It is not surprising that benefits like protection, provision, harmony, and mutuality should provide a strong appeal for self-surrender. Social scientist

Helen Hardacre has identified five reasons that lend persuasive power to the appeal of self-surrender to women:

1. The general message of a return to "tradition" serves as a corrective to the ills of major social change in society, generating fear in both men and women. The tradition feels like a strong anchor in time of storm.
2. In an economic climate in which women are generally relegated to lower-status jobs (this is gradually changing), a woman can experience a much higher standard of living when coupled to a good provider.
3. The differential emphasis on the importance or necessity of a good education for men versus women inhibits women from discovering and exploring alternative values and ways of life.
4. Some women marry and stay in abusive marriages because they fear male reprisals if they do not cooperate.
5. Religious women may fear excommunication from the religious community or supernatural punishment for their failure to submit.[12]

Sociologist Ralph Turner understands the appeal of self-surrender to lie in "the assumption that one has been absorbed into a caring, gratifying entity, both powerful and dependable."[13] That is the promise held out by the kinder, gentler version of the Doctrine of Separate Spheres. A powerful, dependable husband will care for a woman who submits (evidenced by his protection and provision). But Turner also underlines three contingencies of this fulfillment in return for surrender. For women the promise is realized only when there is "reciprocated love, the dependability of the relationship, and new opportunities for gratification that come from the relationship." The question is whether, in exchange for their self-surrender or submission, women consistently experience these three contingencies.

The Problem

Social historian Samuel Huntington, in studying American creedal passion when recruitment to political movements is high, developed a macrosociological analysis of political response that has ramifications for the study of men's and women's experience in hierarchical marriage. It examines possible gaps between our ideals and our reality. For our purposes, if there is a gap, it lies between a man's or woman's commitment to the Doctrine of Separate Spheres in Christian marriage and his or her lived experience within marriage.

Theologian Max Stackhouse distinguishes between a *doctrine* and a *creed*, stating that "a *doctrine* is a teaching, claim, or assertion; a *creed* is a doctrine held to be true, embraced with commitment, celebrated in concert with others, and used as a fundamental guide for action."[14] Using Stackhouse's definitions and Huntington's framework, individual men and women may have accepted hierarchical marital structures not merely as *doctrine* but as a *creed* to which they are heartily and fully committed. At the same time they may see that their experience of marital hierarchical structures does not carry with it the promised fulfillment. In that case, they will experience a gap or a disjunction between their intense belief in the promise and in their personal reality.

In most role strain, people feel uncomfortable without knowing why. Their perception of the gap between the promise and their reality is unclear. If simultaneously they are vague about the gap but also believe intensely in the role, they will *deny* the reality of strain. On the other hand, if they are vague about the gap between the promise and the reality, but they do *not* embrace the doctrine as *creed* (embraced with commitment and used as a fundamental guide for action), they will probably choose to *ignore* the gap. If they clearly see the gap between their commitment and their reality, that clarity can lead in one of two different directions. The person who sees the gap clearly but does not really believe in the doctrine (as creed) will probably become *cynical* about the teaching. He or she puts enough distance between the self and the role to handle the strain. But the person who sees the gap clearly and also believes intensely in the submissive female role as creed will develop an *intense desire to close the gap*.

Huntington further found that for people in this final category (those who see the gap clearly and also believe intensely in the doctrine as creed), this drives them to the following actions:

1. If the gap looms large and the belief is intense, the person begins to question the authority behind the teaching: "Who says so? How can I be sure that person is right?"
2. Taking the ideal seriously, the person then asks, "Why isn't this my experience? What needs to change?" The urgency grows to capture the ideal as reality.

3. If these first two steps do not reduce the tension created by the gap between belief and reality, the person begins to attack the institutions behind the teaching (in this case, the Christian church).
4. When taken to this point, the person begins experimenting with alternatives, and also begins to question other beliefs from the same source.[15]

It is possible to trace these steps enacted in the lives of men and women who have believed with passion in male headship and female submission in an asymmetrical marital relationship, and who have faced the gap between their commitment to the ideal and their experience. When this happens, such persons are impelled to reduce the tension between their beliefs of what the marriage should give them and what they perceive are its deficits. Moral passion fuels their efforts to change either themselves or their situation.[16]

The Worldview of God-Ascribed Hierarchy

Traditional hierarchical marriage has received its legitimation from a worldview in which the sacred frame of reference is God-ordained or God-ascribed hierarchy. Theologian Duane Litfin articulated this worldview:

> The Bible presents a world view . . . based on the assumption that a sovereign, personal God designed an ordered universe to function in a particular way, and the finest achievement of the creature is to discover that design and fulfill it. At its essential level this design is not open to change or redefinition. . . . Feminists find the biblical vision of a divinely ordained male/female hierarchy galling. They have embraced a profoundly unbiblical—indeed antibiblical—ideology and are pressing it on the church.[17]

In this hierarchical worldview men and women are assigned separate spheres within which distinctive roles have been given cosmic significance. As noted in chapter 5, this Doctrine of Separate Spheres received its most dichotomous definition in the early nineteenth century, in which *male* and *female* came to symbolize mutually exclusive oppositions.[18] The Doctrine of Separate Spheres justified ideologically separate roles for men and women. If a woman were a True Woman, she expected a life of self-sacrifice because this was God's will. While details and the rhetoric of the doctrine have changed over the past century (as explored in chapter 5), at its core it remains unchanged because it is legitimated by a cosmic rationale. It is God's design and it is incarnated in Christ's example. The second half of this book (chapters 7–12) tests this assertion by exploring the biblical teachings on marital relationships.

For women the promise of the doctrine is both a carrot and a stick. It includes the assurance of fulfillment for compliance, but beyond the sacred legitimation, it also carries penalties in both this world and in the world to come for those who fail to follow the teaching. John R. Rice put it this way: "The crime wave that plagues America is part and parcel of the rebellion against authority in which every woman who does not submit to her husband has a part."[19] More contemporaneously, the Danvers Statement concludes with this warning: "We are convinced that a denial or neglect of these principles [of male headship and female submission] will lead to increasingly destructive consequences in our families, our churches, and the culture at large."[20] This dual message of divinely ascribed marital roles for women, based on mutually exclusive natures, provides a theodicy of social order—an explanation of the God-given necessity of such roles for the sake of order in all social contexts. It provides men with a divinely sanctioned rationale for a power-over position, and it gives women a way of making sense out of their experience of life when the promise is not fulfilled. Although a woman is promised a rich return in exchange for her self-surrender—God will compensate her in the life to come after death to balance out the deficits of her present situation[21]—the threat enforcing this submission is the double possibility of both personal sorrow and the total breakdown of society if she fails to submit.

Three aspects of this theodicy make it appealing to many. First, as Litfin pointed out, this worldview states that a structured inequality between men and women is fundamental to society, and because God has mandated unequal social structures, they are irreversible. Many Christians believe that a fallen humanity cannot live peaceably without being policed, which means that some persons must have authority over others to keep order in the social system. Since individual needs are not central to what it means to be human, each person must accept his or her place in the cosmic order. Sociologist Max Weber observed that "the sacred is the uniquely unalterable."[22] When particular roles are stamped *sacred*, they are also stamped *unalterable*. What would otherwise be merely a contingency of human existence becomes a manifestation of universal law.

Second is the conviction that what happens to us in this life is relatively unimportant in the light of eternity. We can endure the present life with detachment because it is not a permanent state of affairs. Thus individuals caught in difficult life situations here on earth can be assured of something better in the future if they patiently endure. A woman's submission serves cosmic purposes, and if she carries out her submission with a "gentle and quiet spirit" (1 Peter 3:4), she will be rewarded.

Third, hierarchy gives individuals a place to stand in the order of things. If I know that I am in a divinely ordained place in God's world and purposes, this gives meaning to my life. Together these three elements (divine ordination, the temporal versus the eternal, and a sense of "place") explain, at least in part, the appeal of a hierarchical worldview for women as well as for men. It provides a frame of reference for comprehending the sense of comfort we experience when we think of ourselves as being in tune with God's structure for human life.

Both at the end of the nineteenth century and at the end of the twentieth century, women's changing perceptions of themselves and their entrance into the labor force in greater numbers created heightened anxiety about traditional gender roles. The threat to a traditional balance of power creates such anxiety that complementarians invoke the sacred legitimation of hierarchical order to thwart potential moves toward more flexible gender roles and shared power.

Yet wider cultural forces encourage some women of faith to question the legitimacy of the hierarchical view. Economic factors have led to the rise of dual-career couples within the church on a par with national averages. As such women have become wage earners outside their home, their perception of themselves and their marital status has often undergone significant changes. Some have begun to question their subordination and dependency. While marital ties, once thought to be permanent, are being disrupted by women's increased self-awareness (as happened to great numbers of women in the nineteenth century as well), it is incumbent on Christians to evaluate the effect of hierarchy on women's marital experience.

The Doctrine of Separate Spheres has survived more than 160 years of mutation without losing its central thrust. Whether in a sermon preached in 1837 by a Presbyterian minister in Massachusetts or a diatribe by John R. Rice in 1941 or the idyllic rhetoric of Drs. Piper and Grudem, lauding "two intelligent, humble, God-entranced beings living out, in beautiful harmony their unique and different responsibilities,"[23] at the core of the teaching is male headship and female submission.

In response to an effort to find out what people of faith believe about and experience in Christian marriage, men and women in eleven large conservative churches in various parts of the United States answered questions about the teachings of the Bible in four marital areas—general roles, sex, decision making, and earning and spending patterns.[24] What became immediately apparent in the responses was the gap between what people said they believed and how they actually acted. For example, while more than half of the women in the study said that they believed fully in hierarchical structures for marriage, only 8 percent held hierarchical beliefs in the specific areas of sex in marriage or decision making in marriage.[25] It is possible that the "general belief" is held as *doctrine,* but when it is applied in specific areas of married life, the gap shows that the belief is not truly *creed* in Stackhouse's use of the term. The majority of men and women in this study who embraced the teaching of hierarchical marriage did so as a doctrine but not as a creed.

Beliefs about Sex in Marriage

Social scientists sometimes assume that hierarchical structures for marriage are uniformly negative experiences for wives in subordinate roles. The assumption is that in such a marriage, sex is a man's privilege, a woman's duty. But the data emerging from this study do not support this view. It is true that men and women differed in their focus when describing their beliefs about biblical teachings on sex in marriage. Men were more than twice as likely as women to focus on sex as God's good gift to be enjoyed. On the other hand, women were more concerned about the fences that should be placed around the practice of sex. At the same time, the relationship between general beliefs about gender roles and beliefs about sex in marriage revealed no correlation between the two. While a majority of men and women espoused hierarchical beliefs in general, they were much more egalitarian in the way they interpreted those beliefs in specific areas like sex.

When asked to describe how their experience of sex in marriage conformed to their beliefs about biblical teaching on the subject, the great majority of women stated that their experience fully conformed to their beliefs about what it should be. By contrast, men were nearly evenly divided between those who were ambivalent about their experience in the light of their beliefs, and those who stated that their experience conformed to their beliefs.[26] In general, both men and women in the study gave sex in their marriages high marks.[27]

Women tend to see sex as a part of the fabric of marriage in ways that men may not. In the study women tied satisfaction with sex to satisfaction with emotional warmth in the relationship. For example, one woman responded, "I enjoy sex immensely when I feel intimately loved on a deeper level. At this point in my marriage my husband and I are still struggling to attain that intimacy. For the most part now I feel *used* to meet his sexual needs." Another responded, "I enjoy sex, but I want to feel cherished and I don't." On the whole, however, the experience of sex for men and women in marriage was positive, and very few linked it in any way to teachings about women as "receptors" and men as "initiators."

Beliefs about Decision Making in Marriage

A pervasive theme in the literature of hierarchy concerns decision making. Much of the literature favoring hierarchy in marriage states that there must be a designated tiebreaker in even the most egalitarian relationships, because someone must have the last word. Authors and preachers alike are certain that it is impossible for a couple to function as equals in decision making. But in this study, couples who stated a strong belief in the general principle of hierarchy in marriage did not treat marital decision making hierarchically. While many gave a tip of the hat to the husband's role as tiebreaker in cases of a standoff, 86 percent of the participants described decision making as either completely mutual or as made by the husband after seeking his wife's advice or opinion. Less than 6 percent of the participants said decision making was the husband's responsibility, while merely considering his wife's best interests; and less than 4 percent had a relationship in which the husband made decisions and the wife submitted without being deferred to or consulted.

Age was a significant factor in women's response to the question "What do you believe the Bible teaches about gender roles in decision making in a Christian marriage?" Among younger women (under age thirty), none stated a belief in unqualified equality in decision making, though none called for male decision making without female input. All of these women stated that decisions should be jointly made, but with the husband having "the final say" in cases of disagreement, or the husband has "final say" only after consulting with his wife. Among women over age sixty, 40 percent believed in unqualified equality in decision making in marriage, and none supported male decision making without female input. It was the women in the middle age range (thirty to fifty-nine) whose beliefs about decision making in marriage spread across all categories.

The second question in the decision-making section was "How have you and your spouse handled decision making in your marriage?" While 10 percent of the participants gave strongly hierarchical answers to the question about their *beliefs*, no one in the entire group answered with commensurate responses to this question about *practice*. In every case, decision making was mutual or was made by the husband only after discussing the matter with his wife to get her advice or opinion. Sixty percent of the participants practiced completely egalitarian decision making in the marriage (65 percent of the men and 58 percent of the women). The gap between beliefs and practices was evident. In summary, when beliefs about decision making and practice of decision making in marriage were correlated, only 20 percent of the participants defined their *beliefs* as unequivocally egalitarian, but 60 percent of them defined their *practice* as unequivocally egalitarian.

The third question related to decision making was "How would you rate your overall satisfaction with the way you and your spouse handle decision making in your marriage?" Among the 56 percent of the women who were full-time homemakers, 75 percent were mildly to highly satisfied. On the other hand, among the 39 percent of women who worked full-time or part-time outside the home, 43 percent were dissatisfied with decision making in their marriage.

Among the men, satisfaction with decision making in the marriage correlated with size of income, with satisfaction moving steadily upward with income. Without exception, those with annual incomes under twenty-five thousand dollars were not at all satisfied with present decision making in the marriage; those in the middle range (between twenty-five and fifty thousand dollars) were "somewhat satisfied but with problems" or were "mildly satisfied." Only those with incomes over fifty thousand dollars a year were highly satisfied with decision making in the marriage. This relationship of income to decision making was not significant for the women in the study.

Decision making in a marriage is an important measure of a possible gap between beliefs and experience. The issue of decision making not only highlights an inconsistency between espoused beliefs and practices but throws light on feelings of satisfaction or dissatisfaction with decision making no matter how it is carried out in a marriage.

The Gap between Ideals and Realities

Participants in the study were asked at one point, "Have you ever at any time personally struggled with any of these beliefs [about marital roles] in the context of your own experience of marriage? If so, which beliefs were difficult for you to harmonize with your own experience? How did you resolve the tension?" Forty-three percent of the participants acknowledged that they currently struggled with beliefs directly related to marital hierarchy. Women struggled with having to submit and men struggled with having to take a leadership role they did not feel capable of shouldering. The following responses give some sense of the various ways men and women struggled with the issues.

One man said, "A resounding Yes to have I struggled with any of these beliefs. To be the head of the household—my wife and I have struggled almost from the beginning. What does it mean to be the head of the home? I thought at times I had to make tough decisions and even ignore her or overrule her feelings, her beliefs, her decisions, her wishes, never in the sense of the tyrant, but certainly in the sense of not being respectful of her. . . . I think being the head of the home has been one of the biggest struggles, how that translates on a day-to-day basis—who controls the finances, who controls the checkbook."

Another man stated, "Striving to understand what being a 'leader' means and encompasses has been difficult. The tension resolves as we talk things out and we continue to grow in our young (almost four-year) marriage."

One woman responded: "It's been hard for me to always want to be submissive to my husband, because he's not always been and still isn't much of a spiritual leader and it's also hard to respect someone like that."

Another woman said, "Of course I've struggled with my role at times. It is sometimes difficult to trust that your husband is leading well and has the Lord's interests in mind. I have not personally struggled with a husband who leads in ungodly or sinful directions. But if I did, I would insist on obedience to Scripture as my final authority."

And another spoke about her struggle with submission: "I think probably for most women the hardest area to deal with is the area of submission. It's hard to accept the fact that even though we are equal, we are different and sometimes I might feel like I have the right answer and I don't see why we can't go with my right answer instead of my husband's right answer. And I think that is probably something that most women in evangelical circles struggle with."

Personal Happiness in Marriage

Happiness in marriage is elusive and difficult to measure. Who is able to determine the criteria for assessing happiness? In this study participants were asked to list what, in their opinion, were the most important ingredients of a happy marriage, then to reflect on their own experience of marriage and report the degree to which those ingredients were present for them. In this way they measured their happiness against their own criteria.[28] Perhaps the most telling result of the study came from this group of questions. Three notable gender differences emerged:

1. Men were more than three times as likely as women to describe a happy marriage in terms of mutual self-giving and mutual submission. This is not surprising, given the fact that the men in this study held more egalitarian beliefs about role relationships in marriage than did the women. Mutual self-giving and mutual submission were more salient for the men in the study.
2. Women were 40 percent more likely than men to see happiness lying on the affection dimension. While both sexes agreed that for men this means sex, women were clear that for them it means cuddling, hand-holding, or other gestures of closeness without sex. In fact, while describing a woman's need for "nonsexual affection," a number of women decried the male tendency to interpret any kind of desire for closeness as a signal for sex.
3. Women were more than three times as likely as men to describe happiness in marriage in companionship terms of respect, friendship, laughter, fun, time together, space, understanding, trust, intimacy, sensitivity, devotion, and acceptance.

When participants were asked to reflect on their own experience of marriage and describe the degree to which they had experienced their self-identified ingredients of a happy marriage, the difference between those holding egalitarian and those holding hierarchical beliefs about marriage was startling. Among participants holding egalitarian beliefs about marital roles, *none* rated their own experience of happiness in their marriages as negative or poor. On the other hand, the participants who rated their experience of happiness in their marriages as negative or poor also held strongly hierarchical beliefs about roles in Christian marriage. When men and women identify for themselves the criteria for happiness in marriage, then rank their own experience of happiness in their marriages as fair or poor, it is difficult to defend hierarchical marital structures as "right," despite the idea that such structures provide certitude that one is in step with the universe.

Happiness versus Meaning

Is happiness a valid criterion for measuring a marriage? While happiness is a strongly held value in a large sector of American society today, it is by no means universally embraced as a paramount value among people of faith. Sociologist of religion Peter Berger observed: "It is not happiness that theodicy provides, but meaning. . . . [T]he need for meaning is as strong as or even stronger than the need for happiness. . . . Some theodicies carry no promise of 'redemption' at all—except for the redeeming assurance of meaning itself."[29]

Happiness is not the chief end of life. Many people find that it is better to live with a pain-filled life if it is located in a self-transcending, all-embracing fabric of meaning for the universe. The Christian fear of secular humanism (and, by extension, of feminism and postmodernism) is grounded in a concern that the truly pernicious influences of the wider culture will undermine the right moral commitments that give meaning to life. To choose the self over selflessness is to ally oneself with satanic cultural forces leading inevitably to destruction. The Christian who chooses meaning over happiness can find strong biblical support for such a choice. Yet most people want both happiness and meaning in their marriages and often confuse the two.

Morality and Hierarchy

At its root, whether or not wives are to assume a subordinate role to that of their husband (as leader and provider) is an ethical question, and the answer, either positive or negative, sets up a particular moral framework for relationships within the family. The teaching forms a policy of interpersonal relationship based on the "good" of the community as a whole. In Carl Degler's words: "The historic family has depended for its existence and character on women's subordination . . . [meaning] simply that the family's existence assumes that a woman will subordinate her individual interest to those of others."[30]

The theology of asymmetrical marital structures is a *moral* theology, involving ethical decisions about human relationships. It is predicated on the sinfulness of all humanity and thus the need for some hierarchical structures in every human institution. It is also predicated on the welfare of the group over the interests of the individual. Most people of faith who take the Bible seriously would assent to the fundamental validity of these statements, at least in part. We are indeed sinful people, but whether a hierarchical structure is the only way to manage that sinfulness is questionable. It may discount the internal power and work of the Holy Spirit in our lives. And we *are* to seek community in which the common good becomes more important than the self-serving wishes of individuals. Care must be taken, however, because there are ways in which both of these truth statements can be distorted so that they make a mockery of Christian marriage. Those who promote a theology of asymmetrical marital structures must assume some responsibility for the outcomes of its application in actual families.

Domestic Violence

Spouse abuse is a problem that plagues women at all socioeconomic levels in American society. Mary Stewart Van Leeuwen has noted that after alcohol, zealous, conservative religiosity is the second most stable predictor of domestic violence.[31] Richard Langley and Robert Levy state that "hierarchical marriage constantly teeters on the edge of God's boundary. It operates too close to where temptation is difficult to resist."[32] It is important to state that a great many Christian men are *not* abusers, nor are all hierarchically structured marriages infested with issues of abuse. At the same time, though many people of faith have embraced a softer complementary version of hierarchy, not all have. An alarming degree of spouse abuse still occurs in Christian homes. From case records in a Salvation Army battered-women's shelter serving between 300 and 350 cases each year, it is reported that 23 percent of the clients seen were professing Christians affiliated with evangelical churches.[33]

Recent efforts by some social scientists to study the relationship of spouse abuse and religious belief have measured conservative religiosity by frequency of church attendance or by belief in the inerrancy of Scripture.[34] In using such measures they have not found support for Van Leeuwen's or Langley and Levy's statements above. But conservative Christian couples holding egalitarian views on the marital relationship are often equally committed to the authority of Scripture and to regular church attendance. At issue is the attitude toward power and its use in the family, and this can be seen in decision-making patterns in the home. C. M. Murphy and S. L. Meyer found that wife abuse was nearly three times more likely when the husband dominated decision making than when the wife dominated it, and roughly eight times more likely than in egalitarian marriages.[35] Kirsti Yllo concludes that "regardless of context, violence against wives is lower among couples where there is a relative equality in decision-making . . . In general, domination of decision-making by husbands is associated with the highest levels of violence against wives."[36] Yet female submission to male decision-making is explicitly included in most applications of the doctrine of wifely submission.[37]

In the prescriptive understanding of hierarchy for many Christians, the focus is exclusively on the wife's unqualified submission to her husband, often without limits. Radio preacher John MacArthur has called Christian women to submit, assuring them that God will take care of the results if there is any abuse: if a husband "doesn't obey the Word, submit—submit anyway."[38] Numerous other conservative writers are equally clear that the husband's role is as "leader in the family." He makes all decisions; nothing goes on without his awareness and approval; he is "head" over his wife. This view of the distribution of power has assigned women's abuse to a one-sided suffering for Jesus' sake that gives husbands carte blanche in the home. Such a power differential, as social scientist Donald Dutton has reported, comes from a very legalistic, highly traditional worldview which provides husbands with fertile ground for violent behavior.[39]

John Piper and Wayne Grudem explicitly deny any husband the right to abuse his wife physically, sexually, or psychologically.[40] But men and women may not hear that message in their local church where they are instructed that the husband is the leader (some preachers actually use the word *ruler*) and thus he is the decision maker. It is the wife's place to submit to him without questioning his wisdom. This creates the asymmetrical relationship social scientists have pinpointed as being an invitation to abuse.

When abuse occurs, William Stacey and Anson Shupe report that they "have yet to talk with a[n abused] woman who felt she received much aid from a clergyman."[41] Instead, women in conservative churches and denominations often find little or no sympathy from their ministers. With few exceptions women report that their pastors focused on getting them—not their abusive husbands—to change.[42] This widespread denial of the problem by clergy further legitimates wife battering. Yet, given the *promise* of the doctrine of hierarchy, one would assume that of all people, conservative Christian women would enjoy protection against abuse in the home. In all too many cases, the opposite turns out to be the case. Domestic abuse is not only not barred from Christian homes; it is excused by many clergy and it is sometimes perpetrated by church leaders themselves.

The Crux of the Matter

How are Christians to think about this plethora of sociological and historical data (explored in chapters 2–6) that raises questions about the desirability of marriage? Even more, how are we to deal with the gaps many Christians experience between their idealized concept of marriage and their reality?

When Alexis de Tocqueville wrote about slavery in the mid–nineteenth-century United States, he concluded that there could be no intermediate ground between slavery and complete equality.[43] A "halfway" step toward equality, according to Tocqueville, is inherently unstable and cannot endure. Drs. Piper and Grudem believe they have achieved a viable "middle ground," which they call "complementarity," between harsh hierarchy and freewheeling equality. But Christians dealing with a clear gap between their beliefs about what Christian marriage should be and their personal experience of marriage will not settle for halfway measures for long. If the gap looms large, the more intensely they believe in the creed the more they will attempt to close the gap. The risks in doing so are serious. Such a person will move through the stages outlined by Samuel Huntington: first, questioning the authority behind the beliefs he or she has accepted, then redoubling efforts to capture the ideal as his or her reality. If the person does not succeed, it is likely that the failure will lead to attacking the Christian church and looking at alternatives to previous allegiances. In the process, God's missional goal for Christian marriage may be overlooked or bypassed.

It is possible that as conservative Christians have attempted to sort out issues concerning Christian marriage, they have climbed a ladder leaning against the wrong wall. To continue to talk about hierarchy versus equality can polarize the discussion in unhelpful ways. The issue should not be between groups of Christians but between the people of God and the godless culture's attack on marriage, as explored in chapters 2 and 3. God's call to his people today is to live out marriage as a mission to a watching world. Rather than discussing roles (appropriate versus inappropriate) and structures for Christian marriage, we ought to focus on how we in our marriages are missionaries to the culture in crucial areas of witness. The vision of a good marriage most often described in print and in sermons sometimes accommodates itself to the culture instead of confronting it. This happens in three areas: intimacy, personal self-fulfillment, and love. Until people of faith are freed from erroneous ideas about marriage, the state of matrimony will continue to baffle and disappoint many who have entered it.

Intimacy

First, the very American notion of the primacy of the individual (dating from the eighteenth century's revolutionary fervor) militates against intimacy in marriage. Americans value their autonomy inside and outside of marriage. Paul Ramsey has noted that for most people, marriage is simply a contract in which the two individuals "remain as atomistic as before marriage."[44] We feel the angst of our aloneness. We long for community and intimacy, but our individualism blocks that possibility. People marry, and in theologian Stanley Hauerwas's words, they find themselves in "a relationship between friendly strangers . . . [in which] intimacy is impossible to sustain."[45] We err if we think that marriage will automatically dispel our loneliness as we hold onto our autonomy. Until our mindset includes placing a higher value on "the common good" and accepting the limits imposed by the needs of another person, we will not transcend this self-sufficient, independent individualism. The absence of a strong, practical biblical theology of *community* for the people of God deprives Christians of the rationale and support for going against the tide of the culture's love affair with individualism. (Part 2 of this book develops a biblical theology of community.) If people of faith understood a theology of community, they would be able to bring into marriage a mindset that is focused on the common good.

Self-Fulfillment

The second erroneous idea in the culture's case against marriage, which is seldom addressed in the church, is the belief in the validity of personal self-fulfillment. Hauerwas, speaking from the church, put it this way: "We are encouraged to assume that marriage and the family are primarily institutions of personal fulfillment that are necessary for us to be 'whole' people."[46] He notes two facts we may overlook when caught up in a self-fulfillment ethic. The first is that we often marry the "wrong" person, or we marry the "right" person who changes into the "wrong" person as soon as the wedding has ended. We must learn how to love and care for this stranger to whom we find ourselves married. The second fact is the power struggle that is part of every relationship. Seeking our own self-fulfillment, as the basis of our understanding of marriage, will not in itself sustain a long-term relationship.

When or if the church addresses the issue of self-fulfillment, it sometimes does so by calling for a "selflessness" that denies the self any reality, but we cannot "give ourselves" if there is no "self" to give. A practical biblical theology of personhood as selves created in the image of God for the purpose of imaging God in his world means that we have real selves that are able to serve others in a manner similar to the way the triune God stoops to serve us in provision and empowerment. Such a theology enables those real selves to give up self-fulfillment as an end in itself and find it as a by-product of greater goals.

Love

A third erroneous idea that has crept into the church is the romantic assumption that love is necessary for marriage. The Puritans preached that love would grow in a marriage, but it was not a prerequisite to marriage. Spanish writer and philosopher Ortega y Gasset observed that "people do not live together merely to be together. They live together to do something together."[47] Marriage must have a purpose, a goal, a task beyond "being together." Christian marriage has as its goal the transformation of God's people, beginning with each member of the couple. Successful marriages are never just about two people living under the same roof without fighting. The glue that holds two people together for life must include shared tasks that enable them to prosper and grow together. Though romance is lovely, without shared tasks, it is not enough to sustain a marriage for a lifetime.

A Missional Marriage

Marriage is God's business. It is not just a human affair. As a Christian man and a Christian woman commit themselves to one another for life, *God* is present in that marriage. There is then a connection between two people *and God,* which is the sine qua non for a missional marriage.

Marriage becomes missional in two ways. First, the husband and wife, as bearers of God's image inside the marriage, live so that together they move one another toward fullness in Jesus Christ. Empowered by the Holy Spirit, they reflect God's purposes to one another, telling the truth of God in their actions and words within the relationship.

Second, marriage is missional when husband and wife, being salt and light, reflect God's image in the community through their relationship. In the way they relate to each other, the couple exhibits a credible demonstration of God's power, and their marriage becomes evangelistic. In a postmodern world, words are not enough. In fact words may be a hindrance to the message. But if the content of the relationship is faithful to the God being imaged in the community, it will speak for God and the gospel wherever that relationship is seen.

It is not enough to come alongside struggling Christian couples with seminars on communication or sexual intimacy or how to "fight fair." These may in some cases be helpful, but unless a Christian couple is challenged to live out a missional marriage, the seminars and workshops are mere Band-Aids on a cancer. God has a much bigger agenda for Christians struggling in less than wonderful marriages. The second half of this book now turns to the Scriptures to see what God says about marriage.

Part 2

God's Case
for Marriage

7

Preparing to Hear
God's Case for Marriage

ultural ideas have infected Christian understanding of marriage in subtle ways. Belief in the primacy of the individual, the overriding importance of personal self-fulfillment, and the essential experience of romantic love—all of these ideas stem from cultural presuppositions rather than Scripture. Common usage (including usage by some Christians) gives these ideas the appearance of truth despite the fact that they contain serious error when judged from a biblical viewpoint. In preparing to hear God's case for marriage, Christians need to anticipate that in some instances their present view of marriage owes more to the culture than they may suspect. It is an unsettling reality that committed Christians may believe very unchristian ideas and be unaware of the fact. It is also an unsettling reality that people (including Christians) tend to cling to the familiar even when they suspect that it may not be fully correct.

Many Christians face an additional, rather odd dilemma. Because most Christians value Scripture and have some familiarity with two or three New Testament passages that refer specifically to marriage, they can easily presume a working knowledge of Christian marriage that in reality falls far short of the mark. Christians are not always as familiar with Scripture as they assume they are. In a practical sense, preparing to hear God's case for

153

marriage entails accepting the challenge to learn something that in many instances people presume they already know. Turning to the Scriptures to see what God says about marriage requires more than opening a Bible. It requires an attitude that includes:

- willingness to reexamine the validity of the culture's focus on a happily-ever-after ending to the marital story
- willingness to hear God's case for marriage *from his (God's) point of view* as one part of his goals for his people, rather than as an end in itself or as the chief means of human happiness
- willingness to accept God's case for marriage in the *biblical narrative as a whole* with the resulting necessity to distinguish between God's changeless truth and a cultural expression of that truth
- willingness to explore the concepts of personal transformation and cultural mission as a part of God's case for marriage
- willingness to reexamine God's intent for marriage in the context of the family of God

Consciously choosing such an attitude helps clear out cultural concepts of marriage that we as God's people may have unknowingly allowed to shape our thinking.

The Elusive Happily-Ever-After

One difficulty in understanding God's point of view has been the human desire to ensure a happy ending to every marital story. This is a desire that Christians increasingly (although unwittingly) share with the culture around them.

Following a lecture on marriage and family life, the speaker responded to questions from the audience. A young woman stood. "So you think *God* invented marriage?" she asked, a challenge in her voice and a scowl on her face.

"Yes, as a matter of fact, I do think that," the speaker answered a bit cautiously.

"Well, I don't agree," the young woman said firmly. "It's a human thing. If God wanted to invent something, he would invent something that works. God—if there is one—is too smart to invent something that messes up all the time."

Christians, of course, are reluctant to blame God for a design error in the idea of marriage. But Christians are not fond of the fact that from the beginning God's idea of marriage has not played out smoothly, as God himself reports. Scripture frustrates people who are looking for a promised happily-ever-after formula for marriage. It is almost as though God goes out of his way in the biblical narrative to make the point that in most cases his people *didn't* live happily ever after.

The first family (Adam and Eve) had their problems. Adam demonstrated an unhelpful passivity throughout Eve's confrontation with the serpent in Eden, taking no direct action to support the marital bond and help Eve keep the marriage consistent with God's direction. He adopted a stance of watchful waiting, playing the odds to see what would happen. He said, in effect, "Do your own thing. Talk to that serpent if you want to. I'll watch." In the end, of course, he did far more than watch. When Eve, deceived by the serpent, chose to eat the forbidden fruit, Adam, *knowing full well what he was doing,* purposefully followed her into a place of alienation from God. He gave no indication of reluctance or dissent.

When the first family faced God to give an account of themselves, however, Adam was far from passive. He explained events with an astonishing demonstration of blaming behavior that implicated God as well as Eve. Adam said, in essence, "Listen, God, it's true that I ate some of that fruit. But the real issue here is Eve and you. It was *that woman you* gave me that caused the problem." Adam failed to support the marital bond, he shifted blame to Eve (and God) in self-serving protection of himself, and Adam demonstrated this behavior *before* the gate of the garden closed behind him. He did this on his own initiative. There was no model in Eden to teach Adam these self-justifying skills.

The biblical narrative in Genesis 3 indicates that Adam knowingly participated in the serpent's game, and that Eve, in contrast, was deceived by the serpent (v. 13; see also 2 Cor. 11:3). Nevertheless, Eve's behavior was certainly less than admirable. There is no indication that Eve gave a second thought to the possible implications of her behavior for Adam. The biblical narrative shows Eve in a demonstration of primordial individualism, entering into the debate with the serpent independently, preoccupied with doing her own thing. It is true that Adam was present and chose to watch without volunteering a single word of disagreement or warning. But apart from Adam's choice, Eve also failed to act in a way that supported the marital bond, and she chose her individual options without consideration of the impact on the marriage. No Ozzie and Harriet perfect marriage here, and God's report has reached only the third chapter of Genesis.

The story of the first family does not improve. Banished from Eden, Eve became pregnant and bore a son whom she named Cain. Then she bore a second son, Abel. When the sons were adults, Cain murdered Abel in a fit of jealousy. As punishment God sentenced Cain to be forever a wanderer, carrying a distinguishing mark that warned others of his identity. In the first generation out of the garden, God recorded murder of a sibling and a family separated by the consequences of this violence.

Cain's direct descendant Lamech was a polygamist.[1] In the Genesis narrative Lamech commanded his two wives (Adah and Zillah) to listen as he bragged about killing a young man who had attacked him. Then Lamech threatened terrible consequences for anyone who might seek to avenge the young man's death, providing a bravado encore for his listening wives. Not exactly the Walton family gathered for Sunday dinner.

Soon after the flood, Noah's family demonstrated dysfunctional behavior that resulted in a family tragedy (Gen. 9:20–27). Noah became drunk from the wine from his own vineyard. While he lay naked in his tent, his son Ham entered and looked at him. Ham then told his brothers what they could see if they went into the tent. Ham's brothers (Shem and Japheth), rather than participate in this quasi-pornographic experience, took a robe, and backing into the tent, placed the robe over their naked father.[2] When Noah awakened from his drunken stupor and learned what had happened, he cursed his great-grandchildren (the descendants of Ham's son Canaan) to perpetual servanthood (slavery?) in service to Shem and Japheth.

There is a harsh realism in this story. Certainly from our present understanding of human behavior, this is a family in trouble. *And this is the family God handpicked to be the sole survivors of the great flood.*

Abraham was a man of great faith. It was with Abraham that God initiated the covenant, promising a special son and descendants greater in number than the stars of the heavens. Yet twice in dangerous circumstances, Abraham lied about his wife, Sarah, to save his own skin (12:10–20; 20:1–18). In both instances Abraham placed Sarah at great risk of being incorporated into a king's harem and forced to become a king's sexual partner. Each time, Sarah was saved, but not through Abraham's effort and with no credit to him.

In the story of Isaac and Rebekah, the popular focus is on Isaac's love for his wife. The biblical narrative, however, shows a less-than-ideal family life. Like his father, Abraham, Isaac lied about Rebekah to a foreign king to save his own skin (26:6–10). The king prevented Rebekah from being taken into his harem when he happened to see Isaac fondling Rebekah and deduced (correctly) that she was Isaac's wife, not his sister as Isaac had said.

The Old Testament stories provide a long history of struggling, conflicted families:

- Jacob cheated his brother and deceived his blind old father (Genesis 27).
- Joseph's older brothers envied him and sold him into slavery (37:13–28).
- Abigail had to live with an alcoholic, abusive husband (1 Samuel 25).
- David, the king, took Bathsheba in an adulterous relationship, then killed her husband to cover his sin (2 Samuel 11).
- Tamar, David's daughter, was raped by her half brother Amnon, and her father did nothing to redress the crime (2 Samuel 13).
- And there are the stories of the concubines and the slave women and of marriage by God's people with foreigners that was a part of their slow, steady slide away from Israel's true God.

The Old Testament provides some positive accounts of relationships between men and women, however. Read the passionate celebration of sexual love in the Song of Solomon. Note the tender, gentle love between Hannah and Elkanah. Observe Ruth, the Moabite, faithful to the one true God of Israel. She becomes the heroine in a love story in which a lonely young widow "finds the right man" and becomes an ancestor of the Messiah. Learn from the awesome lady of Proverbs 31 whose family rose up to call her blessed. And through the long "boring" genealogical tables, the biblical narrative records generations of faithful, imperfect families who, despite their quarreling and human sinfulness, together formed the people of God.

The New Testament, like the Old, gives a less than ideal picture of marriage and family life. The controversy regarding divorce, into which the Pharisees sought to entangle Jesus, provides an insight into marriage as it was practiced by God's people in New Testament times. Some religious leaders taught that a man could legitimately divorce his wife if she displeased him for any reason (burned his food while cooking it, for example). Other religious leaders taught that only adultery was legitimate grounds for divorce. Jesus responded to the Pharisees by pointing back to God's original plan in Genesis, saying, in effect, "Your very question shows how far you've drifted from God's intended pattern" (Matt. 19:1–11). Jesus' own human family had their share of trouble. His siblings distrusted him and at one point questioned his sanity (see Mark 3:21).

But in the New Testament, as in the Old, there are occasional glimpses of better things. We learn about the home of Martha, Mary, and Lazarus where Jesus often came to rest. Even here, however, we see conflict between the two sisters (Luke 10:38–42). There was Peter's home in Capernaum where Jesus also went at times to rest. On one occasion he healed Peter's mother-in-law who lived with them (Mark 1:30–31).[3] In the early church Priscilla and Aquila, a remarkable couple of educated, passionate believers, worked together as tentmakers while they ministered together, sharing the good news of the gospel in Rome, Corinth, and Ephesus.

Yet in a real sense, the positives are the exception. The awkward fact is that the biblical narrative is *not* filled with descriptions of wonderful, loving families and happy, soul-mate marriages. Instead, it shows struggling, imperfect people, often in conflict, driven by self-protection and self-serving motives. The Bible makes it clear that whatever God had in mind when he designed marriage and the family, his people have experienced considerable difficulty living out God's idea. When people speak glibly of a "biblical view of marriage," a student of Scripture (or a perceptive postmodern inquirer) may be forgiven for asking, "To which of these stories are you pointing as an illustration?"

During our preparation of this manuscript, a young woman read part of this chapter, then said with a thoughtful look, "There are a lot of places in the Bible where people really messed up, aren't there?" Precisely. Christians are often surprised and perplexed when they discover how unbalanced the biblical narrative is; there are few examples of couples who appear to have a happily-ever-after ending to their story. While some couples, Elizabeth and Zacharias, Mary and Joseph, and Priscilla and Aquila, appear to have been happy and devoted to each other, the biblical narrative does not report these marriages with exclamation points, as though God were saying, "See! That's what I have in mind!"

And there is a second surprise. While it is embarrassing that God's people have demonstrated relatively few "good marriages" (whatever that may mean), it is even more embarrassing that God has made this fact evident with a wealth of embarrassing details. Christians (as well as the inquiring unbeliever) may well wonder what a forgiving God had in mind when he kept such a long, meticulous record of people who did indeed mess up. And they may wonder further what God meant by putting all this messy human imperfection on full display, then claiming these folks as "my people." Clearly, God's concern was for something other than his reputation or the exhibition of a happily-ever-after formula for his human creatures.

In this culture, people (including many Christians) long so intently for the happily-ever-after formula that it is easy to misunderstand God's low-key reporting of "good" marriages and the record of marital struggle included in God's story. As these biblical passages faithfully record the marital difficulty of God's people, they make a vitally important point that is often missed. *Marriage matters to God for some reason in addition to human happiness.* In the face of his people's stubborn resistance and poor marital track record, God continued to pay specific attention to their marriages. God was not indifferent to the muddle his people made of marriage, and he clearly disapproved of many of the ways in which his people behaved (both in and out of marriage). But human failure is not the only point. What is striking in the biblical narrative is God's consistent attention to this most basic of human relationships. Marital difficulties were recorded because (among other reasons) marriage is highly significant in God's plan.

The fact that the biblical narrative contains few happily-ever-after stories intrigued the young woman who read an early draft of this chapter. She went home, thought more about what she had read, then sent us a brief e-mail message: "I don't think I get it." What she didn't get, is, of course, what the culture doesn't get. If God cares about marriage, why doesn't he ensure that the happily-ever-after part of the story comes true every time? Doesn't he care about human happiness? When people initially consult the biblical narrative for information about marriage, they often feel much like the young woman. They know they've read something important, but they are not sure what it was.

Douglas Brouwer offers a helpful comment in regard to this common experience:

> I believe it *is* possible to describe a biblical view of marriage, but getting there . . . require[s] taking a very careful, very thorough look at the Bible. My sense about the Bible is that it says both less and more than we sometimes think it does. The Bible says *less* about marriage in the sense that there are few places where it tells us exactly how to have a successful, satisfying, and God-honoring marriage. . . . We might hope for something much more explicit and direct, but we aren't going to find it. . . . So the Bible says less about marriage than we want it to. But the Bible also says *more* about marriage than we might

sometimes imagine. . . . the Bible has many valuable things to say about marriage—but we'll often find them in unexpected places.[4]

God's case for marriage is compelling. But in considering the scriptural narrative, it soon becomes clear that God chose to make his case for marriage from his own point of view and in full recognition of the long history of marital difficulty that his people have experienced.

God's Case from His Point of View

God has chosen to weave his case for marriage throughout the biblical narrative as a whole, making marriage one part of the long story of God's relationship with his people. In a real sense, God's case for marriage stretches from Genesis to Revelation. No major portions can be safely skipped. One of God's most powerful messages, for example, comes in the book of Hosea, one of the minor prophets. In an impatient culture, this long view can present a challenge.

At the simplest level, meeting this challenge requires that God's people accept the fact that Scripture is *God's* story, after all, and God has a right to tell his story his way and to expect his people to hear it from his point of view. To do this, the listener must lay aside, however reluctantly, the human bias toward centering the search for truth in the human self. In the present individualistic culture, it is difficult to grasp the reality that to hear God, his people must shift their attention away from what they want to hear and focus, instead, on what God wants to say. Shifting to God's point of view is good for the human soul, but it often proves to be a severe stretch for human egos.

Sometimes, to their embarrassment, God's people discover that they are less interested in hearing God's case than in pursuing their own goals. For example, people (Christian and non-Christian alike) come seeking a failsafe method for marriage. And to these formula seekers, God does indeed say less than they may wish he did, as Douglas Brouwer has pointed out. With this realization, even God's people can be tempted to say, "God, your story is a very fine one, but if you are not going to give me a formula for instant happiness, your story is not relevant to my life."

The fact that some of what God says in his story requires cultural translation poses a further challenge. Christians must not only lay aside their personal agenda but also recognize their responsibility to sort their way carefully through cultural differences to the core of God's truth. God's changeless essentials of marriage are packaged differently when they are at work in a wandering desert tribe than when they are operating in the technologically oriented present world.

Hearing God requires that his people think about their own relationship with the present culture as well. The influence of the modern culture encourages Christians to look in their Bibles as good scientists might for a list, a law, a formula. The modern world assumed that "real" truth inevitably came packaged this way. When Christians, thinking like modernists, discover that God's story contains no fail-safe formulas for marriage, it sometimes seems as though God has not spoken at all. God has indeed spoken, as this last section of the book will explore, but God's point of view is not always packaged as a modern thinker might expect.

Desire for a formula is not the only culturally influenced issue. In preparing to hear God's case for marriage, Christians can find themselves listening unwittingly with a very postmodern concern. What, they may ask themselves, is in God's case for *me*? How will God's case make *my* life better? What will make *me* happy and *my* marriage good? God in his mercy is, of course, concerned about his people's lives and marriages. He wants more for his own than they can dream or understand. But hearing God requires his people to shift their perspective from their goals for themselves and to consider marriage in light of God's goals for their lives.

Hearing God's case for marriage is in one sense a straightforward task. Christians need to look at the biblical narrative as a whole, watch out for cultural factors, and adopt God's point of view (as much as is humanly possible). Additionally, Christians need to consider as honestly as they can how the desire for happy endings may shape their understanding of God's story. In practice, each of these factors is more complex than it may sound.

Barriers to Hearing the Biblical Narrative as a Whole

The present culture demonstrates a strong bias toward quick answers. A student in a Bible study group observed rather plaintively, "Sometimes God takes a long time to get to the bottom line." But whatever the challenge to human patience, God has woven his case for marriage throughout his story from beginning to end. God's story is not designed for cut and paste—the biblical narrative must be taken as a whole. Another student said in disbelief, "There's nothing about marriage in Revelation. You're pulling my leg!" It is true that there is not a verse specifically addressed to husbands and wives in the book of Revelation. But Revelation is the end of God's story and it does indeed have something to say about marriage, and most particularly about a happily-ever-after ending. But this is woven into God's story in a way that defies easy labeling.

For this reason, taking the biblical narrative as a whole challenges the bias of the Information Age toward answers that are concrete, specific, and easily accessible. What God says about marriage lies embedded in his *whole* story. Even more, God has integrated his case for marriage not only in the whole story but in the meaning of the whole story. Marriage in God's story cannot be sectioned out into an appendix or a footnote. He does not provide a neatly labeled to-do list for happy marriages. Instead God presents marriage as a part of the complex business of *being* God's people both with God and with each other.

"Is that a bottom line?" one student asked in disbelief.

It is. Much current difficulty comes from Christians' failure to understand that *marriage for God's people is not an end in itself.* (In this failure, contemporary Christians are not far from the disciples who needed to be reminded that God's plan for his people does not include marriage in heaven.) Because marriage is embedded within the experience of God's people, it cannot, in a form of spiritual reductionism, be abstracted into a legalized prescription for marital roles.

In some of Paul's letters to the early church, there are passages specifically addressed to husbands and wives. When Christians think like modernists (viewing truth as limited to the concrete and measurable), they sometimes place an irresponsible emphasis on these passages in the biblical narrative and assume that only these labeled portions of God's story are relevant to God's case for marriage. This misplaced emphasis leads to a serious misunderstanding of God's goal and purpose for marriage in the lives of his people; it distorts the way in which the biblical narrative as a whole speaks to the nature and character of Christian marriage. The gospel account of Jesus and his disciples on the evening of the Last Supper provides a good example of the way misplaced concreteness can limit understanding of God's Word. In this account, Jesus not only told his followers something about marriage—he showed them. *But he didn't mark it concretely: "This is a message for husbands and wives."*

Jesus had told his disciples plainly that he would be killed. They were frightened and confused. At his instruction, they had rented a room and had prepared their last Passover feast together. They sat down to the meal, tense, tired, travel-stained, their feet unwashed. Washing feet was a servant's job, but apparently no servant was available. None of the disciples volunteered for the dirty, demeaning task. They simply sat down and the meal began. But after a while, Jesus quietly got up, took a towel and basin of water, knelt down, and began to wash the disciples' feet. The room grew utterly silent. They knew *who* was eating with them. This Jesus was the Christ, the beloved Son of God, the one some of them had seen transfigured in glory, talking with Moses and Elijah. They knew *what* was happening. This Jesus, the Christ, was kneeling on the floor of a rented room washing their feet. The Messiah himself on his last night with them was washing *their dirty feet*. They knew the *who* and the *what*, but their hearts were not yet clear about *why* he had chosen to do this.

When Jesus came to Peter, Peter could not bear the silence. "Lord," he cried out, incredulous, "are *you* going to wash *my* feet?"

"You don't understand what I'm doing, Peter," Jesus told him gently, "but you will understand later."

"No," Peter objected, "you'll never wash *my* feet."

"Unless I wash you," Jesus insisted even more gently, "you have no part with me."

"Then," responded Peter, "wash not just my feet but my hands and my head as well" (see John 13:6–9).

The room grew silent again. The biblical narrative tells us that when at last Jesus had finished washing the disciples' feet, he returned to his place at the table. When he was settled, he said simply, "Now that I, your Lord and Teacher, have washed your feet, you also should wash one another's feet. I have set you an example that you should do as I have done for you" (John 13:14–15).

Is this about marriage? Is it about husbands and wives? Of course it is. It speaks to the very core of Christian marriage. But because it is not concretely labeled, our modern minds can easily miss it. Christian marriage, if it is anything, is a call for God's people to take Jesus' example into the heart of our everyday, ordinary waking, sleeping, eating, working lives together as husbands and wives. This is an essential of Christian marriage.

What would happen if the ancient rite of foot washing were integrated into a modern wedding ceremony? The bride would probably trip over her wedding gown and the nervous groom would likely spill the water, and the whole affair would certainly ruin the wedding consultant's day. But think what it could mean if in the public context of the marriage vows they take, Christians were to act out in symbolic reality their Christian mandate to serve one another. Certainly washing feet is less glamorous and romantic than lifting the bride's shimmering veil and kissing her. But

God's people are not called to be glamorous and romantic. They are called in radical discipleship to serve one another just as Jesus served his disciples that night—for better or for worse. Is this story about marriage missed in the biblical narrative? Often. And it is frequently missed because people are looking for a concrete marriage label that is not there.

Distinguishing Goal and Purpose from Structure

In God's case for marriage, he distinguishes between his goal and purpose for marriage and the structure of marriage, though both are important. This distinction is not always labeled as such, but failure to make and maintain this distinction risks making nonsense of some important truth. For example, the marriages described in the Old Testament can seem irrelevant to us if we focus solely on their structure, which is foreign to the present culture and difficult for contemporary readers to understand.

For the most part, Old Testament families were large, extended, polygamous kinship groups (although Israel more than its neighboring kingdoms practiced monogamous marriage). These extended families lived and worked together for economic, educational, and protective goals, and their marriages were contracted to promote economic growth and to secure political power and influence. In these family groups, members were intensely loyal to each other, but they also had their share of conflict, deceit, rivalry, and dishonesty. Human passion and sexual attraction were present, as we see in Jacob and Rachel, but romantic love as we think of it was rare and a relatively unimportant factor in forming marriage contracts. Relationships were measured in terms of obligation, respect, duty, and the hard coin of economic gain and political power.

In that culture an individual would not think of living independently of family, and marriage relationships based solely on personal fulfillment were unknown. While divorce was a frequent occurrence, divorce based on "falling out of love with each other" would have made little sense to these ancient people.[5] For us to learn from them requires thinking about people in a world in which belief in individualism and the goal of romantic fulfillment as it is currently pursued were not simply irrelevant—these ideas had not yet been conceived. God's essential truths are eternal and unchangeable, but the ways in which these truths are expressed are shaped by the given culture in which they are embedded.

Some structural factors can change without altering the essentials. For example, no one seriously makes a case for reinstating the bride price demanded by Old Testament marriage contracts as an essential part of Christian marriage. But the risk of contemporary cultural confusion should make us cautious in thinking about structure. For example, in the present culture in which two-career families are common, is maintaining a structure that incorporates a stay-at-home-parent essential to a Christian marriage? Is there something about structure that is independent of culture in the marriages of God's people in all cultures, at all times?

God does indeed have something to say about structure, but it is linked inseparably to God's goal and purpose for marriage. In Old Testament families, God called his people to practice marriage in a distinctive way that marked them as God's people, in contrast to other people around them. In so doing, they were to demonstrate to their unbelieving neighbors something of God's character and faithfulness to them.[6] They were to be faithful to each other (adultery was strictly forbidden), but that structural fidelity functioned as more than a directive for marriage. It served as an expression of God's faithful relationship with his people.

Christians no longer sign a marriage contract specifying a bride price. That specific cultural component has changed, but God's call for Christian marriage to reflect his relationship with his people has not changed. God has not altered that eternal purpose and the structure of sexual fidelity in marriage that expresses that purpose.

Marriage in the Context of God's Story

The biblical narrative comes as a bit of a shock to modern/postmodern nervous systems. The overriding importance of happiness is a cultural given; the postmodern reader assumes that God, if he is indeed good and loving, is primarily interested in ensuring a happy ending to individual human stories. Unfortunately, Christians are not immune to this expectation; some "Christian" prayers at their core are little more than petitions to God to come and be in a human story and give it a happy ending. It is a shock to discover that God has nothing so silly in mind. His intent, thankfully, is the reverse. He longs for us to come and be in his story and to be transformed in the process.

Understanding marriage from God's point of view rests on an understanding of this, God's awesome invitation to all people: "Come, be with me. Be in my story, be my people in my story, in a relationship that will not end." But people come, to borrow from Tolkien's imagery, asking God to come to their personal tea party and make it wonderful. They discover, instead, that God invites them to come with him on a terrible quest—to come with him to cast, at the end, all evil into the cracks of doom, and then make the world beautiful again beyond all dreams.

For the most part, at least initially, his human creatures are not pleased with God's invitation, splendid though it may be. Although people are reluctant to admit this, they would much rather have God at the center of their story than have their story revolve around God and his goals. It would be more pleasant and comfortable, they think, if God would consent to come be in their marriages and make them turn out marvelously to his people's pleasure and the watching world's envy. But most people have an intuitive sense that if they sign on to be in God's story, then like Sam with Frodo, the journey to the end is likely to be one of those adventures that make splendid stories for telling, but in the doing are likely to include some days of slogging through mud with the rain dripping miserably down one's neck.

And they are right to be suspicious. For once into God's story, people discover with what grace and passion God forgives his people for their sin and failure. And they discover as well that it is profoundly unsettling to be forgiven as God does it with an ungrudging generosity that does not count the cost. But people are downright dismayed when they find that God follows forgiveness with a stubborn insistence on transforming his people into a distinctive people who bear his very image. And in God's case for marriage, marriage is a unique human experience in which God's people are called to be the distinctive people of God and distinctively the people of God with each other. God indeed cares about human happiness, but it is happiness linked inseparably with the process of being transformed into the distinctive people of God.

God's case for marriage is not about a prescription for thrills and feel-good. It is not a game plan designed to produce soul mates whose overarching achievement is personal emotional fulfillment. God's case for marriage is based on his goal of the transformation of his people into faithful image bearers. But what Christians discover (often to their surprise) is that once they buy into God's program, personal fulfillment at an undreamed-of level comes as an unlooked-for by-product of old-fashioned obedience and willingness to fit into God's plan.

Marriage and Mission

God's case for marriage entails mission as well as transformation. Anthropologists know that all societies throughout human history have had marriage in some form. From the beginning of the human drama, marriage for all people has been a part of God's story, but marriage for God's people incorporates an utterly astonishing assignment.

First, marriage for God's people is to be transformational. Married couples are to become more like God through the process of being *with each other the living embodiment of what they are with God and he is with them.*[7] In their "everyday, ordinary life—[their] sleeping, eating, going-to-work, and walking-around life" (Rom. 12:1 MESSAGE), they are to *be* the embodiment of God in community with his people. Second, they are to do so with such integrity and fidelity that those who are "not my people" can see and come to know God. In short, marriage in God's plan was designed to be both transformational and missional. It is marriage in this sense of both its transformational and missional aspects that occupies the remainder of this book.

A Christian's understanding of marriage in this sense can be complicated by two other issues that often enter unwittingly into a Christian's consideration of marriage. One is the issue of the uneasy relationship between the Christian mandate and the civil laws of the state; the other is the issue of the discipline of the church itself.

Church and State

Early Christians did not expect Caesar's senators to reflect God's point of view in their laws. American Christians are less clear on this point. For the most part, Christians believe rightly that it is helpful when the state legislates from a value system that is congruent with God's point of view. Traditionally Christians have assumed that civil law shaped on that foundation is more likely to be just and good law, helpful to all. Christians believe that a Christian worldview mediated through civil government contributes to the common good, but many Christians have reshaped this correct belief that their faith can and should make a contribution to the common good into a misguided conviction that Christians can and should compel others to live by their Christian mandate.

In an increasingly pluralistic post-Christian society, Christians need to proceed cautiously.[8] Citizenship in a democracy does not necessarily authorize Christians to compel Caesar to serve Christ. Muddled thinking at this point can confuse Christians' sense of the reality of their true citizenship, which is based in a kingdom not of this world. God's people are *resident aliens* as Hauerwas and Willimon have reminded us. Marvin Olasky, considering the drift of the present culture, has urged Christians to think carefully how they should live in the present Babylon.[9]

When the Supreme Court rules in *Lawrence v. Texas* that sodomy laws are unconstitutional, Christians, who are resident aliens, need to remind themselves that such a decision stems from a logic that is valid in *Babylon*. At the same time, as citizens, Christians may (indeed, they must) give a reasoned response that grapples with the issues of judicial activism—a serious issue in a constitutional democracy. Christians must consider carefully the likely repercussions of this decision for all *resident aliens* living in Babylon. What does it mean for Christian citizens in a constitutional democracy to live in a state in which this ruling now frames the legal regulation of sexual behavior? But in doing this, Christians must remember that they *simultaneously* wear two hats—one a clear heavenly blue and the other bearing the symbol of the civil state. Christians should be very clear with themselves and with others which hat they are wearing when they speak and be careful to frame their statements in the context of *both* civil history and the specifics of the mandate given to God's people. Early Christians worked out a radical sexual ethic and a pattern of Christian marriage in a world in which Roman law supported slavery, the exposure of unwanted newborns (death by abandonment), and homosexual practice. Early Christians changed the world, but they did not do it by lobbying Caesar's senate. Contemporary Christians can learn from the early church both how to live Christianly in Babylon and how to achieve some changes in civil law in the process.

In doing so, Christians must face their own bottom line. When the rules of Babylon and the rules of the Christians' "home country" collide, they must be clear where their loyalties lie. Peter and the apostles facing Rome *and* the religious court of their day said (rather matter of factly, according to the record), "We must obey God rather than human beings!" (Acts 5:29). Then they went out and did so with courage and with little surprise at the often-fatal consequences.

Daniel, living in Babylon, went to the lions' den because he would not pray to the king (Dan. 6:1–23), and there is no evidence that he complained en route: "How dare you do this to me! I am a consultant to the king!" Historically it has never been safe in Babylon, although American Christians have a hard time remembering that. In America Christians have been blessed with an unusually long period of time in which they could live out their faith with minimal civil interference. This may be changing. Our Babylon is now becoming increasingly hostile to God's people. But that is new only in this century. It is an old story in the biblical narrative of the history of God's people and in human history throughout the world.

The point is straightforward in regard to marriage. As Christians prepare to hear God's case for marriage, they must hear it as a mandate for *Christian living* not as an agenda for legislative action. And, whether Babylon approves or disapproves, Christians are called to be obedient to the Christian mandate. As citizens in a democracy, Christians may actively work to encourage civil laws that support marriage and the family. At the same time they would do well to remember the old adage, "He who sups with the devil needs a long spoon." For example, Christians willing to support laws such as Louisiana's tougher divorce laws may get more in the bargain than they want. The state that gathers to itself the power to forbid the dissolution of marriage can by that same power ultimately rule who can and cannot marry.

The deeper question is this: Do Christians really want to ask the state to do for them what they are called in the power of resurrection life in Christ to do for themselves? Do Christians want the law of the state to keep them married by making divorce impossible? Or do they want to keep themselves married by their chosen fidelity to the Christian mandate? It is no bargain to substitute the coercion of the state for the disciplines of the sanctified heart.

Contemporary Church Discipline

A class of young unchurched adults systematically studying the Bible for the first time came to the account of the man who was having sexual relationships with his stepmother (1 Cor. 5:1–5). Initially they were surprised by the man's behavior. To their teacher's amusement, they appeared to think that their generation knew things about questionable sexual behavior that had not even been imagined by those "old-time people in the Bible." They were surprised to find the "new" sins of their generation clothed in old togas, so to speak. But what surprised them most was Paul's response.

"Paul just raised heck," one student said in an amazed voice, "*with that church*!" Precisely. Paul's concern was not just the scandalous behavior. He assumed that everyone was clear that such behavior was unacceptable among God's people. But he was intensely concerned that the church, the local group of believers with whom this man worshiped, had failed to take action regarding his sin.

Church discipline has had a long and complicated history since the crisis of that early Corinthian church. Any person on a church staff knows about the dangerous and slippery interface between church and state at this point in time. Increasingly, church action taken in regard to those who worship with them is subject to review in civil court. The lines are not clear, and the cultural-civil principles of individual freedom frequently overrule the boundaries that churches may choose to draw.

It is difficult for the church in the present postmodern culture to develop discipleship and spiritual maturity in those who come to faith in Jesus Christ. For example, contemporary worship services are effective in evoking participation and praise, but they do not automatically produce disciplined Christian living. In the present "anything goes" culture, it is no easy thing for God's people to hold those who become part of the faith family accountable to serious standards of conduct.

And equally significant, contemporary Christians, for the most part, assume their marriage is a personal matter, and in a functional sense it is none of the church's business. It is easy to imagine objections from Christians to even minimal standards: "What business is it of the church to tell me how to run my marriage?" "Are you going to set up the church police?" "Who cares? Everyone has to work out their own stuff." "Nobody's perfect. I don't think we should judge."

One of the challenging tasks of the contemporary family of God is the nurture of believers into mature Christians whose lives are disciplined and committed to genuine holy living. It is a matter of serious concern that the contemporary church has demonstrated limited ability to promote spiritually disciplined living. (The growing interest in spiritual formation acknowledges this.) And at some levels, the church has been reluctant to acknowledge the connection between this failure and the deterioration of marriage and family life in the Christian community.

Christian marriage is no walk in the park. It requires Christians who are determined to live Christianly at the level of everyday ordinary life. It demands Christians who take with utmost seriousness the responsibility and privilege of forgiveness and who bend to the task of serving others with hearts raised in obedient gladness to God.

The discipline of the church is not merely about what to do when people fail. That, as difficult as it is, is the simplest thing and likely the least important. The vital discipline of the church in regard to marriage lies elsewhere in the ancient disciplines of the spiritual life by which God's people are prepared to walk with him in the power and resilience of the resurrection life. God's idea of marriage has a rather terrifying splendor about it. It is not at all romantic, but (to risk a romantic-sounding phrase anyway) it is an idea that, if Christians catch on to it, will make everyday heroes of us all. But it takes more than six sessions of premarital counseling to be prepared for what God has in mind.

Challenges for Christians

Considered from God's point of view, God's problem does not lie in his case for marriage. It lies in his difficulty in getting a hearing for his case. The biblical narrative indicates that getting people to listen is not exactly a new problem for God. Over the ages he has said, "Listen," and "Hear me, my people," many times, but with limited response. It is possible to think reverently that God himself may have wondered at times if his people had collectively become completely deaf. While at the deepest level God's people are dependent on the Spirit of God to create in them a hearing heart and a desire to obey, at a simpler level God's people can choose to listen. It is their responsibility to prepare to hear God's case for marriage.

This requires God's people to take the biblical narrative seriously, although this perspective goes harshly against the grain of the postmodern society. Christians have no choice at this point, however. Only within the context of God's story can Christians understand their history and themselves. In issues of marriage as in all matters of faith, Christians come to the biblical narrative out of the certainty that God has spoken to his people through the Word and in these last days has revealed himself to us in Jesus Christ.

This point of beginning may seem to be self-evident. But it is not wise to assume that God's people have always understood the fundamental importance of God's story or their part in it. It is even more foolish to assume that God's people have always welcomed his word to them. Furthermore, in ways that may surprise them, Christians may find themselves more the children of the postmodern age than they realized, content to take the biblical narrative as God's Word only as long as it fits the cultural sense of what is true or what they personally want to be true for their lives. In reality, Christians may be less pleased to hear the biblical narrative as *God's* Word when it challenges their comfort or habitual way of thinking. Hearing God's case for marriage means that Christians must be prepared for a challenge to choose. One day as some people dithered around about the pros and cons of Jesus' messiahship, he went to the core of the matter, telling them in essence: "If you will do, then you will know" (see John

7:17). *Preparing to hear God's case means committing in advance to do whatever the Spirit of God enables his people to know.*

Preparation to hear God means struggling to abandon the modern conviction that we as individuals are the most important players in God's drama. The toxic debris from the modern way of thinking combines with the individualism of the postmodern world in ways that make this task a severe challenge. Contemporary Christians tend to read the biblical stories focused on the individuals who attract attention (the rascal Jacob, Hannah praying for a child, Ruth leaving her people, Lydia down by the riverside, Timothy needing some wine for his stomach's sake). These are the "real folks" who interest us. But the *family* of God—God's *people*, the *church*, the *body* of Christ, the *congregation* of the saints, the *great cloud* of witnesses, the very idea of *community*—all these collective nouns of which God seems so fond do not appeal to the contemporary reader. But it is precisely within the context of community that the biblical narrative (including those long pages about messy families in the Old Testament) has a healing word from God. The current culture has produced an epidemic of individualism with countless unconscious, unprotesting victims, many of whom are Christians. God's case for marriage confronts the Christian with God's investment in community and the broader family of God. In hearing God's case for marriage, Christians are challenged to acknowledge their culturally ingrained individualism and ask for grace to hear God's case anyway.

Christians must also deal with the cultural addiction to doing things the easy way. Cultural values suggest that if a task is difficult, if it is challenging, if it requires endurance and resilience to begin again when failure occurs, then there is something inherently, intrinsically wrong with the process. If it is hard, the process is bad. The idea that God might ask his people to do a difficult task, one requiring endurance, patience, and perseverance—the very idea is anathema. When Christians suspect that hearing God's case for marriage might entail being asked to learn the lesson of resilience and develop the ability to fail and pick oneself up and try again, they are inclined to postpone hearing God's case for marriage until another day.

At one level Christians understand that while easy is comfortable, comfortable is not always good. And the cross, Christianity's most basic symbol, does not suggest that "easy does it" has ever been the motto of either God or his saints. But the present postmodern world enflames every small piece of spiritual laziness into a serious temptation. "Feel good—do what feels good," wheedles the consumer-driven culture. "You know it is the right thing to do because it feels so good." In contrast, Paul's message to the Corinthians is radically countercultural. "Run the race to win," he urged them, and encouraged them to discipline themselves as would any serious athlete who runs for the prize. Preparing to hear God's case means accepting the very real possibility that God may invite his people to run—victoriously—a marathon, not to sit leisurely through a matinee.

Most difficult of all, preparing to listen to God's case for marriage means preparing to listen to God, to hear his heartaches, to catch (if only for a moment) a glimpse of God's dream, to understand with what agonizing cost he has dealt with the fragments left from Eden's tragedy. Preparing to listen to God's case for marriage means risking a life-altering glimpse into the heart of God, his infinite love, his incredible dream for these earthlings created in his image, to see (if only for a moment) his design for marriage—not ours.

8

Marriage on God's Terms

What did God have in mind in the beginning? What (in his wonderful new world) was God thinking about when he took the incredible risk of making Adam and Eve male and female and placing them together in the garden? And what (in his bent and broken world) did God think about marriage when his original pair stumbled out of the garden, and the gate swung shut—permanently—behind them? What then?

In the Beginning

What was God thinking about? Actually, rightly understood, he was thinking about himself. What God *did* in creating marriage grew out of who God *is*. And who God *is* is a profoundly relational Trinity: Father, Son, and Holy Spirit, existing in an eternal dance (Greek: *perichoresis*) of love.[1]

The Genesis texts are shadowed from the very outset with the presence of the Trinity: "Let *us* make humankind in *our* image, according to *our* likeness," the record reads (Gen. 1:26, italics added). The plurality in the text requires that the created likeness-to-God (the *imago dei*) in the image-bearers incorporated the relational aspects of God. A fully developed theology of the Holy Spirit cannot be inferred from this Genesis text, but what is clearly present in the text is the eternal reality of relationship and community within the Godhead. God had the idea of togetherness-in-loving-connection because that is what he himself experienced as Father, Son, and Spirit. Marriage is not an accommodation to human limitations. It springs from the very character of God.

The New Testament contains normative teaching about marriage, but both Jesus and the apostle Paul point back to the opening chapters of Genesis as crucial for understanding this central truth about marriage as the togetherness-in-loving-connection of a man and a woman. It is inherent in their creation and in God's purposes for them together as bearers of the divine image. The first chapter of the Bible records these words:

> Then God said, "Let us make humankind in our image, according to our likeness; and let them have dominion over the fish of the sea, and over the birds of the air, and over the cattle, and over all the wild animals of the earth, and over every creeping thing that creeps upon the earth." So God created humankind in his image, in the image of God he created them; male and female he created them. God blessed them, and God said to them, "Be fruitful and multiply, and fill the earth and subdue it; and have dominion over the fish of the sea and over the birds of the air and over every living thing that moves upon the earth."
>
> Genesis 1:26–28 NRSV

Why should this biblical passage be so important? This text is foundational because it describes what God had in mind for humanity created in his image before the world was corrupted by sin. Only as we examine God's intended relationship for the first man and first woman before they sinned can we get a sense of what God has in mind for us as his image-bearers in our world.

In the second chapter of Genesis God is pleased with his creative work and calls it good. God then displays a rather astonishing response, not to Adam (Adam was part of the good creation) but to Adam's aloneness. "It is not good for the man to be alone," God noted with obvious concern. "I will make a helper suitable for him" (Gen. 2:18 NIV).

God began his search for a solution to Adam's problem by bringing to Adam all the living creatures for Adam to name. It must have been enormous fun for Adam—choosing a name for the creature with the long, long neck and funny long legs, and for the creature with the huge flapping ears and ivory tusks. But when the giraffe and elephant were gone, and the parrot had flown away to preen her brilliant feathers in a nearby tree, Adam was still alone. Even when a dog came and lay down at Adam's feet for a nap, Adam was still alone. No suitable helper had been found for him among the living creatures. Adam's relational needs required a special solution, something not yet present in God's creation. God responded with a new creation to meet Adam's relational need.

God caused Adam to fall into a deep sleep, and while Adam was sleeping, God took a part of Adam's body and made a woman. When God brought the woman to Adam, he took one look and burst out in joyful recognition, "This is *one*! This is one *like me*! Bones and flesh from my body! This is one like me!" And it is in the context of Adam's great joy in the one *like him* that the Genesis narrative lays down the foundation of God's basic design for marriage: "For this reason a man will leave his father and mother and be united to his wife, and they will become one flesh" (Gen. 2:24 NIV).

It is the first dawn of humanity. God is pleased with his creation— Adam and Eve, standing newly minted in Eden, so to speak, astonished and delighted with their mutual humanness. And God's plan for them stretched out before them in endless joy. It is to this passage of Scripture that Jesus pointed when he reminded the Pharisees of God's original plan for marriage:

> Haven't you read . . . that at the beginning the Creator "made them male and female," and said, "For this reason a man will leave his father and mother and be united to his wife, and the two will become one flesh"? So they are no longer two, but one. Therefore what God has joined together, let no one separate.
>
> Matthew 19:4–6

The "for this reason" in the Genesis text rests solidly on the *relational* imperative that led to Eve's creation. God did *not* say, "Adam has too much work to do. Let's send help." God did *not* say, "Adam is the important First Man of humanity. Let's send someone to cook and clean for him." God did *not* say, "Adam needs help in making babies." What God *did* say was, "Adam is alone. That aloneness is not good. Let's make someone like him so that he will be alone no longer." And it is to connection, not procreation, that Jesus pointed in his confrontation with the Pharisees: "Haven't you read . . . 'for this reason . . . a man will . . . be united to his wife, and the two will become one flesh'? So they are no longer two, but one. Therefore what God has joined together, let man not separate."

Why did Adam's aloneness so concern God? While it is important to go cautiously here, it is fair to say that God wanted for Adam what he himself experienced within the Trinity—intimate connection with another of his kind. "Let Us make man in Our image, according to Our likeness," the text reads. For that image to be complete, Adam needed to be in relationship, not only with the Creator, whose image he bore, but also with another of his kind, one like him.

In this sense, God's design for marriage grew out of God's own experience of community. Adam and Eve (and the human race deriving from them) carry the *imago dei*. They are the image-bearers, and as such are hardwired for relationship and community. God's design for marriage and family expresses something of who God is as well as his provision for the earthlings he created to carry his image.

As we think about God's purpose for marriage, however, it is helpful to understand that God had two relational goals in mind. God's goal in his creation of the initial image-bearer was to make a person "in his image" so that God and the image-bearer could be in fellowship together. Then prompted by the aloneness of this initial image-bearer, God made another like the first *and* like God so that they could *both* be in fellowship with each other *and* with him.

Adam, carrying the *imago dei*, was in a reflected sense like God and fully able to fellowship with him—God met Adam in the garden and talked with him.[2] And yet at the same time, Adam, made from the dust, was only a created being, and he was alone. Adam needed one like him, a created image-bearer-earthling like himself. Through marriage the created image-bearers were connected to one another and no longer alone. But there is no suggestion that God in any way viewed the connection of the image-bearers with each other as a substitute for their continuing relationship with him.

While God's purpose in marriage was one of relationship and community (the image-bearers with each other and with him), that connection was originally designed as part of God's broader plan to manage his creation and fill the earth with his people. Adam and Eve were to exercise dominion over creation and be fruitful and multiply (Gen. 1:28). Connection and community by design were linked with work and with family.

Anne Atkins notes that Genesis 1 and 2 reveal three things about humanity as male and female.[3] First, the text teaches that men and women are different from one another. God created humanity with a fundamental and necessary physiological distinction (male and female) so that they could carry out the first part of Genesis 1:28—to be fruitful and multiply and populate the earth. In a less easily defined way, "God has made principles of femininity and masculinity to express different things about himself."[4]

Second, Genesis 2 indicates in verses 18–24 that the purpose of this difference was to enable us to connect with one another in a unity that is more than sexual. Verse 18 (and repeated in verse 20) indicates that God created the woman as someone to work alongside the man. The word translated "helper" is the Hebrew word *ezer*, a word used at least nineteen times in the Old Testament. In at least fifteen of those usages, the word refers to God as our helper (for example, Ps. 121:1–2). As *helper*, the woman is not merely standing by her man, handing him a wrench when he needs it. The use of this particular Hebrew word means that he is inadequate without her. "To help" here means "to share the same tasks." Biblical scholar Gilbert Bilezikian notes that "the Hebrew language has four other words for 'helper' that denote subordination. None of those words is used in reference to the woman in Genesis 2."[5] Following *ezer* in the Hebrew text comes a Hebrew word (*knegdo*) meaning "one fit for him," his vis-à-vis, one who is in every way equal to the man and who comes alongside to complete him.

Atkins observes that this duality of the sexes highlights an important fact of our humanity. We are both dependent and interdependent. The aloneness of Adam in Genesis 2:18 was not highlighted to declare his priority in creation but to highlight God's negative judgment on isolation. God created us as sexual beings, equal by virtue of our humanity, related to one another in our createdness, and relating to one another as interdependent creatures.[6]

The third thing we learn from Genesis 1 and 2 is that God gave the man and the woman two tasks—to be fruitful, increasing in number, filling the earth *and* to subdue the earth and rule over it (Gen. 1:28). Note that God did not say to the woman, "It's your place to be fruitful and multiply," and to the man, "It's your job to subdue the earth and rule over it." Both commands came to both the man and the woman. Both are to share in parenting, and both are to share in dominion. We will see this pattern repeated later in both the Old and New Testaments.

God did not create human beings to live in isolation from one another. People need each other and are created to work together. The gender apartheid of first-century Palestine or of the patristic church did not come from God. The Doctrine of Separate Spheres in the nineteenth century overturned this primordial purpose of God that created Eve as Adam's "helper," his vis-à-vis.

At the end of Genesis 2 we read: "For this reason a man will leave his father and his mother and be united to his wife, and they will become one flesh" (v. 24 NIV). Walter Trobisch noted that this is the only statement about marriage that occurs four times in the Bible. Here "it sums up the story of creation. . . . Then Jesus quotes this in Matthew 19:5 and Mark 10:7, after he is asked about divorce. Finally the Apostle Paul relates it directly to Jesus Christ in Ephesians 5:31."[7] In this important passage we discover God's original plan for the structure of marriage in three phases: first, the separation of a man and a woman from their families of origin (leave), second, a commitment of the man and woman to each other (cleave—to use the term from the Authorized or King James version), and third, the construction of a life together, physically, emotionally, and spiritually (become one flesh).

"Leaving" is the legal aspect of marriage, whatever a culture dictates that makes a man and a woman husband and wife. In biblical times (in both Old and New Testaments) a woman would leave her parents and go to her husband, who remained with his clan. But God's statement is that a *man* leaves his father and mother to marry. Trobisch calls this an "unheard-of and revolutionary message" but one that aims toward partnership between husband and wife. Both have to leave home to begin their new life together.

"Cleaving" is the personal relationship in marriage. Just as both have to leave, so both have to cleave—not only the wife to the husband but the husband to the wife (Eph. 5:25–31). Leaving and cleaving belong together. You cannot really cleave if you have not really left. And you cannot really leave unless you have decided to cleave. The literal sense of the Hebrew word for *cleave* is to be glued together. If you try to separate two sheets of paper that have been glued together, you will tear both papers. Cleaving means permanent fidelity.

Third, "becoming one flesh"—the sexual part of marriage—is as essential for marriage as the legal and personal aspects.[8] It is as much within God's will for marriage as is the leaving and cleaving. But to "become one flesh" is more than the physical act of intercourse. It is the sharing of life, not just bodies and material possessions, but thoughts and dreams, joys and sufferings, hopes and fears, successes and failures. In short, it is being one soul as well as one body.

These are the basic components of a marriage. At the end of these first two crucial chapters in the Bible, it is clear that both the man and the woman are created in the image of God and that humanity exists in two parts—male and female. Each is a complete individual, but the text does not stress their individuality or the differences between them. What *is* stressed in the text is their unity and the fact that they are indissolubly bound together. On this basis, God concludes, "For this reason, a man will leave his father and his mother and be united to his wife, and they will become one flesh." Genesis 2 stresses the strength of the reciprocal dependence and mutuality of the man and woman, bound together as one.

A Snake in the Garden

Genesis 2 is not the end of the story. Something catastrophic happened there in the garden. On that world-shattering evening when God came to fellowship with Adam and Eve, he found that the serpent had been there ahead of him. The image-bearers were hidden from him and came only when he called them. It takes little effort to visualize the picture of their shame-filled faces and their pathetic covering of leaves. Human experience makes their guilt and shame all too real. But important as the behavior of the guilty pair is, it is crucial to think carefully about *God's* behavior immediately before his traumatic confrontation with Adam and Eve.

The biblical narrative tells us that God came, walking in the garden in the cool of the day, *looking for Adam and Eve*. It is one of the plainest and most astonishing passages in all of Scripture. God, the great Triune Creator God, came to the garden, looking for the image-bearers he had created so that he could spend time with them. The biblical narrative makes clear God's simple agenda. He just came to be with them.

Of course, God found death and destruction, not companionship. While this story is not usually considered from God's point of view, rightly understood, it is accurate to say that on that night Eden ended for God too. He could never come there again in the old way to walk and talk with the image-bearers, to be there with those he had made to be like himself. God is a partner in Eden's drama. What would he do? Would he still want to be with these broken image-bearers who had gone over to the enemy and betrayed him? Adam's and Eve's guilt and the damage to their relationship with each other and with him were not the only issues. What would God do—he whose holiness and justice require that he deal with sin?

Eden from God's point of view is the great primordial tragedy for him as well as for the image-bearers. Granting the limitations of our human thinking, the biblical account shows that for a profoundly relational God, Eden held a broken heart, a broken dream. God's original plan had been that Adam and Eve would work and play together, have children together, and in the cool of the evening they would share in fellowship with him. But Adam and Eve had changed all that. What would God do?

"What have you done?" God asked the image-bearers as they emerged from hiding. He understood, but the degrees of guilt and responsibility must now be assessed and sentence imposed. Eden had already changed. It was now the first courtroom, and God's role as companion to the image-bearers was now changed to that of the great eternal Judge.[9] When God had clearly established what had happened, he passed sentence on the serpent, on Adam, and on Eve. He cursed the serpent. He cursed the ground.[10] And he declared that in the enmity between Eve's seed and the serpent, Eve's offspring would be victor over the tempter.[11] He briefly described to Adam and Eve something of the world that now lay on the other side of Eden for them: it would contain hard work and pain. He described something of the change in their relationship. It would be marked by conflict in goals and the use of power. And now, at the end, there was death: "You came from dust," God reminded Adam. "Now you shall return to dust" (see Gen. 3:19).[12]

After the sentence, God stopped speaking. Eden had ended for both God and the image-bearers. There was nothing more to say. But in that silence, God made a choice and acted on his choice. The text says, "The Lord God made garments of skin for Adam and his wife and clothed them" (v. 21 NIV).

They were pitiful little garments of skin. But those garments of skin were evidence that God had not given up, and that he would face death itself to keep his relationship with those he had created to be with him and with each other. He had not given up on his original plan that he and the image-bearers would together yet make the family of God.

God had chosen. He would stay with his own. Eden had ended, but God would go with his own. He had chosen the first step down the bitter road to Calvary.

A Tree and a Choice

If God so desired a deep relationship with his image-bearers, why did he not ensure that they would not sin?[13] Would God provide opportunity for Adam to be tempted by placing an attractive tree in the middle of the garden, which he was to tend but from which he should not eat the fruit? Was God playing some kind of game with Adam and Eve, testing them beyond their ability to withstand? To understand that tree, we must understand one more thing about being created in the image of God. In the heart of the universe, the stars move predictably in their cycles. Springtime

and harvest are fixed in the natural course of things. All nature is pro-
grammed to respond as God designed it to respond: Birds fly, fish swim,
and deer run.

In the midst of God's new creation stood a man and a woman who were
created with a difference. They could choose. They could choose to love
God and obey him, or they could choose to turn their backs on God and
go their own independent way. They are the one unprogrammed element
in God's creation. God validated choice and he validated his image in us
by giving us the power to choose. The tree was there in the garden so that
Adam and Eve could voluntarily choose to keep themselves in fellowship
with their Creator, God. In Francis Schaeffer's words:

> The machine can obey God mechanically; when it does, it is doing all that
> God meant it to do. The far-flung system of the universe operates, much
> of it, as a great machine; and as such it fulfills its purpose. That is all it was
> meant to do. But man [humanity] is a different being, made in a different
> circle of creation. He is to love God, not mechanically, but by the wonder
> of choice.[14]

All human loves are bound up in choice. Without the power to choose,
to say that we love has no meaning. We can demand obedience, but we
cannot demand love. That tree gave Adam and Eve the opportunity to love
God meaningfully. True relationships are possible only to the extent that
people can choose to be in them or choose to leave them. The inherently
relational God could not create his image-bearers for relationship to him
without giving them the power to choose against him.[15]

It was true in that long-ago garden and it is true today that all of our
loves are bound up in choice. And marriage today, as it was in that garden,
is an ongoing, day-by-day choice—to leave, to cleave, and to maintain that
one-flesh relationship. Love is not a matter of being swept off our feet. It
is a choice or the beginning of a multitude of choices that we make every
day of our lives, the choice to remain faithfully in a marriage we have
entered before God.

Mending Broken Image-Bearers

For God, marriage is not meant to be simply a social arrangement for
human beings. It is rooted in the relational desire of God for his image-
bearers to share with each other that which is eternally present in him as

Father, Son, and Holy Spirit. But when the essential nature of the image-bearers was altered in the fall, their relationship with each other and with God was broken. And a clear understanding of marriage requires careful consideration of God's relationship to the broken image-bearers, his fallen creation, and his original goal to have a world filled with his people.

God promised that Eve's offspring would be victor over the tempter. From the beginning, it was clear that the serpent was doomed. Eve's offspring would bring about his defeat. Eve had been part of the tragedy, but God in grace and mercy would permit her to be part of the serpent's defeat.

God faced another problem. The image-bearers were bent and broken. While the effects of the fall were not precisely the same for Adam and for Eve,[16] God told them that as a result of their sin, there would now be conflict between them. Adam would exert power over Eve, a relationship unknown in Eden. And the bitter result of Adam's and Eve's choices was quickly apparent. Eve's firstborn son, Cain, murdered Abel, her second son. The created nature of the image-bearers now also carried the image of the evil one.

God knew that the image-bearers were now helpless. There was nothing they could do to undo what they had done, but God could do something. And in his promise to Eve, and in the symbol of the garments of skin with which he covered their shame, God promised that what he alone could do, he would do. He would not leave them, and he knew the cost.

God desired more than that they be redeemed, however; he wanted them restored. He had not given up on the image-bearers, and he had not abandoned his plan for his people. *And despite the bent and broken nature of the image-bearers, he had not altered his original structure for marriage.*[17] This is astonishing.

God knew—who better?—the extent of the damage. He knew that the image-bearers were capable of betrayal; they had betrayed him. He knew that they could kill. Abel's blood, God told Cain, called out to him from the ground. And God knew about the obsession with power and the distortion of desire that were now embodied within the nature of the broken image-bearers. Even knowing this, God left the original *structure* for marriage intact—leave, cleave, and form one flesh.

God left the original *purpose* intact as well. Jesus affirmed this purpose and the original structure in his dispute with the Pharisees: "What God has joined together," Jesus told the Pharisees pointedly, "let no one separate" (Matt. 19:6). *But the joining that God designed was now by default the joining of two bent and broken image-bearers.*

In the face of this reality, the long, discouraging record of imperfect marriages that we find in the biblical narrative begins to make sense. Marriage is not the problem; the nature of people in the marriage is the problem. And God, being wise and sensible, chose his course somewhat in this manner (in paraphrase): "There is nothing wrong with my original idea of connection—the image-bearers connected to each other and to me. That idea doesn't need fixing. But the image-bearers—now that's another matter. There *is* something wrong with them now—tragically, deeply wrong. It's the image-bearers not marriage that will need fixing. So I will keep my original idea of marriage and concentrate on changing the broken image-bearers."

Broken image-bearers do not fix easily. That is part of what God seeks to make plain in the history of his ancient people. God records their stories, generation after generation (until, in fact, we are tired of reading). They marry, then, for the most part, fail at the task of marriage. This makes sense. Marriage was originally designed for God's image-bearers as they once were in Eden. They cannot do it alone as they now are. And they cannot, on their own, change their responses. But God had a plan.

When the gate closed on Eden, the drama of restoration began. God did not alter his *purpose*—a world of his people, intimately connected with him and with each other. And God did not alter his *structure* for intimate connection between broken image-bearers. His desire for them remained the same—a union achieved through leaving, cleaving, and constructing an interwoven life together. But God established an additional goal as well—to restore his image-bearers, to make them once more like him. Nothing at all in the biblical narrative suggests that God fashioned his goal of restoration out of a nostalgic desire to return to Eden's innocence. When God posted the cherubim at the east gate of Eden, *that* way was closed forever to Adam and Eve and to him. God was not naive. He knew from before the foundations of the earth the cost of restoration, and he knew how resistant to restoration these bent and broken image-bearers would be. But God was determined that the lost Eden would one day be replaced with a new heaven and a new earth. He was determined that the broken image-bearers would one day be redeemed and transformed into his likeness and live eternally present in intimate relationship with him. God decided.

As a result, in a way that the world has long found gross and repugnant, part of God's story is covered with blood. From the garments of skin in the garden of Eden to the bloody agony of Calvary, the cost of sin has been blood and death. The image-bearers, having gone over to the enemy, required redemption at a cost that only God could pay.

God's story is marked by his stubborn insistence that his redeemed people *act* like his people, that they image him, that they separate from those who are "not my people" and be distinctively "my people" who are "like me" (the *imago dei*). From Moses exhorting the people of Israel to Paul exhorting the church at Corinth, the message is the same. Here is what Paul wrote:

> Do not be yoked together with unbelievers. For what do righteousness and wickedness have in common? Or what fellowship can light have with darkness? What harmony is there between Christ and Belial? Or what does a believer have in common with an unbeliever? What agreement is there between the temple of God and idols? For we are the temple of the living God. As God has said: "I will live with them and walk among them, and I will be their God, and they will be my people."
>
> "Therefore come out from them and be separate, says the Lord. Touch no unclean thing, and I will receive you. I will be a Father to you, and you will be my sons and daughters, says the Lord Almighty."
>
> Since we have these promises, dear friends, let us purify ourselves from everything that contaminates body and spirit, perfecting holiness out of reverence for God.
>
> 2 Corinthians 6:14–7:1

The interweaving of marriage into God's plan is particularly clear in this portion of the biblical narrative. Paul's directive to the Corinthians not to marry unbelievers and to avoid sexual impurity forms an integral whole with God's call to be his people and God's promise to his people that he will come and be with them. Is this passage about marriage? Of course it is—*all* of it. Here we see God implementing his plan for the restoration of the broken image-bearers. He will be *within* them and they will be the temple of the living God. There can hardly be a greater intimacy than that of God living *within* the believer. Even in Eden there was no connection as close as this. And right in the middle of this restoration process are some clear directions for a believer's relationships with others—believer linked to believer (each now a new creation in Christ with that intimately indwelling Spirit of God), living in sexual purity with each other and in purity before God. God's original design (leave, cleave, and form one flesh) appears here as an integral part of his restoration process that both restores the broken image-bearers and his intimate connection with them and they with each other.

Believers, in their new intimacy with God, made possible by the indwelling Holy Spirit, now live distinctively as God's people (the "come-out" ones, the separated ones). They live distinctively with each other in a union of mutually indwelt ones, marked by purity of life and sexual fidelity. It is an encouragement that the biblical drama provides a glimpse into the triumphant conclusion of God's story. John wrote:

> Then I saw "a new heaven and a new earth," . . . And I heard a loud voice from the throne saying, "Look! God's dwelling place is now among the people, and he will dwell with them. They will be his people, and God himself will be with them and be their God. 'He will wipe every tear from their eyes. There will be no more death' or mourning or crying or pain, for the old order of things has passed away." He who was seated on the throne said, "I am making everything new!" Then he said, "Write this down, for these words are trustworthy and true."
>
> Revelation 21:1, 3–5

While we know that God's story has a wonderful ending, some parts in the middle are grim indeed. And some of the hard parts are about what those bent and broken image-bearers do—or fail to do—about God's original idea of marriage.

In the context of God's plan for redemption, the way in which the meaning and purpose of marriage are woven into God's whole story becomes clear. It becomes evident why, as Douglas Brouwer pointed out, the biblical narrative has considerably less to say about marriage than we wish, if we are looking for fail-safe formulas for human happiness.[18] It has much more to say than we can fully comprehend, however, if we are seeking to understand God's plan to transform the participants in the marriage into his image. God plans to do something more than to undo the consequences of the first pair's sin in Eden. He plans to build something spectacular and wonderful in its place, and marriage is a part of that plan.

God's Design

A biblical theology of marriage begins with who God is and what he experiences in that eternal dance within the Trinity. God's inherent relationality spills over into us who are created "in his image, according to his likeness." Because God's central intention for us is that we enjoy a personal relationship with our Creator and with each other, God designed marriage to fill our "aloneness." He created us male and female to share together the duties of the creation mandate—to be fruitful, multiply and fill the earth, and exercise responsible dominion over God's creation.

The power to choose, which reflects our creation in God's image, has been used against God's purposes for us. The fall, recorded in Genesis 3, ruptured God's relationship with Adam and Eve and their relationship with each other. Despite their choice to disobey God's command and eat the fruit from the tree in the middle of the garden, God has chosen a course of action leading to our redemption and to our transformation from being broken image-bearers to being "sons and daughters of the Most High God." It is a choice that leaves God's blueprint for marriage unchanged, even though the broken image-bearers were unable to live out God's original plan.

Chapter 9 picks up the story of God's plan, centered in Jesus Christ, even as the sound of Eden's gate clanging shut behind Adam and Eve still rings in their ears.

9

Marriage in the Already-But-Not-Yet

ery soon after Eden's bliss ended, many of the broken image-bearers began to indicate that they did not want to be fixed. (This is still true in our broken world.) But some of the broken image-bearers wanted (at least part of the time) to be fixed. God called these broken image-bearers "my people," and he set up a plan for their restoration. This plan from the beginning included Jesus, but God organized his plan in such a way that it was several thousand years before Jesus came. In the meantime, God set up rules for living as his people. These rules had two parts. There were the animal sacrifices for their sins that pointed to Jesus, the Lamb of God who would one day die for their sins. The second part was God's laws for daily living that made God's people his distinctive, holy people.

The biblical narrative indicates that God had several purposes for his rules. One was his desire that his people be like him. For example, he required that his people act justly because he is just. Also God wanted his people to understand how bent and broken they really were so that they would enter into his restoration with their whole hearts.

God's story throughout the Old Testament is a discouraging account of his people walking away from him to worship the false gods of their neighbors. And because they forsook God's law, their relationships with one another (including their marriages) were bent and broken.

The Patriarchal Family in the Old Testament

From early times, the Hebrew family was patriarchal and polygamous.[1] Great power was invested in the head of the household. Polygamy was accepted although Jewish law set some boundaries around it. In addition, the Hebrews and their neighbors practiced concubinage. Sarah, Leah, and Rachel gave their personal maids to their husbands as concubines, and the sons that came from those unions belonged to the proper wife not to the concubine. The son of a concubine could be driven from the house without any inheritance, as we see with Ishmael (Gen. 21:1–21), or if there was no legal son, the son of a concubine could be named the heir.

A household often included several nuclear families. In the period of Abraham, Isaac, and Jacob, the household included the patriarch, his wives and children, slaves, bondservants, and sometimes strangers who had placed themselves under the patriarch's protection. They all lived together in the same camp, occupying numerous tents. Nuclear families were completely swallowed up in the household and had no independent existence. But there was often strong attachment between husbands and wives and between parents and children.

Marriage was not by free choice but most often was arranged by parents. The bride price could be paid in military service, goods, or work. For example, Jacob worked seven years each for Rachel and Leah. Wife-purchase in early times gradually gave way to offering gifts and finally to the formality of the bridegroom placing a coin in the bride's hand. The essential requirement for marriage was an agreement between the fathers. In a later period, the couple as well as their parents had to consent to the engagement.[2]

In early times the wedding involved almost no ceremony at all, usually just a procession and a feast. The bridegroom with his friends went to the home of the bride where she and her companions were waiting for them. The whole party then proceeded to the house of the bridegroom's parents, singing songs along the way. The groom's father gave a banquet, after which friends led the pair to the bridal chamber, and the groom or priest said benedictions. Throughout the centuries, a wedding was essentially a domestic ceremony with neither priest nor magistrate to officiate.

Women were clearly subordinate but in general were respected and loved. Wives were often the devoted and loved companions of their husbands. Genesis 26:8 notes that Isaac caressed his wife, Rebekah, in public. Deuteronomy 24:5 stipulated that a newly married man could not leave to fight in a war or go off on business for one year but was to remain at home to "bring happiness to his wife whom he has taken."

The family was an economic unit, with each member contributing to meet the needs of the household. In general, men tended flocks, tilled the soil, performed religious ceremonies, and carried out political activities and war. Women generally did the spinning and weaving, made clothing, prepared food, organized and conducted housework, and sometimes sold the products of household industry. In early times there was no formal education. Children learned by observing and listening to parents. Proverbs 1–9 gives us a sense of the kind of teaching that went on in Hebrew homes in which both father and mother instructed the children.

As nomadic life gave way to living in fixed housing in towns and villages, the nuclear family became more of a separate unit. While the structure of family life changed, the importance of family in the life of God's people remained constant. Just as chapters 1–9 in the book of Proverbs give us insight into the way fathers and mothers educated their children, so chapter 31 gives us pictures of the economic partnership that characterized Hebrew family life. The Song of Solomon places a seal of approval on good, satisfying sex within marriage. The book of Ruth exposes us to the problems faced by widows but also to the care of communities for them.

Old Testament history speaks far more of the relationships of fathers to sons than of husbands to wives. As noted in chapter 7, in the Bible there are few, if any, ecstatically happy families without problems of one kind or another. Yet the pattern of Genesis 1:28—shared parenting and shared provision—is discernable in the biblical texts. The book of Proverbs, gathering the wisdom of the people of God under the inspiration of God's Spirit, opens with a father teaching his children and reminding his son to listen also to what his mother is teaching him—shared parenting. The book closes with a mother teaching her son, King Lemuel, and her teaching includes a portrait of a good wife actively participating in providing for her family: "She seeks wool and flax and works with eager hands. . . . She considers a field and buys it; out of her earnings she plants a vineyard. . . . She makes linen garments and sells them, and supplies the merchants with sashes" (Prov. 31:13, 16, 24 NIV). The model of shared parenting and shared provision shines through the book.

God's story in the Old Testament traces his interactions with those who chose to be his people and follow his rules for living. And it traces God's interactions with those who chose *not* to be his people. In the New Testament it was time for God to connect with his people in a different way.

The Centerpiece of God's Restoration Plan

From the councils of eternity, Jesus' coming was the centerpiece of God's plan of restoration. Jesus was God-with-us (Immanuel), the God that the broken image-bearers could see and touch, God in a body like theirs. And while he was with them, Jesus had something to say (to teach) and something to do (to redeem through his death and resurrection).

Jesus had something to say about marriage. What he said (in paraphrase) was, "Pay attention! Remember God's original design for marriage. That's what counts!" (Matt. 19:4–6). He said this to the Pharisees who were trying to drag him into an argument over legitimate grounds for divorce. In many ways, Jesus' dispute with the Pharisees was about something far deeper than divorce. It was about the very core of the restoration process.

In first-century Israel, the Pharisees were scrupulously religious. Some have said that they must have been independently wealthy to devote all of their time each day to keeping the minutia of the law. It wasn't just God's law, however. These spiritual do-it-yourself folks took God's rules and added their own rules and regulations to them. Then they evaluated themselves on the basis of their rule keeping. Believing they could be restored—as good as Eden or better—on the basis of their rule keeping, they didn't think they needed God's restoration project. They could do it themselves. For example, God had a rule (a commandment) about sexual purity (Exod. 20:14): "You shall not commit adultery." The Pharisees, the rule-keeping regulators of Jesus' day, had added rules about not speaking to women or being seen in public with a woman, and many other rules besides.[3] On the basis of their keeping all these rules, they then declared themselves Eden-pure sexually.

Jesus, of course, would have none of this and said so bluntly. He pointed out that even though they had kept all of their rules, if their hearts were full of lust, no amount of rule keeping would make them righteous (Matt. 5:28). What counted with God was what was in their hearts. God wanted the restoration of bent and broken image-bearers to move from the inside out. He meant for them to be new creations, redeemed, regenerated. God's goal was not more and better rule keepers. He was after a people who were his people because they were like him.

The Pharisees had made rules about divorce that permitted them to violate God's original plan for marriage. But Jesus cut across the legalisms in which they wrapped themselves. He required a change of heart that would make it unnatural for a man to want to exploit or degrade a woman: "You have heard that it was said, 'Do not commit adultery.' But I tell you that anyone who looks at a woman lustfully has already committed adultery with her in his heart." (Matt. 5:27–28).

He said that the change of heart toward women he required was so hard to achieve that it could be compared to self-mutilation—giving up the myth that lust was okay was as difficult as plucking out an eye or cutting off a hand. But Jesus gave the requirement as a command and promised hell as the alternative to obedience. One of the main reasons for keeping women secluded in Jewish society of the first century was so they would not tempt men sexually. But Jesus turned the problem around by demanding the highest chastity from men.

In Matthew 19:3–6 Jesus responded to the Pharisees' effort to draw him into the rule-keeping debate by pointing back to God's original plan:

> Some Pharisees came to him to test him. They asked, "Is it lawful for a man to divorce his wife for any and every reason?" "Haven't you read," he replied, "that at the beginning the Creator 'made them male and female,' and said, 'For this reason a man will leave his father and mother and be united to his wife, and the two will become one flesh'? So they are no longer two, but one. Therefore what God has joined together, let no one separate."

In effect, the subtext of Jesus' words was, "You're having trouble with marriage because you continue to be bent and broken image-bearers in spite of your rule keeping. And I refuse to pretend otherwise. I will not act as though God's original purpose can be fulfilled simply by a matter of keeping rules. You too need the heart restoration that I have come to bring."

In Matthew 19 Jesus vindicated monogamous marriage and refused to endorse the fall as a basis for defining marriage. Jesus hopscotched over both the old covenant and the fall to base his definition of marriage squarely in Genesis 1 and 2. The bottom line was that in God's plan for restoration, the frame of reference for men and women in relationship is the creation narrative of Genesis 1 and 2. The fall and its consequences are aberrations that were being resolved in the coming of Jesus into the world. Jesus made God's creation statements the standard for Christians, overturning the structures that had been spawned by the fall.

It is not surprising that the Pharisees had trouble with Jesus' teachings about marriage and divorce. In first-century Judaism, as practiced by the scribes and Pharisees, women were held responsible for the evil in the world. They were strictly segregated in their communities, and the rabbis were quite clear about the dangers of letting women out of their secluded existence. Rabbi Eliezer declared, "If any man gives his daughter a knowledge of the law, it is as though he taught her lechery."[4] Jose ben Johnan of Jerusalem declared, "He that talks much with womankind brings evil upon himself and neglects the study of the Law and at the last will inherit Gehenna."[5]

As we watch Jesus move around Israel through the four Gospel accounts, we see him take a firm countercultural stand against such teachings. In a culture in which women were not to be seen, heard, or spoken to in public, Jesus shocked people's sensibilities by speaking to women directly and in public. In John 4:27 Jesus' disciples "marveled" when they found him chatting with the Samaritan woman at Sychar's well. In Luke 8:45 he demands to know and to speak to the woman who touched him in the crowd. And Luke 13:10–16 tells of an incident in a synagogue during the Sabbath service when Jesus addressed, touched, and healed a bent woman. Even on his way to death, he did not hesitate to speak to the many women in the crowd who lamented his death; he presented them to bystanders as models of faith (Luke 23:27–31).

Women as well as men followed Jesus throughout Galilee and down to Jerusalem (Matt. 27:55; Mark 15:40–41; Luke 8:1–3). The overt participation of women in Jesus' later ministry (Mark 15:41) was an audacious precedent in the first-century world. While Jesus related to women with sufficient precautions to avoid creating a scandal, his taking notice of them made a statement about the place of women in God's family.

In Luke 10:38–42 we meet Martha's sister, Mary, who took a position typical of a rabbinic student. She sat at Jesus' feet—something a woman was usually not free to do. Martha, on the other hand, fulfilled the role traditionally assigned to women; she was busy with cooking. When Martha became exasperated with Mary for listening to Jesus rather than helping her in the kitchen, Jesus responded, "Mary has chosen that good part, which will not be taken away from her" (Luke 10:42).

Martha's indignation was fully understandable in the light of her culture. A Jewish woman's role was that of homemaker. She was exempt from rabbinic training and received no merit from learning the Law. When Mary sat down beside the men to learn from Jesus, she overstepped her established role in society. Yet Jesus refused to agree with Martha that Mary's place at that moment was in the kitchen. Jesus would not allow Martha or anyone else to stop Mary from learning along with his male disciples. With his response, Jesus completely reversed the priorities and the consequences of those priorities in ancient Jewish life. Not only did he believe that women should not be exempt from learning Torah, but he knew how much they would benefit from learning God's law.

Jesus had something to say about families as well. (His words got him in trouble, but he said them anyway.) His message (paraphrased here) was a challenge: "Pay attention! The family of God is more important than your earthly family." He started saying this when he was only twelve years old. When Mary scolded him for staying behind at the temple in Jerusalem, he told her, "Why were you searching fo me?" he asked. "Didn't you know I had to be in my Father's house?" (Luke 2:49). When a young man wanted to delay joining Jesus' band of followers so that he could bury his dead father, Jesus responded, "Follow Me, and let the dead bury their own dead" (Matt. 8:22). Jesus challenged the commonly held view that bearing children, particularly sons, was the fulfillment of a woman's life. It was widely believed that the absence of children was a great misfortune for a woman, at times thought of as a divine punishment. A fruitful womb was a sign of God's blessing; the barren womb was a sign of God's curse. But when a woman cried out, "Blessed is the mother who gave you birth and nursed you." Jesus challenged her by replying, "Blessed rather are those who hear the word of God and obey it" (Luke 11:27–28). In effect, it is not a woman's womb (not even Mary's) that is her source of true blessedness. It is her response to the Word of God. New creation by the Word, not procreation by the womb, is the fulfillment of female personhood.

The same idea is clear in Mark 3:32–35 and Matthew 12:46–50:

> A crowd was sitting around [Jesus], and they told him, "Your mother and brothers are outside looking for you." "Who are my mother and my brothers?" he asked. Then he looked at those seated in a circle around him and said, "Here are my mother and my brothers! Whoever does God's will is my brother and sister and mother."
>
> Mark 3:32–35

The difference between Jesus' biological family and his new spiritual family lay in the obedience of his followers to the will of his Father in heaven. This family included anyone who met the condition of obedience.[6] The Jewish oral law stated, "Let the word of the Law be burned rather than be committed to women." Yet not only did Jesus affirm the right of women to be serious followers of his, but he emphasized their responsibility to learn.

In a way that must have utterly confounded his family-centered hearers, Jesus told them bluntly that he had not come to make families peaceful but to confront them with a hard choice: "Anyone who loves their father or mother more than me is not worthy of me; anyone who loves a son or daughter more than me is not worthy of me. Those who do not take up their cross and follow me are not worthy of me. Those who find their life will lose it, and those who lose their life for my sake will find it." (Matt. 10:37–39).

In those last terrible hours on the cross, Jesus cared for his earthly mother, Mary, but did so within the community of his followers. John tells us: "When Jesus saw his mother there, and the disciple whom he loved standing nearby, he said to her, 'Mother, here is your son,' and to the disciple, 'Here is your mother.' From that time on, this disciple took her into his home" (John 19:26–27).

And when, on that glorious resurrection morning, he met Mary Magdalene in the garden, he sent her back "to my brothers" with the news of his resurrection (John 20:17). He was not talking about his biological kin. He sent Mary to that frightened group who, believing that he was the Christ, had followed him to Calvary. *They* were his brothers who were now to be the witnesses of his resurrection life.

In our time, Christians have narrowed their focus on the family to a near-obsessive preoccupation with the tiny, isolated nuclear family. Jesus' focus was on the family of those who were his brothers and sisters because of their obedience to God. In his words and in his actions, Jesus said in effect, "Bent and broken image-bearers can become sons and daughters of God, redeemed, restored, living holy lives in relationship to God and to one another." Years later, the apostle Paul wrote to the Christians in the Greek city of Corinth:

> Therefore, if anyone is in Christ, there is a new creation: The old has gone, the new has come! All this is from God, who reconciled us to himself through Christ and gave us the ministry of reconciliation: that God was reconciling the world to himself in Christ, not counting people's sins against them. And he has committed to us the message of reconciliation.
>
> 2 Corinthians 5:17–19

The Already-But-Not-Yet of God's Plan

When the apostle Paul wrote to the Christians in Rome, he wrote in the light of the resurrection of Jesus, the power of Pentecost, and his own life-altering confrontation with the risen Christ on the road to Damascus. Paul wanted those early Christians to understand the full sweep of God's eternal purpose in Christ for those who love him. All of God's plan for them—their calling, their justification, their being conformed to God's likeness—was so that Jesus might be "the firstborn among many brothers and sisters" (Rom. 8:29).

Paul's letters to those early churches focused on the reality of the risen Christ, the indwelling Spirit, and the pattern of love that was to characterize the family of faith. Paul, once the proud Pharisee, Jewish by birth and training, insisted that it was not biological lineage but obedience of the heart that mattered to God. He called Timothy "my true son in the faith" (1 Tim. 1:2). Titus, Paul said, is "my true son in our common faith" (Titus 1:4). Apphia (probably Philemon's wife) was "our sister" (Philem. 2). And in the marvelous demonstration of the power of transformation within the family of God, Paul entreated Philemon to receive the runaway slave Onesimus back again, this time as "better than a slave, as a dear brother" (Philem. 16).

Peter referred to Paul as "our dear brother" (2 Peter 3:15) and those who were fellow participants in the life of faith as "my brothers and sisters" (2 Peter 1:10). John, explaining the life of love that was to mark the followers of Jesus, wrote: "This is how we know what love is: Jesus Christ laid down his life for us. And we ought to lay down our lives for our brothers. If anyone has material possessions and sees his brother in need but has no pity on him, how can the love of God be in him? Dear children, let us not love with words or tongue but with actions and in truth" (1 John 3:16–18). John was not talking about biological kin but about those who form the family of faith.

Peter, Paul, and the other apostles understood and taught that Jesus was the centerpiece of God's restoration process and that this process was aimed at changing the hearts of bent and broken image-bearers. But they also understood and taught that the connection among God's people, the family of God, was a part of the restoration process.

The story of the runaway slave Onesimus shows, first, God changing the hearts of broken image-bearers and, second, God's people functioning as a part of God's restoration process. Onesimus had run away from his owner, Philemon, a crime punishable by death under Roman law. In Rome Onesimus met the apostle Paul and became a Christian. He was now returning to Philemon, carrying a letter from Paul asking Philemon to accept Onesimus back, now as a Christian brother.

Paul's letter shows that God had already changed the hearts of a number of bent and broken image-bearers. The very Spirit of God now lived within that former old Pharisee Saul who became Paul. The Holy Spirit of God now lived within that once bitter runaway slave Onesimus. It was God's Spirit who enabled Tychicus, Paul's brave and faithful companion, to undertake one more dangerous journey and accompany Onesimus to deliver the letter to Philemon. And it was the Spirit of God who lived within Philemon and Apphia and the members of the church that met in their house. So in Paul's letter we see image-bearers who are being restored as they interact with each other. Some of them had gathered together (including some who were married to each other), and they made a loving space in which their new life together could bloom. And while the greetings in Paul's letter specifically named Philemon, Apphia, and Archippus, the letter was addressed to this collection of image-bearers being restored and the church that met in Philemon and Apphia's house.

"Listen," Paul wrote in essence to Philemon and the church, "Onesimus has become my son. He is very dear to me; he is my very heart. He may have been useless once, but he is different now. The important thing is that he is now a part of the family of God. Take him in—as better than a slave, as a brother."

It must have been incredibly frightening for Onesimus to face going back to confront his past. Philemon's right and power to put him to death were all too real. Think how it may have been that morning as Tychicus tucked Paul's letter into his pack and Paul turned to say good-bye to Onesimus. He might well have said, "Hold on. Be brave. Remember, you are not going back to a slave master. *You are going back to your brother and to the family of God.*" Paul's letter to Philemon is not simply about bent and broken image-bearers being restored. It is that, but it is also about image-bearers who are making a space for one another, and together they are the family of God to which Onesimus could safely come home.

Is the letter to Philemon about marriage? Of course it is. There was a marriage at the center of this drama. The returned slave Onesimus and the church that welcomed him met in the home of Philemon and Apphia. Their relationship and the home growing out of that relationship provided a space for the family of God. But it was not their marriage nor, for that matter, their house that occupied Paul's attention. He was sending his son Onesimus back to Archippus *and* to Philemon *and* to Apphia *and to the church* that met in their house. What warmed Paul's heart was his confidence that Onesimus would be received in love into the family of God.

If anything in life is worth being excited about, this is. Here was Paul, the chief of sinners, as he once described himself. Here was Onesimus, a runaway slave. Here were Tychicus and Archippus and Philemon and Apphia and the church that met in their house—all bent and broken image-bearers, but now *image-bearers being restored*, restored in their connection to God through Christ and restored to connection with each other in the family of God. It is a restoration story that must have made the angels sing.

Life in the community of faith is lived out in what is often referred to as the "already-but-not-yet" tension of the gospel. Gordon Fee describes it in these words:

> God's final salvation of his people has already been accomplished by Christ. In a sort of divine time warp, the future condemnation that we all richly deserve has been transferred from the future into the past, having been borne by Christ (Rom. 8:1–3). Thus we "have been saved" (Eph. 2:8). Since our final salvation has not yet been fully realized, he [Paul] can likewise speak of salvation as something presently in process ("we are being saved," 1 Cor. 1:18) and as yet to be completed ("we shall be saved," Rom. 5:9). "Redemption" is both "already" (Eph. 1:7) and "not yet" (Eph. 4:30), as is our "adoption" (Rom. 8:15 and 23) and "justification" (the gift of righteousness, Rom. 5:1 and Gal. 5:5).
>
> Believers have tasted of the life to come; and the full and final realization of the future is so certain that God's new people become heavenly radicals as they live in the "already" but "not yet" of the present age.[7]

And it is in the tension of the already-but-not-yet of the present age that marriage must be lived out. In a real sense, as bent and broken image-bearers, we have been restored. We are already participants in the resurrection life of Jesus Christ. Yet we are members of that not yet fully realized kingdom where all will be liberated from the present bondage to decay and brought into the glorious freedom of the children of God (Rom. 8:21). And marriage in the already-but-not-yet of the present age reflects both the not yet completed restoration of God's people and the reality of the already present power of Christ's resurrection life.

Marriage Is Not about Power

In the light of the already-but-not-yet life of God's people, marriage is not about power. It is not about forming a hierarchy of privilege or of authority or of importance. It is not about one broken image-bearer controlling another.

Marriage is living out the intimate connection of two broken image-bearers who are in the process of being restored and who are committed to helping one another in the restoration process. It is about two broken image-bearers forming with one another a community of forgiveness that is an embodiment of the gospel and a living demonstration of God's transforming power. Marriage is about the commitment to be, by the Spirit's enablement, Christ present in the life of another person. It is about faithfulness and sexual purity and embracing by faith the miracle of God's restoration process in another person when evidence of that restoration is hard to see. Marriage is about trying again, because God's restoration process makes second chances common sense. It is believing that in the "not yet" moments of ordinary life, the "already" of the resurrection life empowers the Christian to live faithfully, to love, and to forgive.

Marriage Is Not about a Job Description

In the tension of the already-but-not-yet of the present age, marriage does not provide a job description detailing the assignment of the tasks of daily living. Marriage is about helping. It is about doing what needs to be done, and doing it in obedience to the living Christ who, having washed his disciples' feet, told them to follow his example. Marriage is about gifting and honoring differences and trusting the gifting of the Spirit for wisdom and for grace. Marriage is about cleaning and preparing food and earning money and quieting crying children in the night without asking for privilege or exemption from the hard work of life. Marriage is about shouldering each other's burdens, not the Doctrine of Separate Spheres. Marriage is about caring for the poor and giving priority to the family of God. Marriage is about living with the hard fact that Eden is gone forever and someone has to empty the trash.

Also marriage is learning to empty the trash with grace and without keeping records about whose turn it may be, while understanding that whoever's turn it may be, God is busy transforming both of the bent and broken image-bearers that have formed this particular marriage into God's likeness. Marriage is about piety made evident by good humor at the breakfast table and about patience with lost keys and about living with the profound certainty that keeping track of faults or virtues is never necessary. The one who loses his life will find it. In the already-but-not-yet world of the gospel, this fact is as certain as gravity in the "already" and in the "not yet."

Marriage Is Not a Couple's Club

Marriage in the present age is not designed to form a couple's club. Marriage is one form of membership in the family of God, but it is not a license for withdrawal and exclusivity. Leaving, cleaving, and making a life together is God's plan for some *within the family of God*. Marriage is recognizing the members of God's family as brothers and sisters who have a legitimate claim on the marriage for support and encouragement in their journey toward wholeness. Marriage is Priscilla and Aquila making tents and sharing the gospel. Marriage is Philemon and Apphia welcoming Onesimus home. Marriage is being together in the family of God in such a way that the family is enriched by the union, not impoverished by a self-serving coupleness that shuts out the rest of the family. In the already-but-not-yet of the present time, marriage is one way of participating in the "already" family of God that is "not yet" fully realized.

God's Case for Marriage

God's case for marriage, considered in the light of the current culture, is a shock to many Christians. It is a case for Christians, designed for God's people. In a constitutional democracy, like the one in which Americans live, Christians are free to promote marriage as a socially responsible act, a contract that enhances the well-being of children and contributes to the common good. Marriage *is* a socially responsible act, and it *does* enhance the well-being of children. But God's case for marriage does not rest on the ways in which marriage contributes to the common good. It rests on who God is and on God's goals for his people.

Christian ethics, as Stanley Hauerwas and William Willimon have pointed out, are *church-dependent*.[8] They make sense only from "the point of view of what we believe has happened in the life, death, and resurrection of Jesus of Nazareth."[9] Hauerwas and Willimon note that Christian ethics ask people to *do something that is difficult* to do by oneself. And Christian ethics rest fundamentally on Christians' conviction that they are called to be a living witness that Jesus Christ is Lord.[10] When the Alternative to Marriage Project objects to marriage, the argument for marriage cannot be made simply on the basis that marriage is a self-evident "Christian" good for everyone.

> [W]e can speak of marriage as an adventure, but only because for disciples, marriage is now subsumed under the category of an aspect of our adventure in Christ. How on earth could we explain how ordinary people could risk commitment to another person for a lifetime, especially since we have no way of knowing all the implications that this commitment entails? . . . Ultimately there is for us only one good reason to get married or to stay single, namely, that this has something to do with our discipleship.[11]

As we begin to examine more closely in chapter 10 the guidelines for marriage given to New Testament Christians, we do well to remember that these guidelines are for God's people, for those who are being transformed into his likeness in the already-but-not-yet reality of the present age.

IO

Missional Marriage

t is possible that you, the reader, may be thinking, *Wait a minute! It's all well and good to talk about shared parenting and shared provision, or that it's not about roles or power. But what about those verses in the New Testament about the husband being the head of the wife, and the wife being in submission to the husband? That seems pretty clear, and it doesn't exactly fit all that you've been saying in the last three chapters of this book.* Yes, what about those New Testament teachings from the apostles Paul and Peter?

A problem we face as we pick up the Bible and read it for guidance in our lives is knowing how to bring first-century commands and practices across two millennia into the twenty-first century. Which commands and practices were shaped by local customs and are no longer issues in today's world, and which commands and practices are for all people in all times and places and must be kept intact and followed by Christians today? In 1975 *The Other Side* carried an interesting article called "The Temporary Gospel?" in which readers were given a list of fifty commands from the New Testament.[1] They were then asked to decide for each command whether it was permanent (for all people in all places at all times) or temporary (only for the audience to which the command was first given). The commands ranged from "Greet one another with a holy kiss" (Rom. 16:16) to "Do not swear [an oath] at all" (Matt. 5:33–37). Most readers came away from the exercise realizing that some commands in the New Testament are universal or *pre*scriptive and other commands are situational and thus merely *de*scriptive of a particular custom at a given time.

In the New Testament letters, biblical scholars have identified six "household codes," which give ethical directions to husbands and wives, parents and children, slaves and masters about their conduct and attitudes in those relationships.[2] Only two of the six household codes include all three pairs of relationships, and only three of the six codes specifically address the relationship of husbands and wives. In this chapter we will work with only the household codes that instruct husbands and wives.

Around 60 C.E., the apostle Paul wrote letters to the Christians in Ephesus and Colosse. In these two letters he included instructions about husbands and wives, children and parents, and slaves and masters (in that order). The passage in Ephesians is one of the longest of the household codes, and in it Paul focused primarily on the relationships of husbands and wives, with shorter admonitions to children, fathers, slaves, and masters. Here is the part of that household code having to do with husbands and wives:

> Be very careful, then, how you live—not as unwise but as wise, making the most of every opportunity, because the days are evil. Therefore do not be foolish, but understand what the Lord's will is. Do not get drunk on wine, which leads to debauchery. Instead, be filled with the Spirit, speaking to one another with psalms, hymns and songs from the Spirit. Sing and make music from your heart to the Lord, always giving thanks to God the Father for everything, in the name of our Lord Jesus Christ.
>
> Submit to one another out of reverence for Christ.
>
> *Wives*, submit yourselves to your own husbands as you do to the Lord. For the husband is the head of the wife as Christ is the head of the church, his body, of which he is the Savior. Now as the church submits to Christ, so also wives should submit to their husbands in everything.
>
> *Husbands*, love your wives, just as Christ loved the church and gave himself up for her to make her holy, cleansing her by the washing with water through the word, and to present her to himself as a radiant church, without stain or wrinkle or any other blemish, but holy and blameless. In this same way, husbands ought to love their wives as their own bodies. He who loves his wife loves himself. After all, people have never hated their own bodies, but they feed and care for them, just as Christ does the church—for we are members of his body. "For this reason a man will leave his father and mother and be united to his wife, and the two will become one flesh." This is a profound mystery—but I am talking about Christ and the church. However, each one of you also must love his wife as he loves himself, and the wife must respect her husband.
>
> Ephesians 5:15–33, emphasis added

The passage in Colossians is much shorter, repeating the Ephesian code: *"Wives*, submit to your own husbands, as is fitting in the Lord. *Husbands,* love your wives and do not be harsh with them" (Col. 3:18–19 emphasis added).

The third household code discussing husbands and wives comes from the first letter of the apostle Peter and was written some time between 65 and 90 c.e. It is addressed to Jews in Asia Minor (Pontus, Galatia, Cappadocia, Asia, and Bithynia—all in modern-day Turkey). Peter deals with all Christians in relationship to their government, then with servants to masters, then with wives to husbands and husbands to wives. Here is the segment of that code about wives and husbands:

> *Wives*, in the same way submit yourselves to your own husbands so that, if any of them do not believe the word, they may be won over without words by the behavior of their wives, when they see the purity and reverence of your lives. Your beauty should not come from outward adornment, such as elaborate hairstyles and the wearing of gold jewelry and fine clothes. Rather, it should be that of your inner self, the unfading beauty of a gentle and quiet spirit, which is of great worth in God's sight. For this is the way the holy women of the past who put their hope in God used to adorn themselves. They submitted themselves to their own husbands, like Sarah, who obeyed Abraham and called him her master. You are her daughters if you do what is right and do not give way to fear.
>
> *Husbands*, in the same way be considerate as you live with your wives, and treat them with respect as the weaker partner and as heirs with you of the gracious gift of life, so that nothing will hinder your prayers.
>
> Finally, all of you, be like-minded, be sympathetic, love one another, be compassionate and humble. Do not repay evil with evil or insult with insult. On the contrary, repay evil with blessing, because to this you were called so that you may inherit a blessing.
>
> 1 Peter 3:1–9, emphasis added

These are the household codes from which many modern-day ideas about roles in the family have been derived.[3] At this point we must look at the contexts in which the codes were given.

The Mission of Life at Home

Paul and Peter did not give these codes to the early church in a vacuum. Both Greek and Roman societies already had such codes. Aristotle (ca. 400

B.C.E.) had introduced household codes as a necessary part of "order" in the community. For him the collective good (what was best for everyone on the whole) was based on a hierarchical structure in which the government was a model for all other structures in society, including the home. Aristotle taught that the "man is the most rational, the woman is less rational, the child is immature, and the slave is irrational."[4] On the basis of that, he constructed an elaborate system in which only men were capable of justly promoting the laws for society, with women, children, and slaves in carefully defined supporting roles. For Aristotle, this was the only workable system, one with authorities and subordinates.[5] Though his code was written roughly four hundred years before Jesus Christ, the idea of a household code along these lines was still very much a part of Greek thought in the first century.

The first and shortest of the biblical household codes is found in Galatians 3:28: "There is neither Jew nor Greek, neither slave nor free, neither male nor female; for you are all one in Christ Jesus."[6] Try to imagine how that sounded to a Greek or Roman citizen whose ideas about rigid structures between men and women or between slaves and freemen had been shaped by four centuries of assumptions about social status and roles. David Balch notes that such teachings could cause confusion and discord both inside and outside the Christian community: "Wherever Judaism or Christianity made proselytes and changed new converts' religious habits, they were accused of corrupting and reversing Roman social and household customs."[7]

When we look geographically at the six household codes (found in Galatians, Ephesians, Colossians, 1 Timothy, Titus, and 1 Peter), we discover that five of the six were given to churches in Asia Minor (modern-day Turkey); the sixth (directed to Titus) was for the churches on Crete, an island in the Mediterranean south of Greece. Galatia was a large province in central Turkey; Ephesus was on the southwest coast of Turkey, with Colosse about one hundred miles east of Ephesus.[8] Peter wrote to the churches in "Pontus, Galatia, Cappadocia, Asia and Bithynia" (1 Peter 1:1), all in central and northern Turkey.[9] Paul did not include household codes in any of the letters he wrote to congregations in Greece and Italy (apart from the new churches on Crete, which had been left to Titus to organize). It is possible that for reasons of regional customs or differences, some of the churches in Asia Minor required specific teachings on marital and family life. This possibility in no way lessens the importance or force of the codes, but it may point to cultural diversity throughout the Roman Empire regarding marriage and family life. It may also suggest "diff'rent strokes for diff'rent folks."

The apostles were explicit in stating the reason for including the household codes in their letters. When Paul wrote to Timothy, he included these statements in his household code: "Give the people these instructions, so that no one may be open to blame" (1 Tim. 5:7), and "to give the enemy no opportunity for slander" (v. 14). When he wrote to Titus, he wanted young women to behave in such a way "so that no one will malign the word of God" (2:5). When laying down appropriate behavior for young men, he gave as his reason "so that those who oppose you may be ashamed because they have nothing bad to say about us" (v. 8). Peter was concerned that the Christians in Asia Minor be characterized by "such good lives among the pagans that, though they accuse you of doing wrong, they may see your good deeds and glorify God on the day he visits us" (1 Peter 2:12). He continued: "Submit yourselves for the Lord's sake to every human authority. . . . For it is God's will that by doing good you should silence the ignorant talk of the foolish" (vv. 13, 15).

Before anything else, the household codes are missional. When Paul wrote his first letter to Timothy, he stated that leading a quiet and peaceable life in all godliness and reverence "is good, and pleases God our Savior, who wants all people to be saved and to come to a knowledge of the truth" (1 Tim. 2:3–4). All of the household codes are embedded in an apostolic concern for Christian witness. Followers of Jesus Christ are to give no offense to non-Christians in their communities. This is cultural sensitivity in the service of the gospel of God. Because God gave himself to redeem us from every lawless deed (Titus 2:14), we are "to be subject to rulers and authorities, to be obedient, to be ready to do whatever is good, to slander no one, to be peaceable and considerate, and always to be gentle toward everyone" (3:1–2). Wives, husbands, children, parents, bondservants, and masters all must live as resident aliens who are culturally sensitive to those things that might bring reproach to the gospel of Jesus Christ. Peter addresses his code to "foreigners and strangers" (1 Peter 2:11), people who are on their way to heaven and who take care not to offend unnecessarily the citizens of this world.

The family in the first Christian century was patrilineal in which the strongest ties were between brothers and sisters, not between husbands and wives.[10] The father had complete authority over all members of the household. When Jesus taught us to pray to our Father in heaven, the object of our prayers was to be the highest authority in the universe. And when the apostles Paul and Peter spoke often about the relationship of brothers and sisters in the church, they tapped into a primary family image in the

Roman Empire. In New Testament teachings, the church as the family of God reflects in many particulars the structures of the Roman family. At the same time, the household codes significantly modified relationships in the Roman family.

The Great Mystery

The extent of this modification will become evident as we examine Ephesians 5, one of the two lengthy household codes that focused on the relationship of husbands and wives in Christian marriage. In it we find a startling challenge to accepted Roman and Greek thinking about husbands and wives.

Anne Atkins observed: "Our marriages will never illustrate God's love if we ourselves do not. So before telling us how to live as Christian wives and husbands, Paul tells us how every Christian must live."[11] The immediate context of Ephesians 5 is Paul's appeal to all Christians to walk worthy of our calling in Jesus Christ (see Eph. 4:1). That walk includes putting off deceitful lusts like lying, anger, evil speaking, bitterness, wrath, clamor, and malice (vv. 22–31), and it is summarized in Ephesians 5:1–2: "Follow God's example, therefore, as dearly loved children and walk in the way of love, just as Christ loved us and gave himself up for us as a fragrant offering and sacrifice to God." This is the groundwork laid by the apostle Paul for his statement to husbands in verse 25: "Husbands, love your wives, just as Christ also loved the church and gave himself up for her." Paul could later address that to husbands because he had already said it to everyone—to wives, husbands, children, fathers, slaves, and masters. We imitate God by imitating Christ, which means giving up our lives for one another.

Paul then tells all Christians to "be very careful, then, how you live—not as unwise but as wise, making the most of every opportunity, because the days are evil" (vv. 15–16). Being very careful how we live includes "submit[ting] to one another out of reverence for Christ" (v. 21). Because he has now addressed that to everyone—wives and husbands, children and parents, slaves and masters—he can turn to wives and say, "Wives, submit yourselves to your own husbands, as you do to the Lord" (v. 22). In Atkins's words: "Before we can hope to be good husbands or wives we must learn to be good Christians. We must all become self-sacrificing and submissive."[12]

Paul goes on to tell wives: "For the husband is head of the wife as Christ is head of the church, his body, of which he is the Savior" (v. 23). From this verse a doctrine of *headship* has been established, which often misses Paul's point. It is relevant to note that nowhere in Scripture does the word *headship* appear. *Headship* is an abstraction that implies "authority over" in modern common usage; it is not a biblical term nor is it a biblical concept. The Bible says simply that the husband is "head of the wife." If we ask what this means, Sarah Sumner responds, "Scripture doesn't tell us definitively. It tells us instead what it looks like [self-sacrifice]. Thus we have a picture, not a definition."[13] The picture is a metaphor, an analogue to help us understand Ephesians 5:31–32: "'For this reason a man will leave his father and mother and be united to his wife, and the two will become one flesh.' This is a profound mystery—but I am talking about Christ and the church."

How can the two be one? The mystery of marriage is that two—head and body—become "one flesh."[14] Sumner goes on to observe:

> When *head* is defined as "leader" and *body* is defined as "helper," the biblical mystery is lost. What is mysterious about a leader coupled up with his helper? Not very much. Nor is it particularly inspiring. But it is altogether breathtaking to see the biblical picture of body and head joined mysteriously as one.
>
> The picture of "one flesh" communicates volumes of theology. It indicates immediately the organic unity that bonds a husband and wife. How might the divorce rate plummet among Christians if we would recognize that God joins a man and a woman into "one flesh" through the mystery of marriage? It is not so disturbing to imagine a leader breaking up with his assistant. But it is utterly disconcerting to imagine a body being amputated physically from its head. . . . A body belongs to its head and a head belongs to its body. That's why God hates divorce.[15]

The picture of the husband as head is analogous to Christ as head of the church and Savior of the body. Savior? Giving himself for the body? This is a far cry from interpretations of this text that emphasize ruling and authority. Yes, Jesus has authority over the church, but as Paul explores this metaphor further, he describes Christ's work as head of the body, not in terms of authority structures, but in giving himself for the church. Whatever else this metaphor carries, it is not linked to authority. It is about the "head" dying to his own agenda for the sake of the one who is the "body." In Gilbert Bilezikian's words, "Whenever Christ is upheld as the model for husbands to follow, it is not his power, his lordship, and his authority that are presented as the traits to emulate but his humility, his abnegation, and his servant-behavior."[16]

This is the duty Paul assigned to husbands: "Love your wives, just as Christ also loved the church and gave himself up for her" (Eph. 5:25). This word to husbands was highly countercultural. As William Webb noted, "[Paul's] directions toward those on the top of the hierarchy are much more radical within the original culture than what he says to those on the bottom."[17] It was expected that wives would submit to their husbands, but it was not expected that husbands would love their wives in the self-sacrificing manner prescribed by Paul.

Paul goes on with a second argument for husbands: "In this same way, husbands ought to love their wives as their own bodies. He who loves his wife loves himself. After all, people have never hated their own bodies, but they feed and care for them, just as Christ does the church" (vv. 28–29). One flesh—the head lives to serve the body just as the body lives to serve the head. They are inseparable. The way you care for yourself is the way you are to care for your spouse.

It is easy to get caught up in the ongoing debates about "headship" and "authority" in marriage. Much ink has been used and many trees have been turned into paper to disseminate various arguments about the "role relationships" of men and women in marriage. But marriage, according to the Bible, is not about a metaphorical plumber and his female helper. It is about two people indissolubly joined as "one flesh." Paul was not kidding when he stepped back from what he had written and said, "This is a great mystery." We must take it for that.

Heirs Together of the Grace of Life

When Peter wrote the household code in his first letter, he reversed the sequence of Paul's concerns in his letter to the Ephesians. Paul first discussed the whole church, then wives, then husbands, then children, then fathers, then slaves, then masters. Like Paul, Peter began with the whole church, but he then moved to slaves, then to wives and husbands, then back to the whole church. Both codes, however, carry the same motif of submission, set in the context of Christ's example. After addressing slaves and before turning to wives, Peter laid out the motivation for all of our behavior, whether as slaves, wives, or husbands:

> To this you were called, because Christ suffered for you, leaving you an example, that you should follow in his steps. "He committed no sin, and no deceit was found in his mouth." When they hurled their insults at him, he

did not retaliate; when he suffered, he made no threats. Instead, he entrusted himself to him who judges justly. "He himself bore our sins" in his body on the tree, so that we might die to sins and live for righteousness; "by his wounds you have been healed."

1 Peter 2:21–24

Submission (in both Paul's and Peter's household codes) is never mere obedience. The Greek word (*hupotasso*) means to put yourself voluntarily under, and that voluntary act becomes possible because Jesus has already done that for us. This is the servant spirit that turns the other cheek or goes the extra mile (Matt. 5:39–41). Gilbert Bilezikian observed:

> any pagan wife can submit in obedience, but only a Christian woman can submit in servanthood so as to demonstrate the power of the gospel without saying a word and thus win her unbelieving husband [to Christ]. Mere submission to authority has no power to demonstrate the gospel.[18]

Wives are to submit to their own husbands.[19] Then Peter says, "In the same way, you husbands." Just as slaves and wives are to follow Christ's example, so husbands likewise are to do so: "Husbands, in the same way be considerate as you live with your wives, and treat them with respect as the weaker partner and as heirs with you of the gracious gift of life, so that nothing will hinder your prayers" (1 Peter 3:7). One of the major differences between men and women is physiological. Men have more muscle mass and physical strength. A man could use that strength against a woman, and the statistics on battering are tragic evidence of that physical advantage.[20] But Peter tells Christian husbands to live with their wives in the knowledge that they are physically weaker and so husbands are to honor their wives. Why? Because the two are joint heirs of the grace of life. In Atkins's words, "She is more vulnerable than he is on earth, but she is not his inferior in heaven. She is co-heir of the kingdom of God, so she deserves his full honor and respect."[21]

The Bible's Case for Mutual Authority

What about authority? Only one passage in the New Testament explicitly addresses the question of authority in marriage. It is found in 1 Corinthians 7:2–5:

But since sexual immorality is occurring, each man should have sexual relations with his own wife, and each woman with her own husband. The husband should fulfill his marital duty to his wife, and likewise the wife to her husband. The wife does not have authority over her own body but yields it to her husband. In the same way, the husband does not have authority over his own body but yields it to his wife. Do not deprive each other except perhaps by mutual consent and for a time, so that you may devote yourselves to prayer. Then come together again so that Satan will not tempt you because of your lack of self-control.

The only biblical mention of authority in marriage relationships states that it is *mutual* authority. A husband and wife do not "own" their bodies; they own one another's body. Note the parallel: The authority or power that a husband has over his wife, his wife has over him. The relationship is absolutely symmetrical. The immediate context of this passage is at the end of 1 Corinthians 6:18–20:

Flee from sexual immorality. All other sins people commit are outside their bodies, but those who sin sexually sin against their own bodies. Do you not know that your bodies are temples of the Holy Spirit, who is in you, whom you have received from God? You are not your own; you were bought at a price. Therefore honor God with your bodies.

Our bodies belong to God, who made us male and female and who said that in marriage we become one flesh. A woman can fully trust her husband with her body only if she knows that he will treat her body as he would treat his own body—with consideration and care. A husband can fully trust his wife with his body only if he knows that she will treat his body with the same consideration and care she gives to her own body. They are one flesh.

Paul's statement that we are to glorify God in our body and in our spirit, which are God's, is the immediate context for how husbands and wives treat one another's body and spirit. The sexual oneness in 1 Corinthians 7:4 follows (it does not precede) the mutual affection of verse 3. The self-giving in lovemaking is mutual, because the body and spirit of both husband and wife belong first to God and then to one another. Love and trust can grow in such soil. But as noted in chapter 6, true intimacy is not possible to those who come to marriage for purposes of self-fulfillment or merely to ease personal loneliness.

Sex in Christian marriage ought to have about it a rapturous freedom, enveloped in love and consideration that is very different from the images of lovemaking on theater screens. The Old Testament picture of lovemaking is found in the Song of Solomon where the wife exclaims, "My lover is mine and I am his" (2:16 NIV). The poem opens with her longing for him, and throughout the Song we see a man and a woman seeking one another, embracing one another, delighting in one another's company. So the apostle Paul in 1 Corinthians 7:4 says that's how it should be. The husband has authority over his wife's body. She has authority over his body. It is a safety valve to keep us from sexual immorality. But it is more. It enacts the self-giving relationship of Christ and the church, and it embodies what it is to be "one flesh." For this reason, the writer of the letter to the Hebrews is categorical: "Marriage should be honored by all, and the marriage bed kept pure" (13:4).

The Single Life

In a book about marriage, one might get the impression that marriage is the only desirable state. Not so. In the same chapter (1 Corinthians 7), the apostle Paul (who apparently was single) wrote:

> I would like you to be free from concern. An unmarried man is concerned about the Lord's affairs—how he can please the Lord. But a married man is concerned about the affairs of this world—how he can please his wife. . . . A woman is bound to her husband as long as he lives. But if her husband dies, she is free to marry anyone she wishes, but he must belong to the Lord. In my judgment, she is happier if she stays as she is—and I think that I too have the Spirit of God.
>
> 1 Corinthians 7:32–33, 39–40

Chapters 2 and 3 of this book explored the present culture's case against marriage. Thousands of couples today want the pleasures and advantages of marriage without the legal encumbrances. The apostle Paul makes this point in 1 Corinthians 7: "Each of you should live as a believer in whatever situation the Lord has assigned to you, just as God has called you" (v. 17). This is between the passages discussing how Christian husbands and wives are to relate to one another and how unmarried people are to see themselves. So the apostle tells us, live fully in the gifts and calling of God. Has God given you a spouse? Live fully in your marriage. Has God given the freedom of singleness? Live fully in your singleness. Our "walk" is to be in love and in circumspection (Ephesians 5). It is to be without sexual immorality. It is to glorify God in body (1 Cor. 6:20). Within such a framework for our walk, we can live fully and freely, whether single or married. But contrary to today's mores, we cannot take the privileges of the married while remaining single. We are to flee sexual immorality.

Sometimes single Christians find it difficult to embrace and live fully in their singleness, because, as Mary Stewart Van Leeuwen put it, "Despite the fact that Christians pay lip service to the equal value of married and single people, their near-idolatry of the family over the past century has made single Christians feel like second-class citizens at best and moral failures at worst."[22] Yet the apostle Paul notes that marriage complicates service for Christ and sometimes sidetracks Christians from serving God. There is abundant room in the family of God for both single and married people.

Interpreting the Household Codes in a Postmodern World

Some Christians treat the household codes as an "interim ethic," valid only for the times in which they were written. Christian marriage and family life in the first century were hierarchically structured because the wider culture demanded it. The apostles were deeply concerned that Christians not flaunt their new freedom in Jesus Christ and not offend the world outside the Christian community.

But a case can also be made against an interim ethic. Each of the stipulations directed to wives or to husbands had already been mandated for the whole body of Christ. All people of faith are to have submissive spirits. All people of faith are to love one another with a self-sacrificing love. In virtually every case, the rationale for each stipulation was that Christ had already walked that road and his followers could safely walk it as well (Eph. 5:1–2). The example of Jesus Christ giving his life as a ransom for many is the reason that wives submit to their husbands and husbands love their wives in a self-giving manner to the same degree that they love their own body. Peter ended his household code with these words: "Finally, all of you, be like-minded, be sympathetic, love one another, be compassionate and humble. Do not repay evil with evil or insult with insult. On the contrary, repay evil with blessing, because to this you were called so that you may inherit a blessing" (1 Peter 3:8–9). This is not an interim ethic, nor can we treat what preceded it as an interim ethic. The call is to every person of faith—both men and women, bondservants and masters. We do it because Jesus did it, and we follow his example.

What does that look like in the twenty-first century? A Christ-imitating marriage has at least four components. The first is a shared calling, as Peter put it, "knowing that you were called to this, that you may inherit a blessing." Called to what? Called to be of one mind, having compassion for one another, tenderhearted and courteous, not tit for tat. In short, you are called to imitate Jesus in your marriage. Does this mean that you become a doormat? Of course not. Jesus stood up to those who opposed God's work and purposes in the world. But his compassion for others never flagged. He both figuratively and literally turned the other cheek to his oppressors. Our calling is to imitate Christ as we relate to our spouse.

A second component of a Christ-imitating marriage is this: If God sends children into a home, both mother and father share in parenting them. It is no accident that in the household codes directed to parents (Eph. 6:4; Col. 3:21), the instruction to bring up children in the nurture and admonition of the Lord is directed to fathers. The nineteenth-century culture shifted parenting exclusively to mothers, and in most of the twentieth century the church has left it there. But the Proverbs 1–9 pattern of shared parenting is implicit in Paul's words to parents.

A third component of a Christ-imitating marriage is shared dominion or shared provisioning. The creation mandate of Genesis 1:28 established this component in the beginning, and we see glimpses of it throughout the Bible. The Proverbs 31 woman was integrally engaged in helping to provide for her family. She spun thread and wove sashes and linen garments to sell to the merchants. From her profits she bought a field and planted a vineyard. It is significant that a working woman was used as the example of wisdom applied in daily life, summarizing the wisdom of the people of God in the book of Proverbs.[23] Paul's comrades in ministry, Priscilla and Aquila, worked side by side with Paul in both tent making and ministry. Here was an exemplary married couple who shared the responsibility to produce income for the family. And Lydia, another example, carried on her business as a seller of purple.

Someone might object that the household codes do not specifically instruct women to share the task of providing for a family. But we should remember that the household codes spoke directly to problem areas in Christian homes so that followers of Christ would give no offense. Shared provision was so much a part of the daily life for women as well as for men throughout Bible times that it would not have been mentioned unless it were a problem. Archaeologists uncovering ancient homes have identified the rooms where goods were produced and the area where those finished goods were sold to the public. The pattern in Bible times remained the pattern for family life until the Industrial Revolution (see chapter 4), and only then did women shift from production to consumption, relying entirely on what someone else had earned.

Furthermore, shared provision is essential to a good marriage. The central issue is not about paychecks or whether a woman works outside the home or in the home. There are many ways in which wives can participate in providing for the family. At the same time, people of faith sometimes dismiss the human need to be productive, doing work that benefits the family.[24] A theology of work begins with the creation mandate and a God who works and knows our need to work. As noted in chapter 6, marriage must have a purpose, a goal, and a task beyond simply "being together." Shared provisioning that enables a couple to prosper and grow together is a glue that can hold two people together for life. Whether that means waged employment outside the home for the wife is a decision the couple must make.

The fourth component of a Christ-imitating marriage is shared accountability. At the conclusion of the Ephesian household code, addressed to husbands and wives, the apostle Paul comments, "Each one of you also must love his wife as he love himself, and the wife must respect her husband" (5:33). Earlier in the letter, Paul stated that *because we are members of one another*, we must speak truth to one another (4:25) and we must let no corrupt word come out of our mouths (v. 29). A Christ-imitating marriage demands honesty or truthfulness in the relationship so that trust can flourish.

These four components work together to make a marriage *missional*. The household codes give us the daily agenda for a radical, Christ-imitating marriage, which can be a powerful testimony for the gospel to neighbors and colleagues.

A Transforming Relationship

What have we learned from the New Testament household codes? Paul's and Peter's instructions to wives and husbands are both similar to and radically different from the Greek and Roman household codes of the first-century Mediterranean world. The codes reflect the interplay between the non-Christian Roman and Greek cultures and the Christian's freedom in Christ. While the codes mirror in some respects the cultural expectations of their time, they are not merely an interim ethic. Rather, they make concrete in everyday life the ways in which husbands and wives are to imitate the attitudes and actions of Jesus Christ.

Furthermore, while the household codes are sympathetic to the larger culture, they modify the hierarchies of the day by extending the spirit and action of submission to all believers who follow in Jesus' steps. Paul and Peter support submission "to every ordinance of man," including hierarchical marriage, for the purpose of not offending the unbelieving world. At the same time, they depict the husband/wife relationship as "one flesh," the mystery of two becoming one so that each bestows honor on the other in the same way they would their own body. The only marital authority structure in the New Testament letters is a mutual authority over each other's body. Undergirding the relationship of a husband and a wife is love displayed in respect and self-giving.

Christian men and women in the first century may have found the household codes challenging to live by. Men, in particular, would have been startled by the new demands the gospel placed on them in the home. Today Christian men and women may still find the household codes challenging to live by. But today it may be women who chafe at the word *submit*, because they have missed the larger meaning of the household codes for marriage in the twenty-first century. As we study the New Testament passages about marriage, we discover that marriage can be instrumental in the process of sanctification. The two-as-one-flesh relationship provides innumerable opportunities for conflict to erupt. Living with a spouse can be like rubbing up against sandpaper day after day. God uses our relationships to bring us to maturity, to nurture us in our journey toward wholeness. After Eden, God's case for marriage remained unchanged, because bent and broken image-bearers can be redeemed and transformed, and marriage is designed to transform us.

God's case for marriage includes the possibility of our being a daily, living demonstration to a watching world of the relationship of Christ to his bride, the church. Thus our marriages and our radically changed lives are vehicles through which God speaks to the world around us.

11

A Map for Our Postmodern, Post-Christian World

Acartographer in the time of Copernicus must have had a bewildering time of it. It is easy to imagine one of those ancient mapmakers looking irritably at the carefully drawn maps on his wall and thinking, *Not one of these can be used as it is. They must all be changed.*

Redrawing the maps was a task that would have challenged both the cartographer's mind and his pen. He must, for example, draw accurately the curve of the Mediterranean coastline, a curve that had not changed, and yet think and draw that curve into a world that had assumed a startling new position in the universe, an earth that had first moved from flat to round and now to one of several objects rotating around the sun. He faced the task of drawing accurately those things that had not changed but placing them in a world that appeared drastically different and that defied easy description. At least one of those old mapmakers must have muttered to himself, "It's well and good enough for that Copernicus fellow to announce that the earth moves around the sun. It's hard enough to draw a round earth on a flat piece of paper, and now I have to reposition the earth itself."

In thinking about marriage, the present Christian community is much like those frustrated old cartographers. The process of redrawing the marriage maps is not an easy task. Nevertheless, Christians must learn to think differently in a postmodern, post-Christian world, while remaining faithful to God's call to distinctive living.

Postmodern thinking continues to shape the present culture in ways that are not friendly to a Christian worldview, and that makes the culture's case against marriage a persuasive one. For Christians, the challenge at this point is difficult, but it has the virtue of being straightforward. The issue, to use Jesus' description, is one of learning how to be *in* but not *of* the (postmodern) world. Marriage maps are designed to keep God's people on track *in* the postmodern world; they must not lead Christians into a place in which they embrace the value system *of* the contemporary culture.

As Christians, our understanding of marriage rests on the biblical narrative, but this understanding of marriage must be lived out in the postmodern culture, which rejects the idea of truth as a knowable certainty that exists independent of the individual thinker. As Christians, we understand that God's call in marriage is to a faithful, lifelong commitment to the marital relationship. We view Christian marriage as rooted in and responsible to the family and community of God. This concept of marriage must be lived out in the contemporary culture that promotes the autonomy and self-gratification of the individual above the common good. In a culture that views community as subservient to the individual's needs and comfort, Christians are challenged to construct Christian community that will support marriage both as an individual act of faith and as a commitment to the family of God. In the postmodern world Christian marriage is not easy to live or to explain to our neighbors. Christians cannot expect that their pattern of marriage will automatically make sense to the postmodern culture in which it must be lived out.

The present influence of the postmodern world is not the only challenge to biblical marriage. In the past, Christians (particularly evangelical Christians) have been careless students of social history. Now as contemporary Christians begin to correct this neglect and develop a more historically accurate picture of the past, our new knowledge challenges both our distorted sense of how marriage was and our presuppositions about the way marriage, therefore, ought to be.

Earlier chapters of this book, for example, present a historically accurate description of marriage in the Victorian era. History demonstrates that the Victorian pattern of marriage was a nineteenth-century invention, fashioned in response to the economic and social factors of that time. Careful study indicates that these factors had little if anything to do with the Christian mandate for marriage. Further, history reports that, contrary to a romanticized picture, the Victorian model as it was practiced did not work well for thousands of men and women. In light of these facts, Christians cannot in good faith continue to teach the Victorian model of marriage as the biblical model that should command the allegiance of Christians everywhere. Many Christians have believed deeply in the Victorian model and have sought to practice it. History, however, like Galileo's telescope, gives a view of the Victorian era that requires Christians to alter their marriage maps, uncomfortable as the process may be.

In a similar way, a clear look at a piece of more recent history provides another challenge to change. Contrary to nostalgic reconstruction, the decade of the 1950s (like the Victorian age) was not a golden age for marriage. The 1950s were a historic anomaly, a short period in which something resembling a clone of nineteenth-century Victorianism flourished and then disappeared. Like the nineteenth-century original, the twentieth-century copy was a response to economic and social factors. Marriage in the 1950s, however, was not an expression of the scriptural prescription for marriage within the community of faith, even though Christians (and others) may have imagined that it was.

Fear, perhaps as much as faith, has fueled Christians' loyalty to the 1950s marriage map. As social and political chaos accelerated in the closing decades of the twentieth century, Christians (longing for the alleged safe old days) imagined the 1950s as a Christian Camelot, a magic time, much like the fabled original where it never rained until after sundown. In the 1950s' Christian Camelot, there was no rain on the marriage parade. All men became brave, loving husbands; all women became loving, contented housewives; and all children were wanted, loved, and good. Once again history confronts us with an awkward piece of truth. This picture, Stephanie Coontz bluntly told us, is the way we never were.[1] Not only is the world no longer flat—in fact it never was. Christians cannot use the 1950s as a pattern for biblically congruent marriage in the postmodern world.

As we saw in chapters 2 and 3, we live in a culture that is at best indifferent to marriage and at worst outrightly hostile to marriage in many ways. We are rediscovering that Christians are indeed resident aliens here.[2] And living as expatriates in an unfriendly culture, we experience increasing tension between the values of the culture and our loyalties to our heavenly citizenship. While the tension produced by our alien status is not good news from the standpoint of creaturely comforts, it may prove ultimately to be a blessing. The steadily widening gap between the postmodern culture and the life to which the community of faith is called may, in the end, strengthen our resolve about marriage. In the face of a culture making a strong case against marriage, Christians are being pushed increasingly to clarify what we mean by marriage and to rethink our commitment to marriage *in terms of our membership in the community of God's people.*

In the context of this conflict, Christians may find that a good dash of opposition has the potential to clear our fuzzy thinking and help our halfhearted behavior as well, and fence-sitting will be much less comfortable. Do we as Christians agree, for example, with the sexual ethics of the culture? If not, why then do we live by cultural standards? Why is the rate of divorce and the incidence of premarital sex approximately the same for Christians as for the culture at large? Are we or are we not *Christians*? Is or is not the biblical narrative the normative standard for us *as God's people,* whatever the culture may say? When the gap between marriage within the Christian faith and the patterns of the culture becomes so wide that Christians can no longer pretend that it is not there, our choices will not be any easier, but we will see them more clearly.

It is also possible that the growing cultural pressure for Christians to fit in may produce a contrary effect in the long run. Pushed far enough, Christians may reconsider their identity and take the radical step of embracing God's case for marriage. Understanding the implications of their choice, Christians may come to choose marriage as *Christian* marriage, undertaken as God's people under his mandate. In defiance of the culture's worldview, Christians may take seriously the biblical narrative as God's Word to his people, distinctive and normative for all time. We may, so to speak, wake up, call home, and get our instructions from there.

But in this conflict, Christians face the dilemma of the old mapmakers. Charting our path is not a simple matter. We must identify the changeless essentials of the Christian mandate, discard our erroneous assumptions, and redraw our marriage map in ways that recognize the reality of the postmodern world. Christians know that knowledge does not automatically produce discipleship, and Christians understand, sadly, that they do not always practice what they preach. But it is certain that as Christians we will neither preach nor practice the truth if we do not understand the Christian mandate under which we are called to live.

The Changeless Markers on the Marriage Map

What are the essentials of marriage that remain changeless in this postmodern, post-Christian world? Marriage is more than a social institution that may be changed at will. Marriage is God's idea; that does not change. Neither, unfortunately, does the fact of human sinfulness and the fallen world in which marriage must be worked out. In drawing their marriage maps, Christians do well to begin by thinking carefully about these changeless facts.

Marriage as God's Idea

Trends in the culture around us indicate that marriage as a social institution will continue to change and likely decline. Nevertheless, marriage as God's idea for his people has not changed. God's plan remains Genesis-clear. Two people form a committed relationship for a lifetime together, a relationship marked by fidelity and a life of intimate sharing—sexually, emotionally, spiritually, economically. God's idea about marriage has not changed.

Actually, this is rather remarkable. As the culture continues to shift, Christians need to keep in mind how remarkable—and how illogical— God's point of view is from the perspective of the cultural context. Given the relational difficulties with marriage, people might well consider God reasonable if he *had* changed his mind. But as the culture increasingly points to the problems in marriage, Christians are called to remember that God is fully aware of the problems and chooses marriage anyway. It is in this context that the forthright list of marital struggle contained in the biblical narrative becomes comforting. God understands the problems of marriage, but it continues to be a basic part of his plan for his people. If God hasn't given up on marriage, his people certainly need not give up.

Evidence of God's perseverance includes Jesus' teaching about marriage in which he reaffirmed the basic pattern of marriage that God outlined at creation. After Pentecost, Paul referred back to the original plan. There is also experiential evidence in the sociological world. People appear to be hardwired for relationship and have a lifelong need for permanence. It is true that people (Christians and non-Christians alike) are often unable to achieve permanence in their relationships, but the pain and fragmentation of their lives when committed relationships fail are evidence that the postmodern world cannot disregard. Freedom may be the heady wine of autonomy, but commitment—lifelong—is the bread of human relationships that sustains our daily lives.

Human Sinfulness and Failure

Christians must also mark human sinfulness and failure on the marriage map. These human characteristics have not changed. Marking them, however, requires Christians to make a tough reassessment of their willingness to report their tendency to sin and their marriage failures both to other Christians and to the culture around them. In this psychologically obsessed age, Christians are sometimes tempted to do an end run around human sinfulness when talking publicly about their marriages. A listener might conclude that there are no Christians whose marriages are filled with misery, indescribable loneliness, or violence to body and soul. A listener might think that there are no married Christians who are cruel and selfish or mean and sarcastic to those who share their bed and daily life.

In ways that are downright dishonest, Christians sometimes imply, as they talk publicly about Christian marriage, that a marriage license for Christians grants immunity from human sinfulness. It does not. But in an attempt to make their marriages commercials for God, so to speak, Christians sometimes paint a picture of themselves that does not square with the facts. Christians often behave as though they were Brits living in Los Angeles and feeling loyally compelled to deny that London ever has smog.

Christians privately mourn their marital failures and suffer with their personal pain, but they are confused about appropriate ways to report the reality of their lives publicly. Thus Christians often hide, both from themselves and from others, their pain and struggle.[3] Christians are indeed called to be light and salt in the world in which they live, but they cannot do this by assuming a pseudo-identity that hides the reality of their daily relationships. Human sinfulness lives on in Christian marriages, and nothing is gained by attempting to conceal this fact.

Human sinfulness is perhaps never more pervasive, more corrosive, or more brutal than in the form in which it appears in the intimate quarters of family life. In ways that many Christians do not understand, the current focus on the small private nuclear family has given opportunity for sin to flourish in particularly destructive ways. In a general sense, of course, there is nothing new about human sinfulness, particularly in marriage. What *is* new, however, are the powerful ways that this psychologically infected culture has influenced the church to feel self-conscious and embarrassed about this truth in the marriage of Christians.[4] We have permitted cultural pressure to project a public image of the "well-adjusted Christian" to erode our personal honesty about our human sinfulness.[5] Christians know that they are sinful in their marital relationships. They know that living intimately day after day with another sinful person is often difficult and sometimes produces more pain than gain. For the most part, Christians understand that being a Christian does not mean that they automatically become healthy, wealthy, and wise. And it certainly does not mean that Christians always have happy, uncomplicated marriages, full of joy and good will.

Marking sinfulness on the marriage map is not really the problem. The difficulty lies in Christians' reluctance to say plainly, out loud, that as Christians, they too often find marriage difficult. But bearing faithful witness to the transformational reality of life in Christ begins with honesty. The bumper sticker that reads "Christians are not perfect—they are forgiven" conveys great scriptural truth. Wisdom might suggest the addition of another bumper sticker: "Christians do not have perfect marriages—they have marriages in process with God."

Mapping the Already-But-Not-Yet

Another large area on the marriage map has not changed. This is God's transformation area, theologically marked *sanctification*. In the context of daily life, it is the reality of saints-in-process. It is life lived in the already-but-not-yet of God's eternal plan.

The Bible describes the Christian's status this way: "For by one sacrifice he has made perfect forever those who *are being made holy*" (Heb. 10:14). As we discussed in chapter 9, God's definition of who we are as his people contains a dissonant paradoxical duality. We are *already* perfect (eternally perfect by virtue of Christ's *already* completed work on Calvary), but at the same time we are *not yet* perfect. We are *presently being made holy*. It is in the realm of the "not yet," the presently-being-made-holy, that marriage is worked out.

If contemporary Christians have an odd reluctance to be candid about their sinfulness in marriage, they have an even more curious resistance to acknowledge their in-process status. This causes no small difficulty. Christians understand that they are God's people. They embrace the already-reality that they are complete in Christ, who has become for God's people, their righteousness, holiness, and redemption (1 Cor. 1:29–31; Col. 2:9–10). And Christians understand that simultaneously they (like all of God's waiting creation) must live out their lives in the already-but-not-yet dissonance of the present age. Christians can readily understand that *already-but-not-yet people have already-but-not-yet marriages*, and this condition is a fact that cannot be changed on this earth.[6] For the most part, Christians are neither naive nor dishonest. They have no theological reluctance to mark on the marriage map, "union of saints-in-progress." They say to one another only half in jest, "Be patient with me. God is not finished with me yet." They know theoretically that in any marriage there will be human limitations. But while Christians readily mark "union of saints-in-progress" on the marriage map, there are places where in practice Christians have great difficulty acting on their knowledge.

Waiting for the "Not Yet"

As Christians, our first difficulty comes in our *expectations* for our mate, ourself, and the marriage. It is not so much that we deny at the outset the already-but-not-yet. The problem comes when we act as if the "not yet" can become the "already" if we just get the right combination of people or try hard enough. If we just find the right partner or change our partner or change ourselves—be more sensitive, more caring, more spiritual. If we can just change our lives together, have better communication; more and better sex, money, and things; and less responsibility and more leisure time. Sometimes, when things become difficult, we believe that finding a new partner would ensure reaching the "already" in this life. If we could have a mate who is more with it and more attuned to our needs, one who understands us—then the "not yet" would become the "already" in the here and now.

A counselor was dealing with a severely depressed young wife (both she and her husband were confessing Christians, active in a local church). "God does not expect you to be the perfect wife," the counselor said gently. "He knows that you can't do that."

The young woman thought for a moment, then said tearfully, "My husband doesn't agree with that. He thinks I could be a perfect wife—or at least good enough if I just tried harder, and he thinks he deserves that."

Indeed. This young woman was not without problems, but her problems were not the major issue. Expectations, stripped of the biblical context of the already-but-not-yet world of real marriage, were the precipitating factor for the rising conflict in this relationship. Readers will not be surprised to learn that a few years later this young man left his imperfect wife and child for a physically beautiful young woman who was more "spiritually mature," who better understood his needs, and who (he was sure) was the mate God had intended for him in the beginning. It is likely that the high rate of divorce among second marriages will play out with this young man.

No matter how beautiful or spiritually mature this second mate may be, this young man will find himself again in the already-but-not-yet reality of marriage in the present age. And having given himself permission to leave the first marriage, he will likely find it still easier to leave the second.

But in all fairness, the young man's problem is not entirely of his own making. In a culture that pushes self-gratification and self-fulfillment (whatever that may be), his choice was logical. In ways that we may not readily recognize, the culture has influenced us as Christians. Without intending to do so, we sometimes foster a spiritually baptized fable that is both unchristian and psychologically silly. The fable teaches young people that somewhere out there is the perfect mate, a person God has specifically prepared, and when individuals find this "right" person, they will "just know" and will be marvelously, *spiritually* (of course) happy together forever.

A recent advertisement in a publication aimed at Christians centered around a computer-generated program that could help the applicant (for a substantial fee) find a mate who was just the "right" match on twenty-nine different variables (including spiritual compatibility).[7] Marriage, the advertisement inferred, can be fail-safe if you just choose the "right" person. The advertisement tapped into the widespread fable that we (simply because we are Christians) are guaranteed personally fulfilling, trouble-free marriages if we just find the "right" person (whoever that may be) and do it "right" (whatever "right" may be). In subtle and misleading ways, couched in spiritually coded language, Christians tend to suggest that the already-but-not-yet reality is open to change by human means. *Aha!* we say to ourselves, *I know it won't be perfect, but I'll fix it so there's lots and lots of "already" and hardly any "not yet."* Old hands at the marriage business know that marriage does not work out in quite that way.[8]

Our Expectation of God

The second area where we have difficulty with the already-but-not-yet is in our expectation of God. In the Christian life, it usually takes us a while to get past our disappointment and crankiness with God about the necessity of living in a fallen world with fallen people. Once we do, however, we usually develop a personal interest in God's plan to change his people—from vested self-interest if from nothing else.

We discover that God's idea is logical and fairly simple—and it is also set in concrete. God cannot be talked out of his plan to transform fallen, imperfect *not-yet* people into the saints that in Christ he has *already* made them to be. Paul wrote to the saints-in-progress at Rome that they were predestined to be conformed to the likeness of God's Son (Rom. 8:29). But the more we understand, the more we have mixed feelings about God's plan to change his people. His plan includes two things. He provides the opportunity (we get to choose about behaviors and attitudes) and the power (he gives his very Spirit to indwell us and enable us to participate in the process). He takes *already-but-not-yet* people with *already-but-not-yet* marriages and gives his people *through the Spirit's empowering* an opportunity to change. This power is no small thing. It is the very power by which Jesus was raised from the dead (Eph. 1:19–20).

This is where we as God's people often have a problem with the already-but-not-yet, particularly in marriage. We like the idea of being saints and we are quite fond of the *already-saints* part. It is this business of *becoming saints*, of being *saints-in-progress*, that sticks in our craw. We think, *This whole awkward process of participating with God is slow. And the whole awkward process of my mate's participating with God is so totally slow that no motion can be humanly detected. What is needed here is for God to do a spectacular Super-God* kazaam! *And make me—and most particularly, make my mate—into full-blown instant saints.* Of course, then we would like God to follow this instantaneous changing of our mates and us by similarly changing the world into a trouble-free environment appropriate for the saintliness of our instantly wonderful selves. From the standpoint of the biblical narrative, this is a total waste of time and imagination.

God, without exception, has forever firmly declined all invitations to enter the magic business. He simply is not going to do *kazaam!* no matter how much we wheedle and plead. If we are wise, we will look instead at the marriage map and consider sensibly what God has in mind for us in our *already-but-not-yet marriages* between *already-but-not-yet people*. G. K. Chesterton was a man of wit and faith. His comment regarding marriage touches in a memorable way on the issue of what God has in mind:

> When we defend the family we do not mean that it is always a peaceful family; when we maintain the thesis of marriage we do not mean that it is always a happy marriage. We mean that it is the theater of the spiritual drama, the place where things happen, especially the things that matter. It is not so much the place where a man kills his wife as the place where he can take the equally sensational step of not killing his wife.[9]

What God has in mind, as Chesterton clearly saw, is marriage as the stage on which we may choose by the empowering of God's Spirit to act better than we are. But this is not merely putting our best foot forward with God's help. What is at stake is a profound transformation process. We begin to act differently because we are, by God's grace and enablement, becoming different people through the process of the marriage relationship. By our choice and the Spirit's enablement, we do more than simply act better than we once acted. We *become* better than we once were. But this is not magic. It is mystery, but it is also hard work that cuts across the grain of our natural human impulses.

While there is true mystery in the process by which God transforms his people, saints-in-progress do best when they approach this mystery with a large measure of common sense. Marriage does indeed require good communication and cannot flourish without it. Marriage is more satisfying if couples build a caring, considerate sexual relationship. Much of marital satisfaction rests on a couple's problem-solving ability and their skill in conflict resolution. Most marital misery could be alleviated with large doses of courtesy and respect and everyday fairness in the routines of daily life.

Common sense makes clear that since communication, sexual responsiveness, problem solving, and conflict resolution are significant factors in marital satisfaction, couples should learn these skills. Common sense suggests even more strongly that couples *practice* these skills. Courtesy and respect and fairness are both the hallmark of the practicing Christian *and* the essential oil for the machinery of marriage and family life.

But skill and common sense can go only so far. Times of contempt can come. Unfairness and self-justifying denial of wrongdoing can enter the relationship. There may be nights when a shared bed contains an unbounded loneliness and wordless tears. Anger and distrust can seethe in the air, with an atmosphere thick with hatred or raw with pain and disappointment. Sometimes the power to coerce and the desire to do so strain the marital bond to the limit. Sometimes emotional neglect and physical betrayal empty the broken commitment of meaning and hope. Where is God when marriage is like this?

God is present. And God, through the power of the indwelling Spirit, can bring the ability to forgive, the strength to learn new skills, the resilience to endure, and the willingness to begin again. And in the long struggling process, God can transform his damaged image-bearers, step-by-step, bringing them closer to his goal of being like him. Sometimes in ways that astonish us, God can surprise with joy those who in obedience seek to follow him and keep the commitment "till death do us part."[10]

At this point, God's people (particularly those in difficult marriages) may be increasingly inclined to disbelieve God and vote with the culture. We do not really believe that God can change us and change our marriages. We want out. "God wants me happy," we say reassuringly to one another. He certainly could not possibly be interested in my living through something as difficult as this.

There is a piece of truth in this faulty reasoning. God does indeed want us happy, eternally so. Christ died to that end. But in ways contemporary Christians have difficulty accepting, happiness and godliness do not have a linear relationship. God wants us good. He wants us to be like Christ, and the happiness he desires for us is a by-product of that transformation. Living through difficult things is the ordinary, routine laboratory process through which that transformation comes.

Our difficulty in our expectation with God is that we are full of wishful thinking. We want him somehow to *transcend* our human condition and the human condition of our mate so that the long arduous *transformation* process is not necessary. Again, this is an odd mistake because there is something right about it, a piece of legitimate hope tangled in our wishful thinking. The biblical narrative promises that he will indeed transcend our human condition, but that comes at the end of the road. In the meantime, the *already-but-not-yet is not a temporary assignment. It is who we are. It is who we will be every day of our marriage here on earth.* "What we will be," John writes soberly, "has *not yet* been made known." But (in rising triumph) then "we *shall be* like him, for we shall see him as he is" (1 John 3:2, emphasis added). *Then. Then.*

The Need of Spiritual Skills

We have another difficulty living with the already-but-not-yet. Getting through hard things takes spiritual skills that we often do not have. The classical spiritual disciplines of prayer, meditation, fasting, study, solitude, submission, service, confession, and worship are tools through which the enabling Spirit of God reaches to change us, and thus to change our circumstances and relationships.[11] Most of us do not have these tools nor do we understand their significance. Contemporary, hurried Christians have been slow to understand, for example, that mastering the skill of centering prayer is a practical, powerful preparation for dealing with an environment filled with intense anger or latent rage. It is not an esoteric exercise for a wannabe mystic. The spiritual discipline of confession is a powerful immunization against blaming others. And the discipline of meditation is an irreplaceable tool for keeping our emotional and spiritual balance. No matter how difficult the circumstances, our options appear different—enormously different—if we can review them in God's presence, in the quietness of his love.

Then there is the absolutely bedrock business of forgiveness. A gifted young marriage therapist recently remarked, "I would be out of business in a year if my clients acquired the deep intentional practice of forgiving one another along with the practice of making amends for the wrongs they had committed." Forgiveness is not simple, either to understand or to do.[12] We confuse forgiveness with trying to forget an injury. We ignore issues of justice. We behave as though forgiveness were a matter of a minute, the snap of our fingers. Forgiveness is none of these things. Archbishop Desmond Tutu, writing from free South Africa in which the struggle to deal with the bitter wrongs and hatred of the past continues, reminds us:

> Forgiveness is taking seriously the awfulness of what has happened when you are treated unfairly. It is opening the door for the other person to have a chance to begin again. . . . Forgiveness is not pretending that things are other than they are. Forgiveness is not cheap. . . . When you say to me, "I am sorry," in my Christian understanding I am then constrained by the Gospel imperative to forgive. Yet, this is not the end of the story. You see, if you have stolen my pen and you say you are sorry, and I forgive you and you still retain my pen, then I must call into question the authenticity of your contrition. I must—as a part of the process of reconciliation, of forgiving, of healing, of the willingness to make good—appropriate restitution. . . . Forgiveness does not mean amnesia. . . . Those who forgive and those who accept forgiveness must not forget in their reconciling. If we don't deal with our past adequately, it will return to haunt us.[13]

Forgiveness is possible in the presence of the forgiving Christ and the empowering of the Spirit. When we are willing to forgive and be forgiven, to make and receive amends, reconciliation becomes possible in circumstances that can utterly amaze the unbelieving onlooker.[14]

"You're going to forgive *that*?" an incredulous young man asked his Christian friend in regard to a terrible marital wound.

"Yes," the young Christian replied. "In the first place, God forgave me. Besides, there are lots of other reasons too. It's better this way."

Paul Coleman, discussing the process of forgiveness in marriage, summarized it this way: "Forgiveness is more than a moral imperative, more than a theological dictum. It is the only means, given our humanness and imperfections, to overcome hate and condemnation and proceed with the business of growing and loving."[15] Precisely. Forgiveness sets us free and transforms us a bit in the bargain.

Marriage and the Family of God

In our redrawing of the marriage map, we must reconsider the relationship of marriage to the family of God, that collection of saints-in-process that God calls the church, the real and mystical body of Christ. Our present map has a serious flaw. We have treated marriage as though it were an independent sovereign nation and as though the family of God were something like the United Nations—an advisory group to which an individual marriage-nation may choose or not choose to belong, and whose advice an individual marriage-nation may choose or not choose to take. This does not reflect the biblical picture of the relationship of the individual marriage to the church.[16]

If we think of modern maps, the truth of the relationship of individual marriages to the church is more like a map of the United States or Canada, both of which have political subdivisions (states or provinces) that are organic parts of the larger whole. People in marriages are indeed a unit of their own, with their own sovereignty, but the individuals in the unity and the unit itself *have an organic connection with the church.* Together we form the body of Christ, the family of God. And we must consider, as Rodney Clapp has phrased it, whether indeed the family of God is "first family." Have we, like the old mapmaker, confused things?

To rethink the relationship between marriage and the family of God makes us uncomfortable. We must reconsider how we have glorified the small nuclear family. We must examine the ways in which unconsciously we bend our ideas of church to fit our emotional investment in the value of the individual and our passionate belief in the autonomy of individual believers. But at its core, this issue is not about power or autonomy. It is about our identity as members of the family of God, and the need for us in marriage to be in relationship with something bigger than ourselves.[17] And in a parallel reciprocal way, it is about the need of the family of God to have the marriages of its people open to the legitimate claim of the church at large for the support and nurture of *all* who are part of the family. We cannot sustain a biblical view of the importance and function of marriage apart from the family of God. In this sense it becomes apparent that a sound theology of marriage stands or falls on the way in which singleness is viewed in the context of the biblical mandate.[18]

Hauerwas and Willimon tell a story that helps us think about marriage and the family of God with greater clarity. They include in their story a young pastor who was initially unclear about the way in which this connection is designed to work:

> Nancy [the young pastor] had spent a great deal of time with a couple in her church, Tom and Sue, who were having great difficulty. Sue was an alcoholic. She had been in and out of AA and a number of treatment programs, all to no avail. For ten years Tom had been patient and supportive of her, but Sue's alcoholic binges were becoming worse and Tom was becoming aware of the effects the illness was having on their two children.
>
> Late one night, Tom called Pastor Nancy over to his house saying, "Sue is drunk again and I can't stand any more of it."
>
> All week Tom had been doing the housework, looking after the children, and trying to hold down his difficult job. Nancy felt that Tom had at last reached his limit.
>
> "I'm an ordinary, everyday person," Tom said. "I just can't take any more. What can I do?"
>
> Nancy had complete sympathy for him. "Tom, I know that you have gone a second and third mile with this thing. I don't blame you a bit. If you were to kick Sue out right now, nobody would blame you."
>
> "But we're married. I promised to love her for better or worse," said Tom.
>
> Nancy assured Tom that no reasonable person could expect him to keep his marriage vows under such circumstances. Besides, it might be best for Sue and the kids if he made a break.
>
> "You said that I've gone the second mile," said Tom. "Does Jesus put limits on how far we're to go?"
>
> Nancy tried to reassure Tom that there were limits. Jesus said lots of things, but we also must take the actual situation into account. We must be realistic. After all, Nancy wasn't a conservative or a fundamentalist. She knew how to help her people take Jesus with some interpretive sophistication.
>
> Nancy left Tom that night in great despair. Tom saw no way out of his situation. He could not bring himself to leave Sue, but he had no confidence that he could survive. Nancy was sure that she had been the good, understanding, open pastor. Perhaps, with continued support, she would enable Tom to "do what was necessary."
>
> All might have been left like that were it not for Alice Jones. Alice called Nancy the next day to see if she had heard that "Sue is drunk again." Alice was the president of Tom and Sue's Sunday school class and was fully aware of the situation. Nancy recounted for Alice the conversation she had had with Tom, thinking that Alice might be helpful in enabling Tom to overcome his hesitation about getting out of the marriage.

"Tom's right when he says that he can't bear this thing alone. He's reached his limit," said Alice. "He's not a particularly strong person to begin with. And that's what bothers me."

"What bothers you?" asked Nancy.

"It bothers me that he's expected to bear all this alone. Here he's got two children, a job, and a drunken wife. He's a good enough man not to break his promise to his wife but not a good enough man to keep a promise to a drunk," said Alice. Alice was never one to mince words.

"So where does that leave us?" asked Nancy.

"Right," said Alice. "Where does that leave *us*? We've been talking about this as if it were Tom's problem. If it's his problem, I'll tell you right now, he can't handle it."

"So?"

"So, what the heck do we have a church for, anyway? I'm fed up with this fooling around. All talk, no action. I say I call the Sunday school class together and we quit wringing our hands and take over."

"Take over?"

"Right. Let's let Tom know that we're not just behind him, we're *with* him. We can handle the meals. We can help with the kids. That's no problem. Besides, the hospital has just started a new program for alcoholics. The month of treatments costs $8,000. I say that we pay half and tell Sue that, if she doesn't go, we'll help Tom get that divorce. Threat worked with my brother-in-law, who was also an alcoholic."

. . . Nothing the gospel asks of us—compassion, promise-keeping, child-bearing, healing—is expected of us as loners. We exist as family, as a colony that enabled ordinary people like Tom to be saints. Too eagerly, Nancy had forsaken the story, a story Tom was not yet willing to forget, a story about forgiving seventy-times-seven and being faithful even in suffering. . . . It took Alice Jones to wonder what sort of people they would need to be in order to enable Tom, a weak man even though he was good, to be a disciple.[19]

If in the postmodern world we are to assert the radical call of biblically congruent marriage for God's people, then how can the family of God support marriage among its own? Faithfulness is indeed one of the things that the gospel asks of us, but as Hauerwas and Willimon note, it does not ask this of us as loners. In the story, Alice Jones had the question right: What kind of people must we be *as the family of God* so that, despite human weakness, those among us who are married may be faithful promise keepers?

And in the postmodern world, what kind of people must we be *as the family of God* to call those who are married away from the smallness of their couple-centered existence into the work of the kingdom to care for the body of Christ? A young woman requested that her Bible study group pray for wisdom regarding a decision she and her family were making:

"I just think we [her immediate family] should take Andrea in," she said thoughtfully. "It would be hard for us all, and there would be some things that we couldn't do that we'd like to do. And it would be an expense. There isn't anyone that would help financially. But she needs parenting." She hesitated, then added, "I think that's what it's all about. We are responsible for more than just ourselves."

Like Alice, this young woman had her map right. Marriages need the context of the family of God for meaning, accountability, and support. And in turn, the family of God has a legitimate claim on the marriage for support and nurture of those in God's family on their journey toward wholeness. We are indeed responsible for more than those whose ties to us are biological. It is not difficult to hear Paul saying to Onesimus, "Don't worry. You're going home to your family now. They'll welcome you there."

Every good map marks clearly those places with potential risk of harm— white water, unpaved roads, areas under water at high tide. In the cultural shifts ahead, as values and customs of society change, Christians may find themselves in new situations requiring careful navigation. Ethical and legal issues related to marriage already raise new questions. And in a culture not faith-friendly to Christians, the missional part of marriage becomes more difficult and more important. These places of possible risk should also be flagged on the marriage map.

12

There Be Dragons Here

The old mapmakers were careful folk. When they came to the vast unknown areas of their changing world, they hesitated. The unknown was there—of that they were certain—but they were unsure how it should be marked. To leave it unmarked was irresponsible. The lives of sailors and the survival of their frail ships depended in part on those maps. But how to mark something not yet explored, with boundaries not yet charted?

A professor brought an antique map to geography class one day. On the vast reaches of the Atlantic Ocean off an oddly shaped coast of Africa, the old mapmaker had written in impeccable Latin: "Large water here." But many of the old mapmakers were not content with simply labeling those unexplored seas. Unknown dangers lay hidden in those waters. And so on many of the ancient maps, the vast uncharted oceans carried an additional note: "There be dragons here."

There be dragons here for us as well in the years ahead as we seek to define and practice Christian marriage. And while naming a dragon is not the same as slaying him, it is still a useful activity.

Defining Christian Marriage

When we attempt to define Christian marriage, we may meet up with the *dragons of muddled thinking*. There are at least eight of these beasts.

The first rears its head when we evangelical Christians fail to define our terms carefully. Moreover, when evangelical Christians think and talk about marriage, we are often inconsistent, and at times we are guilty of lazy logic. We add to our sins by sometimes handling the biblical narrative in ways that are historically and theologically questionable and hermeneutically unacceptable. The issue at stake is a clear understanding of Christian marriage, and it involves far more than semantic quibbles. Some of this difficulty stems from theological differences between Christians and from the complexity of the issues that surround a biblically sound understanding of marriage. But a large portion of our difficulty comes from these other sources.

The second dragon of muddled thinking lurks very close when we confuse the biblical goals and purpose of Christian marriage with issues of its social structure. This confusion has contributed, for example, to the general failure to recognize shared calling, shared parenting, and shared provisioning as it has appeared in the biblical narrative from the beginning.

The third dragon of muddled thinking breathes out fire when we regard history as irrelevant to our present practice of the faith. Our glorification of the Victorian model or the Ozzie and Harriet stories of the 1950s are examples of the problems that can result from this failure to understand and learn from history. When we are not grounded in facts, the things we imagine to be true shape our lives without our conscious awareness. The 1950s were not a glorious trouble-free time for marriages, regardless of what was portrayed on a television screen.

When we "people of the Book" demonstrate an inclination to read personal values and theological presuppositions into the biblical narrative, without acknowledging that what we find in the text may well be what we have brought to the text, the fourth dragon of muddled thinking threatens. In dealing with issues that are emotionally sensitive (marital roles, for example), this mistake hardens positions and strains relationships. It makes progress in true understanding of the issues difficult. Kevin Giles, vicar of St. Michael's Church in North Carlton, Australia, has reminded us that no social order should be taken as God-given and inviolable.[1] Yet we use psychological categories that permit us to frame our questions in a way that presupposes the answer we wish to find. For example, Stanley Hauerwas, in his discussion of abortion, demonstrates the way framing the question has been part of the problem in our debate on this painful issue.[2]

The fifth dragon of muddled thinking is a culture that overvalues emotional response as a source of truth. At times we walk precariously near the edge ourselves. We adopt the postmodern belief in the truth-revealing power of emotional response, but we conceal our defection by baptizing our thinking in religious terms—if it *feels* biblical, it *is* biblical; if it *feels* spiritual, it *is* spiritual. Fidelity to the biblical narrative makes that approach unacceptable for Christians. Truth-by-feel-good (including *spiritual* truth-by-feel-good) is a technique with which the postmodern culture may tempt us, but it is a point at which we would be most unwise to yield.

The sixth dragon of muddled thinking lies in the shadow of the modern age now passing. We sometimes yield to black-and-white thinking. We develop a "one right way" to do it (the "law" of Christian marriage), then we measure people and their marriages by their conformity to the law we have developed. The distinctiveness of Christian marriage cannot be defined by a "law" that prescribes a how-to-do-it formula or by insistence on power-oriented definitions of social roles. Christian marriage is a choice. The essential core of Christian marriage is a commitment to be Christ present in the life of one's partner through the leave-cleave-one-flesh structure of Genesis. That is not a formula to do. It is a way of life to be.

We suffer from a lack of sufficient biblical theology to guide our thinking, and this is the seventh dragon of muddled thinking. Christians who are active members of the Roman Catholic, Orthodox, or Anglican communions can be guided by the doctrinal understanding and traditions of those churches. The Protestant free-church division of the church, and more specifically those who form the evangelical arm of the Protestant church, have a much smaller body of biblical theology to form a foundation for teaching and personal practice. Some very good work has been done. More is needed.[3]

Lack of material is not simply a matter for academic concern. A counselor was dealing with a young woman who was engaged to marry. She was severely diabetic and grappling in premarital counseling with the issue of contraception. She had consulted her physician and was dissatisfied with the manner in which her medical doctor had reviewed her options. The counselor recommended that the young woman consult her pastor about the doctrinal position of her church. Then, on the basis of this doctrinal statement, she and the counselor would attempt to work out the ethical issues posed by the personal circumstances of her life. The young woman reported back to the therapist, "The pastor said it's my personal decision. The church thinks I have the right to choose." Indeed, but is this all that the church (of whatever denominational persuasion) has to say or needs to say in language and inexpensive materials to which God's people have ready access?[4]

The eighth dragon of muddled thinking is the knotty issue of the relationship between the church and state in regard to marriage. Although Christians don't always think clearly at this point, there is a growing urgency that we do so. Christians live in a given civil society, unless they reside on a floating iceberg in international waters, and even there maritime law is likely to reach. With rare exception, civil government regulates the *contract* of marriage. Before the wedding, the couple (Christian or non-Christian) is required to secure a license, which is a permit from the state to marry. Following the wedding, the couple is required to share property and indebtedness in ways that are regulated by the state. Certain parental responsibilities are state regulated as well. The marriage is taxed by Caesar's formula and Caesar regularly collects his coin, forcefully if necessary. This licensing-taxing-regulating arrangement is complex and has serious implications. A logical and theologically responsible dialogue regarding cohabitation or divorce is not possible without straight thinking about the state and marriage. The following questions show some of the ways these issues are tangled together.

- Is it possible for two confessing Christians to marry with ecclesiastical blessing (a ceremony conducted and blessed by ordained clergy) and the state's license and, despite their personal faith, not have a *Christian* marriage? What is the relationship between the ecclesiastical blessing, the state's license, the personal faith of each individual, and *Christian* marriage? Which trumps which and why?

- Suppose two confessing Christians profess before state-licensed clergy their intent to form a permanent, committed relationship into which children will be welcomed, but they do not secure a state license. Is their relationship, then, an instance of sinful cohabitation rather than *Christian* marriage? Does the state license make the essential difference between cohabitation and *Christian* marriage? The state license certainly determines cohabitation on the tax rolls of the state and the recording pencil of the census taker. But past this first certainty, the issue is not so clear.

- Consider this scenario: Suppose that two confessing Christians are married with state license by a justice of the peace, without a licensed clergy blessing. Does their personal piety plus compliance with state regulations result in a *Christian* marriage? Does their personal faith make unnecessary any public confessional act of commitment before the body of the church?

- And to add to already muddled matters, what is the significance of sex in all of this? Is a marriage not a marriage until consummated sexually? Consider the case of a couple, both confessing Christians, who pledged privately to each other by candlelight and a glass of wine to "be together forever" and then promptly went to bed together. Are they married "in the eyes of God," to use a quaint old phrase? Could they later say accurately if oddly, "We've been married for quite a while, but this year we've decided to have a wedding at Christmas"?

- If one member of a couple publicly married with state license by licensed clergy is a confessing Christian and the other is not, then what is the status of the marriage? (The Corinthian Christians were concerned about this issue. In the Corinthian family of faith there were "mixed" marriages in which only one of the couple was a Christian.)

- And to examine a common practice (one which fuels the lucrative wedding industry), suppose two individuals, neither of whom is a confessing Christian, secure a state license to marry, then find a church in which licensed clergy agree to marry them. After the wedding, they adopt a "Christian" structure for their relationship—that is, they form an exclusive and distinctive unit (they *leave* their families of origin), they are monogamous and sexually faithful to each other (they *cleave* to one another), and they make a sexual union and build a family (they form a *one-flesh* relationship). They may even attend church on religious holidays and send their children for moral instruction to a local Christian education program. Is this a *Christian* marriage? At this juncture, some witty reader is certain to be muttering, "If it looks like a duck and walks like a duck, is it a duck?" Precisely the point, if inelegantly put.

- Even the act of adultery is not so simple to understand as one might initially think. If a partner in a committed cohabiting couple is sexually unfaithful, is that unfaithfulness an act of adultery? If not, why not? Does adultery by definition require physical unfaithfulness in a relationship regulated by a state license? And how does intentionality and human will interact to define the ethical significance of the physical act of unfaithfulness? For example, compare these two acts of sexual unfaithfulness. Two adults, each of whom is a confessing Christian, are only marginally attached to a local church. Their lives pivot around their work. They are successful, mid-thirties business acquaintances, both married to spouses with whom they share limited time and decreasing interests. The two decide to have an affair. Under the guise of business, they organize a weekend away together. After a romantic dinner and some fine wine, they go to bed together.

That's the first example. Now the second example: This couple is quite young, each twenty-two years old. They are struggling economically and are already parents of two small children. They grew up in the church, but now they attend only episodically. The crucial incident occurs at a New Year's Eve office party. The young husband, an admittedly immature Christian, strongly under the influence of alcohol, finds himself in a strange bed with an office secretary. His partner in this act is not a believer. She is an unmarried woman whom he knows only casually and who at the time is also strongly under the influence of alcohol. When he awakens, he is not exactly sure what transpired. Are these two acts morally and ethically equivalent?

Jesus insisted that intention and the state of the heart be taken into account when judging a matter. In what ways does mental impairment (for example, the result of drugs, alcohol, or intellectual limitations) limit culpability or alter the significance of adultery to the marital bond? And in what ways does the *failure of the people of God* (the local group of saints-in-process) *to nurture and support the marriage* limit the culpability and significance of an individual act of adultery? Am I my brother's keeper?

Premarital sex is commonplace, even among Christians. The skyrocketing rates of cohabitation include Christians. The frequency of sexual infidelity is disheartening and destructive. Now the majority of young adults (Christians and non-Christians) expect that divorce and remarriage lie somewhere in their future, and statistics make that expectation a strong probability. In the face of current cultural trends, Christians must develop greater clarity in our thinking. What essentials define marriage in contrast to cohabitation? How do we know a *Christian* marriage when we see one? Once a *Christian* marriage is formed, can it be broken? If so, how? And what does it mean for *the people of God* to live in a marriage as the embodiment of Christ's sacrificial-servant relationship with the church? There is real danger in muddled thinking. There be dragons here.

Marriage as Mission

A second drove of dragons has taken up residence in our thinking about the mission of marriage. For Christians, marriage is one of the ways in which we are called to make disciples. We don't often think of marriage in this way, but in the shifting, changing postmodern culture in which we live, Christian marriage delivers a powerful message to the unbelieving culture around us. The message may be negative or positive, but it is heard, for better or for worse. In this sense, marriage is an unavoidable missionary enterprise of the church.

Years ago there was a television program called *Mission Impossible* about a brave, creative team of high-tech adventurers. Each segment of the series began with a teaser—the team watching a tape that gave glimpses of characters and scenes from the upcoming script. The teaser closed with the deep, mysterious voice on the tape announcing, "Your mission, if you choose to accept it, is . . ." an impossible task that the heroes would, of course, accept and complete successfully in the following sixty minutes.

Surveying the dragons with which they are surrounded, Christians may think that marriage is one mission they choose *not* to accept. But unlike the old television series, marriage as mission is not an assignment that Christians are free to reject. When Christians sign on for marriage, they sign on for marriage as mission, like it or not, understand it or not. A friend reading this chapter noted that the dragons are nonetheless hungry for all our failure to anticipate their presence. And this is perhaps the first important thing for Christians to consider in the matter of marriage's missional mandate. Marriage is indeed the stage where important things happen, as Chesterton observed; it is the theater of the spiritual drama. The surrounding world knows this. People watch Christians at work, at play, and for better or worse, in their marriages. And while they are not free to decline their mission, Christians can do something about decreasing the likelihood that a dragon will make lunch of them along the way.

Christian marriage requires more than human resources. It requires community connection (in the family of God). And it requires the special energy source that belongs to Christians alone—the resurrection life of God within them. Only God's power is sufficient here. While the joy and achievement possible in Christian marriage are truly wonderful, its challenges are sobering. Realistically, Christian marriage, like old age, is not for sissies.

When we begin to think about Christian marriage as mission to the postmodern culture, we face an additional set of challenges. From the outset we face the difficulty posed by our residential status. Though we are residents of this world and participants in this culture, we are, at the same time, not citizens of this world; we are citizens of another, with a higher loyalty to a kingdom not of this world. It is that kingdom from which we take orders and the interests of which we serve. We undertake our disciple making while living in this dual status—as participants in the culture but with loyalty lying beyond the culture. In ways that can be dangerous, we live counter to the values and demands of the culture in which we live. We are resident aliens, expatriates in an increasingly hostile culture.

In the tension of life as expatriates, however, we are not called "to keep our heads down" or to "keep a low profile." Instead, we are called to live with a terrifying transparency in the open light of the culture. People do not light a lamp to put it under a bushel, Jesus pointed out to his disciples. No, instead "let your light shine before others, that they may see your good deeds and praise your Father in heaven" (Matt. 5:16). And Jesus practiced what he preached. He was himself the light set on a hill. When they came to seize him that last terrible night, he did not resist them. He did, however, point out to them the irony of their hypocritical behavior, reminding them that he had sat every day openly in the temple courts teaching. They had not arrested him there; they had waited to come under cover of darkness to take him as though he were a rebel or a criminal. Life in the open can be dangerous. But it is our mission. Jesus calls us into life in the open under the watching eyes of a hostile world.

The purpose of our mission is straightforward. It is our task to live as a radical alternative to the culture in a way that persuades individuals in the watching culture to choose allegiance to the Christ whom we serve. Paul, writing to the Corinthians, explained, "We are therefore Christ's ambassadors, as though God were making his appeal through us. We implore you on Christ's behalf: Be reconciled to God" (2 Cor. 5:20). Christians have not always agreed about the best way to undertake this task.

Christianizing the Culture

At various times in history, Christians have invested a great deal of effort in attempting to change the culture. Good things have happened as a result of such efforts, but in practice they have often produced unintended consequences, with serious problems. Christians have discovered that to fit in and Christianize the culture, they have had to cut a deal that ultimately produced strong pressure on them to compromise the essentials of the faith. In bending over to speak to the world, they fell in, to use an image from Hauerwas and Willimon.[5] Many Christians think that the distressing powerlessness of the church in the present, thoroughly secular culture reflects, at least in part, a misguided effort by the church to fit into the culture rather than to live as a radical alternative within the culture.[6] As a result, it is now commonplace to speak of North America as a mission field.[7]

But the danger of fitting into the culture aside, this option ultimately fails, no matter how well intentioned it may be, because it is a substitute for our biblical mandate. We are not called to reform the culture as such. We are called, rather, to transform the world by living out a radical alternative that the world cannot know apart from the lives of God's people. We are God's transformed-and-being-transformed people. We live triumphantly in the already-but-not-yet of the present age through the reality of the indwelling Christ and the empowering presence of the Holy Spirit. Certainly we will influence the culture. How, in view of the resurrection reality, can we not do so? For God's people, influence on the culture is a by-product of their transformed lives. Those early Christians made disciples and, as a result, the world around them was turned upside down.

Withdrawal from the Culture

From time to time another problem has emerged out of an opposing but equally misguided strategy. Christians have practiced a withdrawal from the culture, an isolationism through which they have sought to immunize themselves to infection from the culture in which they live. This strategy has also produced some highly problematic and unintended consequences.

First, this effort is based on an illusion. As Christians we are participants in the culture and are shaped by the culture, whether we wish to acknowledge this or not. Failure to see the inevitable interchange between Christians and the surrounding culture is dangerous. It leads us to avoid the self-examination that protects us from unconscious absorption of the culture's values and goals. Lois Barrett gives an example of the way in which the postmodern value of individualism has reached into the church but remains unidentified:

> Church becomes defined apart from community, in terms of individual choice, individual morality, individual self-actualization, and individual decisions about where to obtain the best spiritual goods and services. All too typical is the woman who, after attending worship and disliking the sermon, asked her visiting friend, "Now tell me, what did you get out of that worship service?" The woman was taken aback when the friend replied, "That's not a question I ask myself. I ask myself, 'Did this community of God's people worship God today?'" It never occurs to many people to define worship in terms other than meeting individual needs, or to put God rather than personal satisfaction at the center of worship. This situation is the result not

just of people's individual perversity, but of the pervasiveness of the power of individualism that tries to determine not only the answers but also the way one shapes the question.[8]

Theology has not been immune to difficulties arising from unrecognized cultural influences.[9] Kevin Giles notes that those theologians who, holding a "high" view of Scripture, used Scripture to support slavery in the nineteenth century, "never considered the possibility that self-interest was corrupting their theologizing."[10]

But the strategy of isolation stumbles ultimately because it revises our biblical mandate. We are called to be God's people *in* the world, an unavoidable alternative, a visible presence, a persuasive voice. We are mandated to do good deeds with the goal that people may see and give glory to God who is in heaven.

Two women out shopping paused to look at an elegant pair of shoes artfully displayed in the window of an upscale shoe shop. One woman commented to her companion, "Just look at those shoes! It takes an Italian to make a shoe like that." As God's people, we are called to live within the culture in such a way that the watching world may see our lives and say, "Now it takes a Christian to make a marriage like that."

Christians are called to engage the culture at key points where the difference between them and the surrounding culture points to the nature of God and the redemptive reality of our life in Christ. Barrett notes, for example, that a local congregation listening to sermons that deplore crime may faithfully reflect God's call for right relationships between people. But it is as the church works to establish economic opportunities in communities in which crime is the main escape route from poverty that the church has engaged the culture in a way that is not only faithful but is a light to the world, a city set on a hill.[11]

Locating the key points at which we are called to engage the culture is sometimes a difficult task. But in the postmodern world, marriage certainly is one of these key points. Such engagement with the culture, however, is risky. As Barrett notes, one of the most difficult human tasks is to be different from another and yet stay in relationship with the other.[12] But we are called to engage the culture regarding marriage because it is one point where we may visibly display the redeeming reality of our life in Christ. It is possible for Christians in a world obsessed with sexuality and sensual gratification to model an unself-conscious sexual purity that presents an attractive, if radical, alternative to the culture. Out of the resurrection life that is ours, Christians can demonstrate a lasting commitment to each other that points to our enabling life commitment to Christ. And can we not in the face of the watching world bend to serve one another in marriage in a way that points to the Savior who taught us that to lose one's life is to gain it in the end? As the family of God, we model the community for which the postmodern world longs, but which it cannot reach.

Celebrating Our Mission

Marriage is a vital missional endeavor in the postmodern church. But there are dragons here. Already we have bent over and fallen in, to use Hauerwas and Willimon's phrase.[13] Look at our rate of divorce, our rate of premarital sex, our rate of sexual infidelity and domestic violence. At these points we look like the culture around us rather than like God's transformed-and-being-transformed people. But we know that by God's enabling grace, this can be changed—not easily, but it can be changed, once we see where we have drifted and the dangers in the drift.

At the same time, there are encouraging trends. Churches take the task of premarital preparation of couples more seriously. Mentoring couples, who support new marriages and assist struggling couples, are making a practical and positive difference. Greater interest in spiritual formation focuses on the process of growing mature Christians, able to live with grace and effectiveness in any life circumstance. We are beginning to understand the cultural issues more clearly and to think about Christian marriage as the distinctive that it is. But we are still slow to see clearly our responsibilities as the family of God to support the marriages of couples around us.

The authors both grew up at a time when the church's commissioning of missionaries who were "being sent" was a joyful and solemn day of celebration in the church. It was also an expression of deep, long-term mutual commitment. They were "our missionaries." We would support them, and they would go.[14]

A wedding today is a sending ceremony, but most churches are not intentional and clear about both the sending and the subsequent support that will be needed. At a recent wedding, one of the authors watched the rose petals rain down on the laughing couple as they ran down the church steps, and she thought, *There go our missionaries to the postmodern world. They've had Sunday school and youth group and church membership classes. We have given them six sessions of premarital counseling. Today we have showered them with love, best wishes, and rose petals. Is this enough to ward off the dragons*

*and enable them to be effective missionaries in the world to which they go? And
how do we support them now?*

What the Church Has Done Right

The church has not survived these tumultuous years unmarked, nor has
it avoided at several crucial points an unfortunate contamination by the
culture. But in all fairness, the closing decades of the twentieth century did
not prove to be an easy time to function as salt and light. The church has
had difficulty framing a redemptive word in the language of the culture
and winning a hearing for that word.

We must also acknowledge that as marriage has increasingly fallen on
hard times, we have become entangled in the wreckage. We confused our
history and thought that fidelity to a historical model was fidelity to Scripture. We made the error of confusing style with substance. We thought
that if we prescribed rigid roles, we could conserve and honor the essence
of Christian marriage. We thought that faithfulness to our mandate to be
God's people required us to stay in the same place, when God's calling has
been to carry with us the essence of the faith, the uncompromisable essentials of Christian marriage, and to move on into the postmodern world
as salt and light in this culture. And we have sinfully assigned significance
to the human family that rightfully belongs to the family of God, the living
community of faith. We have made our share of errors. And yet—and yet,
we have done some things right, and they are things we need to continue
to do.

We need to celebrate the survival of the church by God's grace and empowerment. It remains one of the sturdy institutions in our civic society.
The community of the faithful provides a source of hope and a ground of
beginning for the reexamination of the essence of Christian marriage and
the encouragement of its practice.

In the context of the sexual revolution and the experimentation with
"alternate patterns of family," the church has continued to insist that marriage is fundamental both to human happiness and to a decent civil society.
We were right to do so, and in the face of the present ills of society, we
may be forgiven a human impulse to say, "We told you so."

Further, we have insisted that Christian marriage is more than an arbi-
trarily chosen social arrangement. We have argued that people are hardwired by God's design to need and want the stability and security that a
permanent, monogamous commitment to a partner brings. Our position is

a strong one. In her letter in chapter 2, the cohabiting young mother unintentionally makes our point. Her rejection of marriage as a legal contract comes in the context of her passionate, pain-filled anger at the destruction of the marriage bond through divorce that she had experienced in her family of origin. In contrast to her parents' divorce-oriented pattern, she described her own life's fiercely protected structure. Her life, she insists, will be characterized by bonding with one mate; faithful, lifelong commitment to that mate; a child to be protected at all costs from disruption of that bond; building a house, making a home. Listen to her again:

> My decision not to marry does not indicate a desire for a life of debauchery and half-formed commitments. Quite the opposite. With our new baby, our nightly sit-down dinners, and our impending mortgage, my boyfriend and I are hardly bucking the system. . . . But we're looking for more than just a party, a round of toasts, and a validity stamp from Uncle Sam to get us to that golden anniversary.[15]

She and her boyfriend are, of course, bucking the postmodern culture in a way they do not realize. They have adopted a pattern of permanent, monogamous, child-valuing relationship that sounds astonishingly close to an idea God had a very long time ago. We *were* right. We *are* right. We need to continue to say that marriage as a permanent monogamous relationship is a part of the original design and that people do best in relationships that reflect that design.

As the church, we have insisted that marriage is a responsibility with binding obligations in which the "rights" of a given individual must at times be superseded by the needs of another. This has earned us considerable criticism and some ridicule in a culture addicted to individualism and intoxicated with the concept of self-gratification. We have insisted further in an equally unpopular fashion that children are not objects to be placed in a will-call department until some adult has the time and inclination to pick them up. They are fragile and vulnerable and our hope for tomorrow. Their needs must at times trump adult comfort and pleasure, and the state cannot substitute for their parents in their care, their nurture, and the shaping of their values.

We have been right on both counts. Our society has only begun to reap the bitter fruit of inadequately socialized children who have grown to adulthood without attachment to a family unit. And already we experience the consequences of a society governed largely by adults with little or no capacity to commit to the welfare of others when there is cost to themselves in that commitment.

We have been "most" right where we have been most countercultural. In the face of the culture's obsession with self-gratification, we have called for commitment to the welfare of others. Even when "the thrill is gone" and marriage becomes hard work, we encourage couples to make and keep vows. Embracing the paradox of marriage, we believe that Christian marriage demonstrates the truth that Jesus taught—that losing one's life can be gain. By definition Christian marriage is, we believe, the intentional surrender of the individual to the commingling of two lives. Two become one, yet remain two, each the more complete for the lost individuation, the freer for the lost autonomy. In marriage, we believe that the self that is lost is found again, the more complete self in the paradoxical context of its loss. In this postmodern culture, however, we understand that our idea of Christian marriage is an unthinkable concept, something that cannot be thought and therefore cannot be done.

In the tension of the already-but-not-yet world in which we live, we understand something else. Christian marriage, no matter how imperfect our practice, is doing what is right, whatever the cultural opposition may be. And in Christian marriage we have the opportunity to embody for a watching world the reality of God's loving, powerful presence in the life of his people.

Appendix A

Survey Questions

DESIGNED BY ALICE MATHEWS

The survey questions used in the research project with eleven large churches in five parts of the United States in 1994–95 were grouped in eight triads of three questions each, with each triad focused on a particular subject.

Triad 1: Christian Experience

1. How would you describe what it means to be a Christian?
2. How did you become a Christian?
3. How do you nurture your Christian life now?

(This triad of questions allowed the investigator to ascertain the level of evangelical belief about Christian conversion.)

Triad 2: Biblical Teachings about Marriage

1. What do you believe the Bible teaches about the roles of men and women in Christian marriage?

2. As you think about your beliefs about Christian marriage, where or how did you arrive at these beliefs? Please include in your description any books, seminars, classes, or individuals that played a key role in helping you form your beliefs about Christian marriage.

3. Have you at any time personally struggled with any of these beliefs in the context of your own experience of marriage? If so, which beliefs were difficult for you to harmonize with your own experience? How did you resolve the tension?

Triad 3: Sexuality in Marriage

1. What do you believe the Bible teaches about sex in marriage? You may want to include in your response what you believe the Bible teaches about roles and appropriate limits in expressing sexuality.

2. As you think about your own experience of sex in marriage, how has your experience conformed to or deviated from your beliefs about what sex in marriage ought to be?

3. How would you rate your overall satisfaction with your experience of sex?

Triad 4: Decision Making in Marriage

1. What do you believe the Bible teaches about gender roles in decision making in a Christian marriage?

2. How have you and your spouse handled decision making in your marriage?

3. How would you rate your overall satisfaction with the way you and your spouse handle decision making in your marriage?

Triad 5: Work and Money Matters in Marriage

1. What do you believe the Bible teaches about who should earn and who should spend money in a marriage?

2. If you have most recently been in a one-wage-earner marriage, how have you and your spouse handled spending decisions? Who spends most of the money and how? If you have most recently been

in a marriage with two wage earners, how have you and your spouse handled spending decisions?

3. If in the course of your marriage you moved either from a two-wage-earner to a one-wage-earner marriage, or vice versa, how has this shift impacted the way you and your spouse relate?

Triad 6: Resources in Time of Need

1. If you have experienced times of frustration or difficulty in your marriage, where have you turned for moral support or helpful advice?
2. In what ways has your church been a resource for you in times of need?
3. What kinds of support would you have liked but did not find available to you?

Triad 7: Overall Happiness or Fulfillment

1. What do you believe are the most important ingredients in a happy marriage?
2. Which, if any, of these ingredients do you think may be different for men or women? Why would this be true?
3. As you reflect on your own experience of marriage, to what degree have you experienced these ingredients of a happy marriage?

Triad 8: Personal Sacrifice in Marriage

1. What are the personal sacrifices a person ought to expect to make when entering into marriage?
2. Are these sacrifices different for men and women? If so, in what ways?
3. As you reflect on your own experience of marriage, how have you personally experienced and adjusted to these sacrifices?

Appendix B

The Six New Testament Household Codes

Galatians 3:28 (48–57 C.E.). This brief code is considered to be the earliest and most succinct: "There is neither Jew nor Greek, neither slave nor free, neither male nor female; for you are all one in Christ Jesus."

Ephesians 5:15–6:9 (60 C.E.). Ephesians is the longer exposition with the parallel code to the Colossian Christians being an abbreviated version.

Be very careful, then, how you live—not as unwise but as wise, making the most of every opportunity, because the days are evil. Therefore do not be foolish, but understand what the Lord's will is. Do not get drunk on wine, which leads to debauchery. Instead, be filled with the Spirit, speaking to one another with psalms, hymns and songs from the Spirit. Sing and make music from your heart to the Lord, always giving thanks to God the Father for everything, in the name of our Lord Jesus Christ.

Submit to one another out of reverence for Christ.

Wives, submit yourselves to your own husbands as you do to the Lord. For the husband is the head of the wife as Christ is the head of the church, his body, of which he is the Savior. Now as the church submits to Christ, so also wives should submit to their husbands in everything.

Husbands, love your wives, just as Christ loved the church and gave himself up for her to make her holy, cleansing her by the washing with water through the word, and to present her to himself as a radiant church, without stain or wrinkle or any other blemish, but holy and blameless. In this same way, husbands ought to love their wives as their own bodies. He who loves his wife loves himself. After all, people have never hated their own bodies, but they feed and care for them, just as Christ does the church—for we are members of his body. "For this reason a man will leave his father and mother and be united to his wife, and the two will become one flesh." This is a profound mystery—but I am talking about Christ and the church. However, each one of you also must love his wife as he loves himself, and the wife must respect her husband.

Children, obey your parents in the Lord, for this is right. "Honor your father and mother"—which is the first commandment with a promise—"so that it may go well with you and that you may enjoy long life on the earth."

Fathers, do not exasperate your children; instead, bring them up in the training and instruction of the Lord.

Slaves, obey your earthly masters with respect and fear, and with sincerity of heart, just as you would obey Christ. Obey them not only to win their favor when their eye is on you, but as slaves of Christ, doing the will of God from your heart. Serve wholeheartedly, as if you were serving the Lord, not people, because you know that the Lord will reward each one of you for whatever good you do, whether you are slave or free.

And masters, treat your slaves in the same way. Do not threaten them, since you know that he who is both their Master and yours is in heaven, and there is no favoritism with him.

Colossians 3:15–4:1 (60 C.E.).

Let the peace of Christ rule in your hearts, since as members of one body you were called to peace. And be thankful. Let the message of Christ dwell among you richly as you teach and admonish one another with all wisdom through psalms, hymns and songs from the Spirit, singing to God with gratitude in your hearts. And whatever you do, whether in word or deed, do it all in the name of the Lord Jesus, giving thanks to God the Father through him.

Wives, submit yourselves to your own husbands, as is fitting in the Lord.

Husbands, love your wives and do not be harsh with them.

Children, obey your parents in everything, for this pleases the Lord.

Fathers, do not embitter your children, or they will become discouraged.

Slaves, obey your earthly masters in everything; and do it, not only when their eye is on you and to curry their favor, but with sincerity of heart and reverence for the Lord. Whatever you do, work at it with all your heart, as working for the Lord, not for human masters, since you know that you will receive an inheritance from the Lord as a reward. It is the Lord Christ you are serving. Those who do wrong will be repaid for their wrongs, and there is no favoritism.

Masters, provide your slaves with what is right and fair, because you know that you also have a Master in heaven.

1 Timothy 5:1–22; 6:1–2 (63–65 C.E.). Paul included household codes in two pastoral epistles—1 Timothy and Titus.

Do not rebuke an older man harshly, but exhort him as if he were your father. Treat younger men as brothers, older women as mothers, and younger women as sisters, with absolute purity.

Give proper recognition to those widows who are really in need. But if a widow has children or grandchildren, these should learn first of all to put their religion into practice by caring for their own family and so repaying their parents and grandparents, for this is pleasing to God. The widow who is really in need and left all alone puts her hope in God and continues night and day to pray and to ask God for help. But the widow who lives for pleasure is dead even while she lives. Give the people these instructions, so that no one may be open to blame. Anyone who does not provide for their relatives, and especially for their immediate family members, has denied the faith and is worse than an unbeliever.

No widow may be put on the list of widows unless she is over sixty, has been faithful to her husband, and is well known for her good deeds, such as bringing up children, showing hospitality, washing the feet of God's people, helping those in trouble and devoting herself to all kinds of good deeds.

As for younger widows, do not put them on such a list. For when their sensual desires overcome their dedication to Christ, they want to marry. Thus they bring judgment on themselves, because they have broken their first pledge. Besides, they get into the habit of being idle and going about from house to house. And not only do they become idlers, but also busybodies who talk nonsense, saying things they ought not to. So I counsel younger widows to marry, to have children, to manage their homes and to give the enemy no opportunity for slander. Some have in fact already turned away to follow Satan.

If any woman who is a believer has widows in her care, she should continue to help them and not let the church be burdened with them, so that the church can help those widows who are really in need.

The elders who direct the affairs of the church well are worthy of double honor, especially those whose work is preaching and teaching. For Scripture says, "Do not muzzle the ox while it is treading out the grain," and "Workers deserve their wages." Do not entertain an accusation against an elder unless it is brought by two or three witnesses. Those who sin are to be rebuked publicly, so that the others may take warning. I charge you, in the sight of God and Christ Jesus and the elect angels, to keep these instructions without partiality, and to do nothing out of favoritism. . . .

All who are under the yoke of slavery should consider their masters worthy of full respect, so that God's name and our teaching may not be slandered. Those who have believing masters should not show them disrespect just because they are fellow believers. Instead, they should serve them even better because their masters are dear to them as fellow believers and are devoted to the welfare of their slaves.

These are the things you are to teach and insist on.

Titus 2:1–15 (63–65 C.E.).

You, however, must teach what is appropriate to sound doctrine. Teach the older men to be temperate, worthy of respect, self-controlled, and sound in faith, in love and in endurance.

Likewise, teach the older women to be reverent in the way they live, not to be slanderers or addicted to much wine, but to teach what is good. Then they can urge the younger women to love their husbands and children, to be self-controlled and pure, to be busy at home, to be kind, and to be subject to their husbands, so that no one will malign the word of God.

Similarly, encourage the young men to be self-controlled. In everything set them an example by doing what is good. In your teaching show integrity, seriousness and soundness of speech that cannot be condemned, so that those who oppose you may be ashamed because they have nothing bad to say about us.

Teach slaves to be subject to their masters in everything, to try to please them, not to talk back to them, and not to steal from them, but to show that they can be fully trusted, so that in every way they will make the teaching about God our Savior attractive.

For the grace of God has appeared that offers salvation to all people. It teaches us to say "No" to ungodliness and worldly passions, and to live self-controlled, upright and godly lives in this present age, while we wait for the blessed hope—the appearing of the glory of our great God and Savior, Jesus Christ, who gave himself for us to redeem us from all wickedness and to purify for himself a people that are his very own, eager to do what is good.

These, then, are the things you should teach. Encourage and rebuke with all authority. Do not let anyone despise you.

1 Peter 2:11–3:9 (ca. 65 C.E.).

Dear friends, I urge you, as foreigners and strangers in the world, to abstain from sinful desires, which war against your soul. Live such good lives among the pagans that, though they accuse you of doing wrong, they may see your good deeds and glorify God on the day he visits us.

Submit yourselves for the Lord's sake to every human authority: whether to the emperor, as the supreme authority, or to governors, who are sent by him to punish those who do wrong and to commend those who do right. For it is God's will that by doing good you should silence the ignorant talk of the foolish. Live as free people, but do not use your freedom as a cover-up for evil; live as God's slaves. Show proper respect to everyone, love your fellow believers, fear God, honor the emperor.

Slaves, in reverent fear of God submit yourselves to your masters, not only to those who are good and considerate, but also to those who are harsh. For it is commendable if you bear up under the pain of unjust suffering because you are conscious of God. But how is it to your credit if you receive a beating for doing wrong and endure it? But if you suffer for doing good and you endure it, this is commendable before God. To this you were called, because Christ suffered for you, leaving you an example, that you should follow in his steps.

> "He committed no sin,
>   and no deceit was found in his mouth."

When they hurled their insults at him, he did not retaliate; when he suffered, he made no threats. Instead, he entrusted himself to him who judges justly. "He himself bore our sins" in his body on the tree, so that we might die to sins and live for righteousness; "by his wounds you have been healed." For "you were like sheep going astray," but now you have returned to the Shepherd and Overseer of your souls.

Wives, in the same way submit yourselves to your own husbands so that, if any of them do not believe the word, they may be won over without words by the behavior of their wives, when they see the purity and reverence of your lives. Your beauty should not come from outward adornment, such as elaborate hairstyles and the wearing of gold jewelry and fine clothes. Rather, it should be that of your inner self, the unfading beauty of a gentle and quiet spirit, which is of great worth in God's sight. For this is the way the holy women of the past who put their hope in God used to adorn themselves. They submitted themselves to their own husbands, like Sarah, who obeyed Abraham and called him her master. You are her daughters if you do what is right and do not give way to fear.

Husbands, in the same way be considerate as you live with your wives, and treat them with respect as the weaker partner and as heirs with you of the gracious gift of life, so that nothing will hinder your prayers.

Finally, all of you, be like-minded, be sympathetic, love one another, be compassionate and humble. Do not repay evil with evil or insult with insult. On the contrary, repay evil with blessing, because to this you were called so that you may inherit a blessing.

Notes

Foreword

1. Joseph C. Aldrich, *Lifestyle Evangelism: Crossing Traditional Boundaries to Reach the Unbelieving World* (Portland: Multnomah, 1981), 20–21, italics in original.

Chapter 1 Laying a Foundation

1. Yet as thousands of couples in today's culture live together without a state license (called *cohabitation*) to avoid, at least in part, the interference of civil government, the state is preparing to execute an end run around the licensing procedure. In response to a request from a Judges Advisory Panel, the prestigious American Law Institute (ALI) recently issued a 1,200-page report proposing laws parallel to present divorce laws that would govern the breakup of long-term cohabiting relationships. The proposed legal code would provide for distribution of property and wealth, the care of minor children, and in specified instances, payment of alimony. This report made the front page of the November 29, 2002, *New York Times*.

2. F. Alford-Cooper, *For Keeps: Marriages That Last a Lifetime* (New York: M. E. Sharpe, 1998).

3. Robyn Parker, "Why Marriages Last: A Discussion of the Literature" (research paper, no. 28, Melbourne 3000 Australia: Australian Institute of Family Studies, July 2002), 24, at www.aifs.org.au/.

4. Stanley Hauerwas and William Willimon, *Resident Aliens: Life in the Christian Colony* (Nashville, TN: Abingdon Press, 1989).

5. Readers may want to read H. Richard Niebuhr's *Christ and Culture* (New York: Harper Torchbooks, 1951), which examines the various stances discussed here and in the paragraphs that follow.

6. Constantine the Great (I) converted to Christianity in 312 C.E. on the eve of a battle. He established toleration of Christianity throughout the empire with the Edict of Milan in 313. In 324 he defeated the Eastern emperor and moved his capital to Constantinople. He had become the emperor in 306 and died in 337.

Chapter 2 Marriage in the Postmodern Culture

1. The Alternatives to Marriage Project (ATMP) was recently initiated in response and reaction to the Rutgers National Family Project. The ATMP web site—unmarried.org/family.html—provides information about the organization and regular updates regarding their activities and publications. ATMP can also be reached through Alternatives to Marriage Project, P.O. Box 991010, Boston, MA 02199. One of the ATMP publications is a list of "famous" people who are in cohabiting relationships. Among others, the list includes Oprah Winfrey and Stedman Graham, engaged since 1992 and still unmarried; Goldie Hawn and Kurt Russell, together since 1984 with no plans for marriage. The list sends an indirect but unmistakably clear message: Look at the numbers of rich and famous, the "cool" people, who no longer find marriage relevant.

2. The eighth annual National Symposium on Family Issues held at the Pennsylvania State University, October 2000, provides an example. The theme of the symposium was "Just Living Together: Implications of Cohabitation for Children, Families, and Social Policy." The conference proceedings reflected broad acceptance of cohabitation. Concern was focused on "making cohabitation work," i.e., providing public policy and social assistance so that cohabiting participants, including children, were given adequate support. The tone and content of the symposium are incorporated in Alan Booth and Ann C. Crouter, *Just Living Together: Implications of Cohabitation for Children, Families, and Social Policy* (Mahwah, NJ: Lawrence Erlbaum Associates, 2002).

The influential Jewish Public Forum in January 2000 hosted the seminar "The Future of Family and Tribe" and included Dorian Solot, executive director of the Alternatives to Marriage Project, as a major participant. Solot's presence as a speaker does not, of course, indicate that the Jewish Forum endorsed without qualification her point of view. Her presence does, however, reflect the degree to which people and organizations of social significance are considering cohabitation as a potentially acceptable alternative to marriage. Materials published under the auspices of the Jewish Public Forum, including Solot's paper, can be secured at http://www.clcl.org/jpf88.html.

3. Ari L. Goldman, religion editor at the *New York Times*, spent a sabbatical year studying at Harvard Divinity School. In his book *The Search for God at Harvard* (New York: Ballantine, 1992), Goldman reports his disillusioned sense that God was not very evident on the prestigious Ivy League campus. In contrast, Kelly Monroe in her book *Finding God at Harvard* (Grand Rapids, MI: Zondervan, 1997) reports the stories of forty-two people—students, faculty, staff—at Harvard, who in that highly skeptical intellectual climate have indeed come to know God in a life-changing relationship. The two books together give an interesting insight into the post-Christian climate that characterizes the present campus and others like it. The anti-Christian climate characterizing private institutions is present as well at public universities. Finding God at the University of California (Berkeley), for example, is not a comparatively easier task than finding God at Harvard.

4. The ATMP position paper "Affirmation of Family Diversity" carries a long list of distinguished signatories, including as a representative example Constance Ahrons, director, Marriage and Family Therapy Program; professor of sociology, University of Southern California; board member of Council on Contemporary Families. The position paper and list of signatories are available at http://unmarried.org/family.html or through Alternatives to Marriage Project, P.O. Box 991010, Boston, MA 02199.

5. Jean Bethke Elshtain, "Families and Civic Goods," in *Marriage and the Common Good* (proceedings from the twenty-second annual convention of the Fellowship of Catholic Scholars, Sept. 24–26, 1999), ed., Kenneth D. Whitehead (South Bend, IN: St. Augustine's Press, 2001), 108–9.

6. Robert Bellah, Richard Madsen, William M. Sullivan, Ann Swidler, and Steven M. Tipton, *Habits of the Heart: Individualism and Commitment in American Life* (Berkeley, CA: University of California Press, 1985).

7. Carl Degler, *At Odds: Women and the Family in America from the Revolution to the Present* (New York: Oxford University Press, 1980).

8. Stanley Grenz, *A Primer on Postmodernism* (Grand Rapids, MI: Eerdmans, l996).

9. Thomas L. Friedman, *The Lexus and the Olive Tree* (New York: Random House, 2000), xvi.

10. Ibid. Friedman is the Pulitzer Prize–winning foreign affairs columnist for the *New York Times*. In *The Lexus and the Olive Tree* he describes the new electronic global economy that is reshaping world affairs. Friedman's analysis of the post–Cold War international economy, its challenges, and its dangers makes clear the irreversible changes that have already occurred.

11. Don McLean, "American Pie" at http//www.mbhs.edu/-bconnell/cty/American-pie.plain-lyrics.

12. The album on which "Bye-Bye, Miss American Pie" was recorded was released in 1971; the song reached number one on the charts in 1972. Today, more than three decades after McLean composed and sang this song, there are still multiple web sites, such as *American Pie Historical Interpretive Digest*, on which "interpretations" of the ambiguous lyrics are debated. See, for example, Brendan's American Pie Archives at http//www.mbhs.edu/~bconnell/american-pie.html contains additional resources and information.

13. Stephanie Coontz, *The Way We Never Were: American Families and the Nostalgia Trap* (New York: Basic Books, 1992).

14. For readers who want a clearer understanding of modernity, see Peter Berger's chapter in *Religion and the Sociology of Knowledge: Modernization and Pluralism in Christian Thought and Structure*, ed., Barbara Hargrove (New York: Edward Mellen Press, 1984), 335–49.

15. Lewis Carroll, *Through the Looking-Glass and What Alice Found There* (New York: Random House, 1946), 94.

16. David E. Daye, "The Influence of Postmodernism on the Family: A Biblical-Sociological Analysis" (master's thesis, Trinity Evangelical Divinity School, May 2002), 9.

17. Stanley J. Grenz, *The Social God and the Relational Self: A Trinitarian Theology of the Imago Dei* (Louisville, KY: Westminster John Knox Press, 2001), 97. Grenz provides a careful analysis of this 1,500–year history with a meticulous documentation of primary sources, 58–97.

18. Lewis Carroll, *Alice's Adventures in Wonderland* (New York: Random House, 1946), 49–50.

19. Grenz, *The Social God and the Relational Self*, 136.

20. See M. Gay Hubbard, *Women: The Misunderstood Majority* (Dallas: Word, 1992; reprint, Eugene, OR: Wipf and Stock, 2003), 104–15.

21. Hara Estroff Marano, "The New Sex Scorecard," *Psychology Today* 36, no. 4 (July-Aug. 2003), 38–49.

22. James Hitchcock, commenting on this message of the culture, notes that sexual expression viewed from this perspective makes any idea of betrayal meaningless. See James Hitchcock, "The Sexual Revolution—A Case Study," Online commentary, Aug. 30, 2002, *Women for Faith and Family* at http//www.wf-f.org/JFH-SexualRevolution.html. For an article opposing the postmodern view without specific reference to a Christian worldview, see Jonathan Keats, "The Other Woman," *Salon*, at http://www.Salon.com/miot/feature/1999/11/17/anti-mistress/print.html.

23. Tom Brokaw, *The Greatest Generation* (New York: Random House, 1998).

24. Grenz, *The Social God and the Relational Self*, 136.

25. Grenz, *A Primer on Postmodernism*, 8.

26. Daye notes that postmodern communities are "more than just the gathering of similar individuals. They are truth creators, reality interpreters, and ironically power structures and authorities in their own right. . . . [But the] authority of the group lasts only as long as a person *chooses* to submit to its authority" ("The Influence of Postmodernism on the Family," 10–11, italics in original).

27. Richard Rorty, "Pragmatism," in *The Consequences of Pragmatism* (Minneapolis: University of Minnesota Press, 1982), 166, quoted in Grenz, *A Primer on Postmodernism*, 157.

28. Stanley J. Grenz, *A Primer on Postmodernism*, 9.

29. Barbara DaFoe Whitehead, "Dan Quayle Was Right," *Atlantic Monthly* (April 1993) at http://www.theatlantic.com/politics/family/danquayl.htm.

30. Ibid., 40.

31. Ibid., 40–41.

32. Hauerwas and Willimon, *Resident Aliens*, 64–65.

33. *Fast Company* 41 (Dec. 2000), 8–9.

34. Grenz, *A Primer on Postmodernism*, 9.

35. Elshtain, "Families and Civic Goods," 115.

36. Rodney Clapp, *Families at the Crossroads* (Downers Grove, IL: InterVarsity Press, 1993), 51.

37. Ibid., 52.

38. Ibid., 57. Clapp's chapter "Advanced Capitalism and the Lost Art of Christian Family" is an excellent analysis of consumerism and the ways in which Christians become complicit in the marketplace approach to life and relationships, 48–66.

39. See Hauerwas and Willimon, *Resident Aliens*, 33, 77–78.

40. Quoted in Clapp, *Families at the Crossroads*, 57.

41. Clapp, in *Families at the Crossroads*, includes a list of thinkers across the philosophical spectrum from left to right who view with concern the ways in which the marketplace mentality is shaping our culture and our lives, 187–88.

42. Ibid., 59.

43. Barbara Dafoe Whitehead and David Popenoe, "Why Men Won't Commit: Exploring Young Men's Attitudes about Sex, Dating, and Marriage," *The State of Our Unions: The Social Health of Marriage in America* (2002), 3, 5–7, online at http://marriage.rutgers.educ/TEXTSOOU2002.htm.

44. Clapp, in *Families at the Crossroads*, notes that Milton Friedman and the Chicago School of Economics has seriously proposed that the marketplace should serve as the moral code defining all our lives, 59, also note on 187–88.

45. Elshtain, "Families and Civic Goods," 115.

46. Joan Williams, *Unbending Gender: Why Family and Work Conflict and What to Do about It* (New York: Oxford University Press, 2000), 112–13. Williams provides a detailed analysis of the ways in which corporate demand for the "ideal worker" distorts all aspects of relationships between men and women. See also Juliet B. Schor, *The Overworked American: The Unexpected Decline of Leisure* (New York: Basic Books, 1992). Schor's study of consumerism documents the "cost" of consumerism to individuals and to families and discusses some alternative strategies being used to deal with the power of the consumer-oriented culture. Also see Juliet B. Schor, *The Overspent American: Upscaling, Downshifting, and the New Consumer* (New York: Basic Books, 1998).

47. Quoted in Elshtain, "Families and Civic Goods," 113.

48. Ibid., 114.

49. Quoted in Clapp, *Families at the Crossroads*, 184–85.

Chapter 3 The Culture's Alternatives to Marriage

1. Barbara Dafoe Whitehead and David Popenoe, "Changes in Teen Attitudes toward Marriage, Cohabitation, and Children, 1975–1995," Next Generation Series, National Marriage Project (Piscataway, NJ: Rutgers University, 1999), online at http://marriage.rutgers.educ/pubteena.htm.

2. Barbara Dafoe Whitehead and David Popenoe, "The State of Our Unions: The Social Health of Marriage in America, 2001," National Marriage Project (Piscataway, NJ: Rutgers University, 2001), online at wysiwyg://8/http://marriage.rutgers.educ/TEXTSOOLU2001.htm.

3. David Popenoe, "Marriage Decline in America" (testimony before the Subcommittee on Human Resources, Committee on Ways and Means, United States House of Representatives, Washington, DC, May 22, 2001), authors' emphasis added.

4. Signatories to the position paper are available on the Alternatives to Marriage web site http://unmarried.org/family.html or through Alternatives to Marriage Project, P. O. Box 991010, Boston, MA 02199. Signatories include individuals in positions of influence. One among many others, for example, is Constance Ahrons, director, Marriage and Family Therapy program and professor of sociology, University of Southern California, and board member of the Council on Contemporary Families.

5. Elizabeth Graham, "We're Moving in Together," *Today's Christian Woman* (Sept.–Oct. 2002); access online at http://www.christianitytoday.com/tcw/2002/005/6.70.html/.

6. Barbara Dafoe Whitehead and David Popenoe, "Sex without Strings, Relationships without Rings: Today's Young Singles Talk about Mating and Dating," essay from *The State of Our Unions, 2000: The Social Health of Marriage in America,* the National Marriage Project, online at http://marriage.Rutgers.educ/Publications/pubsexwostrings.htm.

7. Whitehead and Popenoe, "The State of Our Unions," authors' emphasis added.

8. Larissa Phillips, "The Case against Matrimony," *Mothers Who Think, Salon* at http://salon.com/mwt/feature/1999/11/18/unmarried/print.html.

9. Barbara Dafoe Whitehead and David Popenoe, "Why Men Won't Commit: Exploring Young Men's Attitudes about Sex, Dating, and Marriage" in *The State of Our Unions: The Social Health of Marriage in America, 2002,* online at http://marriage.Rutgers.edu/TEXTSOOU2002.htm.

10. Quoted in Diana R. Garland, *Family Ministry: A Comprehensive Guide* (Downers Grove, IL: InterVarsity Press, 1999), 547–48.

11. Judith S. Wallerstein and Sandra Blakeslee, *Second Chances: Men, Women, and Children a Decade after Divorce* (New York: Ticknor and Fields, 1989). Stephanie Coontz is among critics of Wallerstein's initial research procedures and conclusions, arguing that her reported effects of injury were misleading and oversimplified. But a follow-up study by Wallerstein, correcting some methodological problems, appears to confirm her findings. See Judith Wallerstein, Julia Lewis, and Sandra Blakeslee, *The Unexpected Legacy of Divorce: A Twenty-Five Year Landmark Study* (New York: Hyperion, 2000).

12. Wallerstein and Blakeslee, *Second Chances,* 297–308; see also Wallerstein, Lewis, and Blakeslee, *The Unexpected Legacy of Divorce,* 75.

13. The rate of divorce among couples married twenty years or more rose dramatically during the divorce revolution and continues to rise, although divorce rates overall have tapered off slightly. The impact of parental divorce on adult children is relatively unstudied, perhaps because adult children are commonly presumed to be unaffected by their parents' divorce. Available material indicates, however, that adult children are strongly affected. See Noelle Fintushel and Nancy Hillard, *A Grief Out of Season: When Your Parents Divorce in Your Adult Years* (Boston: Little Brown, 1991). See also Stephanie Staal, *The Love They Lost: Living with the Legacy of Our Parents' Divorce* (New York: Delacorte Press, 2000).

14. Wallerstein and Blakeslee, *Second Chances,* 308.

15. E. Mavis Heatherington and John Kelly, *For Better or for Worse: Divorce Reconsidered* (New York: W. W. Norton, 2002).

16. Phillips, "The Case against Matrimony," 3.

17. These survivors of parental divorce are plagued not only with the fear of repeating their parents' marital failure but also with the task of attempting to build a successful marriage

without a model. Wallerstein et al. noted that they face a predicament comparable to "becoming a dancer without ever having seen a dance" (*The Unexpected Legacy of Divorce*, 75).

18. Larry Bumpass, J. A. Sweet, and A. Cherlin, "The Role of Cohabitation in Declining Rates of Marriage," *Journal of Marriage and the Family* 53 (1991): 913–27.

19. In one section of the Rutgers National Family Project, the author suggested that if women were interested in marriage, they should consider withholding sexual relations until after marriage as an inducement for men to make a legal commitment to the relationship: "If a woman truly wants a man to marry her, wisdom dictates a measure of playing hard to get." The scornful response of the Alternatives to Marriage Project was terse and to the point: "We'd hoped that we have moved beyond this kind of dishonest game-playing" ("What's Wrong with the Work of the National Marriage Project?" at http://www.unmarried.org/10problems.html).

20. Jessie Bernard has written an insightful history of the way the "good provider" role has altered in recent history; see Jessie Bernard, "The Good Provider Role: Its Rise and Fall," *American Psychologist* 36 (January 1981): 1–12.

21. In their expressions of concern about women in marriage, evangelical churches and parachurch organizations are more likely to focus on the alleged theological responsibility of the woman to "submit" than on the man's theological responsibility to demonstrate at least minimal levels of love by controlling his fists. For example, a very large Protestant denomination recently made part of their statement of faith the requirement that a woman submit "graciously" to the loving leadership of her husband. Nothing was said about her options if he chose to enforce his "loving" leadership with his fists. Still less was said about the denomination's provisions to deal with the man if violence occurred. Such disregard of women's safety is not lost on the present generation (men and women) when they consider the option of marriage.

22. See for example the frequently cited study, Jan E. Stets, "Cohabiting and Marital Aggression: The Role of Social Isolation," *Journal of Marriage and the Family* 53 (1991): 669–80. Stets's study was cited in *Focus on the Family* (Aug. 1995), 2–4, and then in turn by John N. Clayton on the web site http://doesgodexist.org/MayJun96DataSupportsWisdomOfBiblical Family. Clayton says, "Males beating female partners are 'at least twice as common among cohabitors as it is among married partners,'" lifting this statistic from Stets's study without reference to Stets's qualification of the finding. Charles Colson, on *Breakpoint* (Washington, DC, March 20, 1995) spoke on "Trial Marriages on Trial: Why They Don't Work," and cited an alleged U.S. Justice Department report that women are sixty-two times more likely to be assaulted by a live-in boyfriend than by a husband; available online at http://multimag.com/mag/nmc/column12.html. These data have entered the street wisdom of evangelical Christian circles without careful examination, simply because of its citation by Colson on *Breakpoint*. On a similar "Christian" web site, physiciansforlife.org/cohabitation.htm, authors in unsigned articles assert flatly, "Those who live together before marriage abuse each other more often and more severely than dating couples or married couples." The authors then cite without discussion or qualification twelve studies reporting increased levels of violence related to cohabitation; the discussion contains no acknowledgment that poverty, mental health, levels of drug usage (including alcohol), or issues of safety also contribute to the statistical incidence of violence in cohabiting relationships, facts of which physicians would presumably be aware. The direct inference was that cohabitation itself was the crucial (and only) precipitating factor. See "Psychological Reasons [to avoid cohabitation]" at members.aol.com/cohabiting/pysch.htm. Such inappropriate use of statistics severely decreases the credibility of Christians' objection to cohabitation.

23. The work of the Rutgers National Marriage Project (NMP) is not immune to the difficulties inherent in the complex factors present in social research regarding cohabitation. For example, in "What's Wrong with the Work of the National Marriage Project?" Dorian

Solot from The Alternatives to Marriage Project (AtMP) quotes the NMP Report, "Should We Live Together? What Young Adults Need to Know about Cohabitation before Marriage," as summarizing (page 12 of the report), "Some research has shown that aggression is at least twice as common among cohabitors as it is among married partners." The research cited is that of Stets, "Cohabiting and Marital Aggression," and Solot of AtMP, then points out succinctly (and accurately), "They've misrepresented this research. The study they cite here, by Jan Stats[sic], actually found that the probable cause for the 'aggression' is the demographic profile of the average cohabitor (young, black, and more likely to have depression and alcohol problems). Although the National Marriage Project would like the reader to believe that the aggression is because they're not married, it's more likely because of these other factors, which are all linked more with poverty than with marital status. Again, correlation is not the same as causation" (Alternatives to Marriage Project, "What's Wrong with the Work of the National Marriage Project?" at www.unmarried.org.10problems.html).

24. For the most part, we have a distorted historical view of women's sexuality and the struggle to control fertility. See Degler, *At Odds*, 210–48.

25. Most people are startled when reminded that it is only approximately thirty years since the Supreme Court ruled that the State of Connecticut could not prevent the sale of contraceptive products to married couples (*Griswold v. State of Connecticut*, 1971).

26. In an interview with Dave Tianen of the *Milwaukee Journal*, quoted by Amy Benfer, *I Do—Kind Of* (*Salon*, at archive.salon.com/mwt/feature/2001/08/15/9-do/index.html), Benfer's analysis of the ambivalent response of some radical feminists to the choices of others to marry shows another face of shifting social values.

27. The music that the general populace makes and listens to gives an insight into the issues with which the culture is dealing, as Peter Fortunale pointed out in "Goin' to the Chapel," an examination of marriage theme songs that made it to the Top 40 hits from the beginning of the rock-'n'-roll era (1955) up to the present, at www.poppolitics.com/articles/printerfriendly/2000-06-19-we.

28. John Hartford, words and music, "Gentle on My Mind," (New York: Ensign Music, 1967), used by permission.

29. John Denver, words and music, "Leavin' on a Jet Plane," (New York: Cherry Lane Music, 1967), used by permission.

30. Stanley J. Grenz, *Sexual Ethics: An Evangelical Perspective* (1990; reprint, Louisville, KY: Westminster John Knox Press, 1997). This is a scholarly but readable exploration of sexual ethics and the essentials of Christian marriage.

31. Ibid., 96.

32. Pepper Schwartz, *Peer Marriage: How Love between Equals Really Works* (New York: Free Press, 1994), 31.

33. Christians, of course, view marriage as an essential cannot-leave-behind basic for God's people. Marriage for Christians becomes, as a consequence, an increasingly countercultural act in the present world.

34. The objection to marriage voiced by those over sixty commonly includes the difficulty marriage poses for the fair negotiation of family trusts, wills, and the distribution of property, and the disruption of relationships with the "first" family. "We do just fine the way it is," a seventy-plus cohabiter reported. "Otherwise Ed [her partner] would think he has to treat Jane [her adult child from a previous marriage] as a daughter, and believe me, that would never work."

35. I. A. Morris, *The Heterosexual Male* (Thousand Oaks, CA: Sage, 1997), 47.

36. Gender roles, such as husband/wife roles, are difficult to study in themselves because one cannot know what happens in a relationship when the husband/wife roles are absent. Such a study would require proof that something that is *not* there be causally linked to something else that is there.

37. The point here is to present as fairly as possible the culture's case against marriage.

38. Arlie Hochschild with Anne Machung, *The Second Shift* (New York: Avon Press, 1989). The current printing includes two appendices (titled Afterword, 1990, and Afterword, 1997) that deal briefly with Hochschild's initial findings in the context of current trends and statistics.

39. The ways in which couples rationalized and explained the compromises and solutions they had worked out varied widely. Hochschild's study of the men who did and did not share housework indicated that more crucial than men's and women's beliefs about the proper *spheres* of labor were couples' beliefs about the right degree of men's and women's *power* (*The Second Shift*, 222).

40. Arlie Russell Hochschild, *The Time Bind: When Work Becomes Home and Home Becomes Work* (New York: Metropolitan Books, Henry Holt, 1997), 197–203.

41. Studies of cohabiting couples are only now beginning to examine ways in which they negotiate household work and child care in light of the competing demands of the work world. It appears probable that these studies will find that while cohabiting couples have avoided state licenses, they have not avoided the problems that challenge couples whose life together encompasses two jobs, the responsibilities of home and housekeeping, and care of children. Life for such couples, married or cohabiting, cannot be made simple.

42. Rates of cohabitation are being pushed upward by members of the over-sixty group who choose not to marry. Reasons frequently include loss of social security and retirement payments. Reliable studies of this group are still quite limited. Keep in mind, however, that cohabitation is not merely a "youth" phenomenon.

43. Obviously, to emphasize marriage as the primary source of the tension and struggle that accompany change in gender roles is an oversimplification. It results in serious distortion of the complex interface between marital roles and the broad currents of social change, including change in the world of work. Joan Williams examines the complexity of role change in the context of work in *Unbending Gender: Why Family and Work Conflict and What to Do about It* (New York: Oxford University Press, 2000).

44. Jessie Bernard, "Women's Mental Health in Times of Transition," in *Women and Mental Health Policy*, ed. L. E. Walker, Sage Yearbooks in Women's Policy Studies 9 (Beverly Hills, CA: Sage, 1984), 191.

45. U.S. Bureau of the Census, *Statistical Abstract of the United States*, 117th ed., cited in Margaret W. Matlin, *The Psychology of Women*, 4th ed. (Fort Worth, TX: Harcourt Brace, 2000), 236–37.

46. Williams, *Unbending Gender*, 48–54.

47. Jerry Jacobs, *Gender Inequality at Work* (Thousand Oaks, CA: Sage, 1995), 172.

48. Matlin, *The Psychology of Women*, 250.

49. Williams, *Unbending Gender*, 50.

Chapter 4 The Myth of the Victorian Ideal

1. The Victorian age was so called because it paralleled the long (sixty-three-year) reign of Queen Victoria over the British empire from 1837 to 1901. She brought morality to the British throne, in contrast to the vices of earlier monarchs. Thus private virtue and public honor became hallmarks of her rule.

2. The ideas of the Doctrine of Separate Spheres are explored in detail in this chapter and in chapter 5.

3. Degler, *At Odds*, 152, 159–60.

4. Ibid., 166. Degler reports that this upsurge was completed by 1920, the year in which there were about 8 divorces for every 1,000 married couples, compared with 4 in 1900 (a jump of 100 percent in two decades). But as recently as 1960 the rate was only 9.2 per 1,000 married couples, or a mere 15 percent rise since 1920. The National Center for Health Statistics

reported the 2001 U.S. divorce rate at 0.40 percent per capita. See www.divorcereform.org/rates.html.

5. "Our Divorce Laws," *Watchman* 61 (February 12, 1880): 52, cited in Betty DeBerg, *Ungodly Women: Gender and the First Wave of American Fundamentalism* (Minneapolis: Fortress, 1990), 68.

6. T. DeWitt Talmage, "Clandestine Marriage," *Christian Herald and Signs of Our Times* 9, no. 5 (Jan. 28, 1886): 52–53, cited in DeBerg, *Ungodly Women*, 59. This periodical had a circulation of 250,000 by 1910; Talmage edited it until the early 1920s.

7. John Milton Williams, "Woman Suffrage," *Bibliotheca Sacra* 50 (April 1893): 343, cited in DeBerg, *Ungodly Women*, 46.

8. Louisa Mae Alcott (1832–1888) worked as a seamstress, servant, teacher, nurse, and writer, living mainly in Concord, Massachusetts; quoted in Ann Douglas, *The Feminization of American Culture* (New York: Avon Books, 1977), 406–7.

9. Throughout the nineteenth century most colleges and universities refused to admit women. To make an equal university education available to women, some women first sought university training in Europe, then returned to the United States to begin colleges specifically for women. In the mid–nineteenth century Oberlin College in Ohio opened its doors to a limited number of women, and by 1870 some state universities and private colleges allowed a small quota of women to matriculate. But not until the formation of the women's colleges (Mount Holyoke in 1837, Vassar in the 1860s, Smith and Wellesley in the 1870s, Radcliffe in the 1890s) did a college education become widely available to women.

10. Sara Evans, *Born for Liberty: A History of Women in America* (New York: Free Press, 1989), 147.

11. "Athletics for Girls," *Western Recorder* 86, no. 5 (Dec. 8, 1910): 8, quoted in DeBerg, *Ungodly Women*, 55.

12. "Wanted—More Mothers," *King's Business* 12, no. 2 (Feb. 1921): 107–8, quoted in DeBerg, *Ungodly Women*, 43.

13. Laurel Thatcher Ulrich, *Good Wives: Image and Reality in the Lives of Women in Northern New England 1650–1750* (1980; reprint, New York: Random House Vintage Books, 1991), chapter 2, "Deputy Husbands," 35–50.

14. See Sara Evans, *Born for Liberty*, 27–34. Women's everyday work in the early colonies consisted of building and maintaining the fire, processing and preparing food, milking cows, making cheese and butter, gathering eggs, feeding chickens, brewing cider and beer, slaughtering animals, rendering tallow to make candles, smoking bacon, and managing the vegetable garden. A woman might also spin thread and weave cloth for clothes and quilts for the family, and she might sell or barter surplus eggs or butter in the village.

15. At a death, the full household inventory, down to the last spoon, was listed and filed at the county courthouse, giving historians a clear idea of what people had in their homes.

16. Evans, *Born for Liberty*, 35.

17. It began among the Presbyterians in Pennsylvania and New Jersey in the 1730s and later spread to New England among the Congregationalists (Puritans) and Baptists. There it started with a revival in Jonathan Edwards's Northampton church in 1735, then spread with a preaching tour by the English Presbyterian George Whitefield in 1740.

18. Evans, *Born for Liberty*, 56–57.

19. Ibid., 49.

20. Women attacked merchants (especially those with loyalist leanings) whom they suspected of hoarding. When they met resistance, they seized the goods, sometimes leaving the amount of money they felt was proper. Abigail Adams describes an incident in 1778: "A Number of Females, some say a hundred, some say more assembled with carts and trucks, marched down to the 'Ware House' belonging to one eminent, wealthy, stingy Merchant."

The women wanted the coffee they believed he was hoarding, and when he withheld the keys, "one of them seized him by his Neck and tossed him into the cart." Once in possession of the keys, they "opened the Warehouse, Hoisted out the Coffee themselves, put it in [hand]trucks and drove off. . . . A large concourse of Men stood amazed silent Spectators." The Revolutionary War offered women increased opportunities to act politically and aggressively from within their role as housewives. Cited in Evans, *Born for Liberty*, 54.

21. Ibid. Lucy Flucker Knox wrote to her husband in 1777 that after the war she wanted to continue to exercise her own judgment and participate in their affairs. "I hope you will not consider yourself as commander in chief of your own house—but be concerned . . . that there is such a thing as equal command" (Mary Beth Norton, *Liberty's Daughters: The Revolutionary Experience of American Women, 1750–1800* [Boston: Little, Brown, 1980], 212–24, cited in Evans, *Born for Liberty.*)

22. In 1776 Abigail Adams wrote her husband, John, that the new laws being made should curb the "unlimited power" of husbands over wives. She threatened that "if particular care and attention is not paid to the ladies, we are determined to foment a rebellion and will not hold ourselves bound by any laws in which we have no voice or representation," cited in Evans, *Born for Liberty*, 56.

23. See Evans, *Born for Liberty*, 57, for an additional discussion of this.

24. The earliest schools for girls in the 1780s and 1790s were founded by men to teach girls to read, write, cipher, and learn the domestic and social graces, such as needlepoint and singing. In the early nineteenth century, Catherine Beecher, Mary Lyon, and others organized schools for girls that had more serious aims and curricula.

25. Evans, *Born for Liberty*, 72.

26. Ibid., 65.

27. The earliest practical steam machine was that of Thomas Savery, 1698, improved on by Thomas Newcomen in 1705, and given true industrial use by James Watt in 1769. *Encyclopedia Britannica* 21, 352–53.

28. At the same time that women flocked to jobs in the factories, Evans reports that "home-produced textiles grew dramatically even as the factory system made its beginning. In 1809 women at home produced 230,000 yards against only 65,000 yards produced in factories" (Evans, *Born for Liberty,* 60).

29. The early mills and factories were generally stiflingly hot in summer, glacial in winter, crowded with people and machines, with fetid air filled with lint or particles that led to lung diseases. Sanitation was minimal, and the work often caused illness and early death.

30. Evans, *Born for Liberty*, 68.

31. For a full discussion of this, see Degler, *At Odds*, chapter 12, 26–51. Today most Americans assume that the personal happiness and affection between husband and wife provide the best foundation for marriage. But that was new in 1800. Previously, permitting a marriage on the basis of personal or individual preference or whim rather than on the basis of family needs and prospects threatened a family's holdings and its long-term future. By 1800 parents came to consider personal, individual happiness the goal of marriage.

The idea of love was not new to the nineteenth century, of course. Puritan preachers had put a new emphasis on affection within marriage. But the Puritan idea was not that love should be the origin of marriage, rather that time would bring love into the relationship. By the end of the eighteenth century, the notion of a marriage of companions emerged. This new expectation of affection actually introduced a new element of discontent into marriage.

32. For a fuller discussion of this, see Degler, *At Odds*, chapter 3, 52–65.

33. Evans, *Born for Liberty*, 68.

34. Before the nineteenth century, children were considered little adults. Often they were apprenticed out as early as age six to other families to learn a skill or trade. Modern readers may be shocked by comments recorded by colonial parents about their children, showing a

lack of affection and concern for them. The nineteenth century changed that perception, and adults began to realize that children are not merely little adults and they deserve not only physical care but solicitude and love as well. Some historians call the nineteenth century "the century of the child" because of this shift in thinking about children. For a fuller discussion of this, see Degler, *At Odds*, chapters 4 and 5, 66–110.

35. For a fuller discussion of this, see Degler, *At Odds*, chapters 8, 9, and 10, 178–248.

36. Mary Wollstonecraft, *A Vindication of the Rights of Women*, chapter 4, "Observations on the State of Degradation to Which Woman Is Reduced by Various Causes" at www.bartleby.com/144/4.html.

37. An extended discussion of this can be found in Barbara Berg, *The Remembered Gate* (Oxford: Oxford University Press, 1978), chapters 4 and 5. One might argue that because the middle class at no time comprised more than 10 percent of the U.S. population in the nineteenth century, the middle-class family model of separate spheres would be irrelevant to the vast majority of families in America. However, it was touted from pulpit and press and became the ideal to which the working classes aspired.

38. For a full discussion of the Cult of True Womanhood, see Barbara Welter, *Dimity Convictions: The American Woman in the Nineteenth Century* (Athens, OH: Ohio University Press, 1976).

39. Historian Barbara Berg noted, "woman's impact supposedly flowed from the instruction she gave her children," citing Rev. Winslow who asserted that "upon woman depends the destiny of the nation! For she is rearing up senators and statesmen." Though secluded, dependent, and emotional, a woman received the persistent guarantee that she played an important role in society by remaining within the confines of her dwelling (*The Remembered Gate*, 78). Henrik Ibsen's *A Doll's House* (1879) captured the social expectations for Norwegian middle-class women in the late nineteenth century, parallel to American women's experience.

40. Welter, *Dimity Convictions*, 34.

41. Quoted in Welter, *Dimity Convictions*, 37–38.

42. Ibid., 41.

43. Benjamin Wadsworth, *The Well-Ordered Family* (Boston, 1712), cited in Barbara Epstein, *The Politics of Domesticity: Women, Evangelism, and Temperance in Nineteenth Century America* (Middletown, CT: Wesleyan University Press, 1981), 30.

44. From the Colonial Society of Massachusetts *Publications*, XXVII, 370; quoted in Edmund Morgan, *The Puritan Family: Religion and Domestic Relations in Seventeenth Century New England* (1944; reprint, New York: Harper Touchstone, 1966), 54.

45. Epstein, *The Politics of Domesticity*, 31.

46. Morgan, *The Puritan Family*, 31.

47. *Western Recorder*, January 1886, quoted in DeBerg, *Ungodly Women*, 44.

48. Quoted in DeBerg, *Ungodly Women*, 44–45.

49. Ann Douglas, *The Feminization of American Culture* (New York: Avon Books, 1977), 12.

50. Ibid., 6.

Chapter 5 Accommodation to the Culture

1. Broverman constructed a list of 122 personality variables, then gave that list to three separate groups of mental health professionals. She asked the first group to choose those words that characterized a mature healthy adult male, the second group to choose those words that characterized a mature healthy adult female, and the third group to choose those words that characterized a mature healthy adult, sex unspecified. The result was that the lists from the first and third groups were very similar, but the list from the second group was their polar opposite. A woman could not be both a mature healthy adult and a mature

healthy woman at the same time, if the choices made by the participating mental health professionals were accurate.

2. This partial list is taken from Virginia Sapiro, *Women in American Society* (Palo Alto, CA: Mayfield Publishing, 1986), 260.

3. DeBerg, *Ungodly Women*, 14–17.

4. While authors may vary in the details, much of the recent literature of the various men's movements at the beginning of the twenty-first century identifies these same issues as crucial to a sense of masculinity. See, for example, Leon Podles, *The Church Impotent: The Feminization of Christianity* (Dallas: Spence, 1999), and Robert Bly, *Iron John* (New York: Perseus, 1990). A helpful discussion of various approaches to masculinity can be found in Kenneth Clatterbaugh, *Contemporary Perspectives on Masculinity: Men, Women and Politics in Modern Society* (Boulder, CO: Westview Press, 1997).

5. Berg, *The Remembered Gate*, 73.

6. Charles Butler, *The American Lady* (Philadelphia: Hoagan and Thompson, 1836), 27, quoted in Berg, *The Remembered Gate*, 76.

7. From *The Princess*, part V, by Tennyson.

8. M. M'Gee, "Woman's Place in the Kingdom," *Western Recorder* 80, no. 32 (July 6, 1905): 12, quoted in DeBerg, *Ungodly Women*, 44.

9. Welter, *Dimity Convictions*, 21.

10. This concept is rooted in the Reformed Calvinist thought of the Puritans who saw companionship, mutuality, and a certain equality of the sexes as signs of God's grace. Theologian Max Stackhouse put it this way: "The Puritans universalized the covenant view of sex and the family by making it a part of the very foundation of creation. . . . After the Fall, according to the Puritans, chaos tended to break into the covenantal relationship. . . . The fact that paternalistic authority is required to prevent chaos, in the Puritan view, did not compromise the deeper principle of coarchy and coequality in theory. It did compromise it in practice" (Max Stackhouse, *Creeds, Society and Human Rights: A Study in Three Cultures* [Grand Rapids, MI: Eerdmans, 1984], 95–100).

11. Glenna Matthews, *"Just a Housewife": The Rise and Fall of Domesticity in America* (New York: Oxford University Press, 1987), 3.

12. Evans, *Born for Liberty*, 22.

13. Stephanie Coontz, *The Social Origins of Private Life: A History of American Families 1600–1900* (London: Verso, 1988), 93–94.

14. Epstein, *The Politics of Domesticity*, 63.

15. Berg, *The Remembered Gate*, 112.

16. DeBerg, *Ungodly Women*, 18.

17. Epstein, *The Politics of Domesticity*, 62.

18. DeBerg, *Ungodly Women*, 18.

19. For statistics on women in the workforce at the end of the nineteenth century and into the twentieth century, see Degler, *At Odds*, chapter 15, "Women's Work: The First Transformation," 362–94; also Evans, *Born for Liberty*, 156–60.

20. Barbara J. MacHaffie, *Her Story: Women in Christian Tradition* (Philadelphia, PA: Fortress, 1986), 36–37.

21. William Acton, *The Functions and Disorders of the Reproductive Organs in Youth, in Adult Age, and in Advanced Life: Considered in the Social and Psychological Relations* (Philadelphia, 1865), 133, quoted in Berg, *The Remembered Gate*, 84.

22. Wives were trained to comply with their husbands' sexual wishes, but they were also trained to think of themselves as passionless. At the same time, the number of available prostitutes soared in the nineteenth century.

23. Degler, *At Odds*, 280.

24. Quoted in Ruth Tucker and Walter Liefeld, *Daughters of the Church: Women and Ministry from New Testament Times to the Present* (Grand Rapids, MI: Zondervan, 1987), 103.

25. Ibid., 164.

26. Ibid., 177.

27. Evans, *Born for Liberty*, 40.

28. Ann Douglas notes that in 1775, prior to the American Revolution, nine of the thirteen colonies had "established" churches/denominations in which citizens were required to attend and maintain the state-supported church. See Ann Douglas, *The Feminization of American Culture* (New York: Alfred Knopf, Avon Books, 1978), 24.

29. Ibid., 23–24.

30. For a fuller discussion of this, see DeBerg, *Ungodly Women*, 21–22.

31. Peter N. Stearns, *Be a Man! Males in Modern Society* (New York: Holmes and Meier, 1979), 51; cited in DeBerg, *Ungodly Women*, 22.

32. DeBerg, *Ungodly Women*, 23. In this paragraph DeBerg quotes Julie A. Mattaei, *An Economic History of Women in America: Women's Work, the Sexual Division of Labor, and the Development of Capitalism* (New York: Schocken Books, 1982), 103–6.

33. Welter, *Dimity Convictions*, 85.

34. Albert G. Lawson, "Why Are There Not More Men in Our Churches?" *Watchman* 73, no. 38 (Sept, 22, 1892): 1, quoted in DeBerg, *Ungodly Women*, 75.

35. Leonard Sweet, *The Minister's Wife*, 232–35, quoted in DeBerg, *Ungodly Women*, 86.

36. "Iron in Her Blood," *Herald and Presbyter* 83, no. 27 (July 3, 1912): 2, quoted in DeBerg, *Ungodly Women*, 87.

37. Matthews, "Virility in the Ministry," *Western Recorder* 94, no. 38 (June 26, 1919): 2, quoted in De Berg, *Ungodly Women*, 87–88.

38. Quoted in DeBerg, *Ungodly Women*, 88–89.

39. Douglas W. Frank, *Less than Conquerors: How Evangelicals Entered the Twentieth Century* (Grand Rapids, MI: Eerdmans, 1986), 215.

40. For a helpful discussion of this, see Carroll Smith-Rosenberg, *Disorderly Conduct: Visions of Gender in Victorian America* (New York: Oxford University Press, 1985), 245–96.

41. Vida Scudder, who entered Smith College in 1880, reflected in the 1930s on women's education: "I must regard the success of colleges for women as one of the few triumphs of idealism. . . . I do not know for what reason this throng of educated women has been released into the larger life, just in the period when an old order of civilization is passing away, and the new order emerges in confusion. . . . But I recognize that in general they mean for civilization the introduction of a new element; and for women, a change not only of social opportunity but of psychological make-up, resulting from a transformation of status, actual and prospective, which is no less than epoch-making" (*On Journey*, 63–64, quoted in Smith-Rosenberg, *Disorderly Conduct*, note 5, 343).

42. Welter, *Dimity Convictions*, 41.

43. See discussion in DeBerg, *Ungodly Women*, chapter 5, "Fundamentalists and the Flapper," 99–117.

44. Evans, *Born for Liberty*, 175.

45. World War I, like the 1960s era of the Vietnam conflict, was a period of profound social upheaval. Many conservative Christians had already embraced a premillennial eschatology that had the side effect of creating an indifference to work for world betterment. But as World War I began, liberal theologians accused the conservatives of being unpatriotic because they did not actively support the war effort in print and from the pulpit. Conservative theologians rethought their stance on political involvement and concluded that had they attacked corrupt German theology fifty years earlier, the world war could have been avoided. They emerged with a paradoxical position: The world could not be saved, but Christians were the world's only cultural hope to slow the slide into perdition. As the war ended, they determined to save

American society. See George Marsden, *Fundamentalism and American Culture: The Shaping of Twentieth-Century Evangelicalism, 1870–1925* (New York: Oxford University Press, 1980), 152.

46. John R. Rice, *Bobbed Hair, Bossy Wives, and Women Preachers: Significant Questions for Honest Christian Women* (Wheaton, IL: Sword of the Lord, 1941), 67–68.

47. Charles C. Ryrie, *The Place of Women in the Church* (New York: Macmillan, 1958), 67–68.

48. James B. Hurley, *Man and Woman in Biblical Perspective* (Grand Rapids, MI: Zondervan, 1981), 148.

49. Evans, *Born for Liberty*, 304.

50. John Piper and Wayne Grudem, eds., *Recovering Biblical Manhood and Womanhood: A Response to Evangelical Feminism* (Wheaton, IL: Crossway, 1991), 35–36.

51. Ibid., 46.

52. A helpful discussion of six men's movements in the United States is found in Clatterbaugh, *Contemporary Perspectives on Masculinity: Men, Women and Politics in Modern Society* (Boulder, CO: Westview, 1990).

53. The seven promises are as follows:

1. To honor Jesus Christ through worship, prayer, and obedience to God's Word
2. To form and participate in an accountability group with other men
3. To practice spiritual, moral, ethical, and sexual purity
4. To build strong marriages through love, protection, and biblical values
5. To support the mission of the church
6. To reach beyond any racial and denominational barriers to demonstrate the power of biblical unity
7. To be obedient to the Great Commandment and to the Great Commission

54. Ed Cole, *Maximized Manhood* (Springdale, PA: Whitaker House, 1982), 147, quoted in John P. Bartkowski, *Remaking the Godly Marriage: Gender Negotiation in Evangelical Families* (New Brunswick, NJ: Rutgers University Press, 2001), 42.

55. Cole, *Maximized Manhood*, 63.

56. Podles, *The Church Impotent*, 164.

57. Ibid., 169.

58. Ibid., 196.

59. Lois Barrett, "Missional Witness: The Church as Apostle to the World," in Darrell L. Guder, ed., *Missional Church: A Vision for the Sending of the Church in North America* (Grand Rapids, MI: Eerdmans, 1998), 112.

Chapter 6 New Wineskins for New Wine

1. The term *hierarchy* is being used here rather than *complementarity* because it more clearly describes any relationship that is not equal in every way.

2. An excellent exposition of the benefits to women of such self-surrender can be found in Piper and Grudem, eds., *Recovering Biblical Manhood and Womanhood*, 45–52.

3. Judith A. Miles, *The Feminine Principle: A Woman's Key to Total Fulfillment* (Minneapolis, MN: Bethany Fellowship, 1975), 42.

4. Piper and Grudem, eds., *Recovering Biblical Manhood and Womanhood*, 196.

5. This teaching is normative in the majority of conservative Christian churches in North America.

6. Gene Getz, *The Christian Home in a Changing World* (Chicago: Moody, 1972), 28.

7. Jerry Falwell, ed., *The Fundamentalist Phenomenon* (Garden City, NY: Doubleday Galilee Original, 1981), 111.

8. Piper and Grudem, eds., *Recovering Biblical Manhood and Womanhood*, 53.

9. Larry Christenson, *The Christian Family* (Minneapolis, MN: Bethany Fellowship, 1970), 32–33, 37.

10. Piper and Grudem, eds., *Recovering Biblical Manhood and Womanhood,* 35–54.

11. Ibid., 52–53.

12. Helen Hardacre, "The Impact of Fundamentalisms on Women, the Family, and Interpersonal Relations," chapter 6 in *Fundamentalisms and Society: Reclaiming the Sciences, Family, and Education,* eds., Martin Marty and R. Scott Appleby (Chicago: University of Chicago Press, 1991), 141–43.

13. Ralph Turner, "The Real Self: From Institution to Impulse," *American Journal of Sociology* 81 (1976): 1005.

14. Stackhouse, *Creeds, Society, and Human Rights,* 2.

15. Samuel P. Huntington, *American Politics: The Promise of Disharmony* (Cambridge, MA: Harvard University Press, 1981), chapter 4, "Coping with the Gap," 61–84.

16. The authors have known women who, because of their moral passion to experience the promise embedded in teachings on hierarchical marriage, have in the end abandoned their marriages and have also abandoned the institutional church when they concluded that the authorities who taught them the creed of marital hierarchy cannot be trusted. For an extended exploration of the phenomenon of women who become "subjective knowers" and abandon their past lives, see Mary Belenky, et al., *Women's Ways of Knowing* (New York: Basic Books, 1986), chapters 3 and 4.

17. Duane Litfin, "Evangelical Feminism: Why Traditionalists Reject It," *Bibliotheca Sacra* 136 (July–Sept. 1979).

18. Readers interested in pursuing this idea may wish to read DeBerg, *Ungodly Women,* and Welter, *Dimity Convictions.*

19. Rice, *Bobbed Hair, Bossy Wives and Women Preachers,* 36.

20. Piper and Grudem, eds., *Recovering Biblical Manhood and Womanhood,* 471. The Danvers Statement is the 1987 document setting forth the rationale, purposes, and affirmations of the Council on Biblical Manhood and Womanhood; this document appears in the Piper and Grudem book, pp. 469–72.

21. For a full discussion of this, see Rodney Stark and William Sims Bainbridge, "Networks of Faith: Interpersonal Bonds and Recruitment to Cults and Sects," *American Journal of Sociology* 85 (1980); also by the same authors, *The Future of Religion: Secularization, Revival and Cult Formation* (Berkeley, CA: University of California Press, 1985).

22. Max Weber, *The Sociology of Religion,* trans., Ephraim Fischoff (1922; reprint, Boston: Beacon Press, 1963), 9.

23. Piper and Grudem, eds., *Recovering Biblical Manhood and Womanhood,* 52.

24. This research was carried out in 1994–95 as part of dissertation research. See Alice Palmer Mathews, "Prescription and Description: The Gap between the Promise and the Reality in Women's Experience of Hierarchical Marriage," (Ph.D. diss., Iliff School of Theology and University of Denver, 1996). A complete list of the twenty-four questions asked in this study can be found in appendix A.

25. The imposed voluntary nature of the sampling procedure in this study may have skewed the data because more than one-third (35 percent) of the women were in the 20–39 age bracket, and 56 percent of the women identified themselves as full-time homemakers. Age correlated with beliefs, showing that older women are significantly more egalitarian than are younger women (p<.05). This inverse relationship of age and hierarchical beliefs about roles in marriage may reflect a differential experience of marriage. Older women may have had life experiences that make them less willing to espouse hierarchical beliefs about role relationships in marriage. Or younger women may be more eager to live up to the ideal and so embrace it more willingly. Regarding the full-time homemakers, with 70 percent of all women between ages sixteen and fifty-five in the work force, the percentage of full-time

homemakers in this study does not follow national averages. The men in the study, on the whole, were significantly more egalitarian than the women.

26. Curiously, for men in the study, age at the time of Christian conversion correlated with the conformity of their experience of sex in marriage to their beliefs (p<.005). Men converted before age twenty were much more satisfied with their experience of sex in marriage, whereas none of the men converted after age twenty described their experience of sex in marriage in strongly positive terms. It is possible that the earlier conversions meant earlier exposure to church teachings on sexuality and thus lessened the gap between beliefs and personal experience for them. No such conversion/age difference showed up among the women in the study.

27. For both men and women (p<.05), education correlated with the enjoyment of sex in marriage. Those with college or postgraduate degrees were more likely to rate their marital sex lives as highly satisfying; in this study 57 percent of the men and women participants held college degrees.

28. The result was a composite list of eighty-five characteristics that were then sorted into an ordinal scale of seven general categories ranging from nonrelational on one end of the continuum to highly relational "ingredients of a happy marriage." The scale thus moved from minimal relationality between spouses to high relationality.

29. Peter Berger, *The Sacred Canopy: Elements of a Sociological Theory of Religion* (1967; reprint, Garden City, NY: Anchor Books, 1969), 58.

30. Degler, *At Odds,* vi–vii.

31. Mary Stewart Van Leeuwen, *Gender and Grace* (Downers Grove IL: InterVarsity Press, 1990), 170, 244.

32. Richard Langley and Robert Levy, *Wife Beating: The Silent Crisis* (Boston: Beacon Press, 1983), 105; quoted in James Alsdurf and Phyllis Alsdurf, *Battered Into Submission: The Tragedy of Wife Abuse in the Christian Home* (Downers Grove, IL: InterVarsity Press, 1989), 80.

33. Holly Wagner Green, *Turning Fear to Hope: Help for Marriages Troubled by Abuse* (Nashville: Thomas Nelson, 1984), 184, 44.

34. See, for example, Annette Mahoney, Kenneth Pargament, Nalini Tarakeshwar, Aaron Swank, "Religion in the Home in the 1980s and 1990s: A Meta-Analytic Review and Conceptual Analysis of Links Between Religion, Marriage, and Parenting," *Journal of Family Psychology* 15, no. 4 (December 2001): 559–96; Christopher Ellison, John Bartkowski, Kristin Anderson, "Are There Religious Variations in Domestic Violence?" *Journal of Family Issues* 20, no. 1 (January 1999): 87–113.

35. Julia Babcock, Jennifer Waltz, Neil S. Jacobson, and John M. Gottman, "Power and Violence: The Relation Between Communication Patterns, Power Discrepancies, and Domestic Violence," *Journal of Consulting and Clinical Psychology* 61, no. 1 (1993): 41.

36. Kirsti Yllo and Michele Bograd, eds., *Feminist Perspectives on Wife Abuse* (Newbury Park, CA: Sage, 1984), 316–17; see also Richard Gelles and Murray Straus, *Intimate Violence: The Causes and Consequences of Abuse in the American Family* (New York: Simon and Schuster, 1988), 92.

37. See John MacArthur, *The Family* (Chicago: Moody Press, 1982); see also Paul Meier, Frank Minirth, and Frank Wichern, *Introduction to Psychology and Counseling* (Grand Rapids: Baker, 1982).

38. MacArthur, *The Family,* 31. MacArthur reasons that a woman is constantly after a man's God-given power because she is fallen and does not understand that "God designed men to be stronger." He sees marriage as "potential warfare" and begins a chapter in his book *The Family* by quoting the English Field Marshall Montgomery: "Gentlemen, don't even think about marriage until you have mastered the art of warfare," 52.

39. Donald Dutton, *The Domestic Assault of Women* (Boston: Allyn and Beacon, 1988), 68.

40. Piper and Grudem, eds., *Recovering Biblical Manhood and Womanhood,* 470.

41. William Stacey and Anson Shupe, *The Family Secret* (Boston: Beacon Press, 1983), 105.

42. Alsdurf and Alsdurf, *Battered Into Submission*, 106.

43. John Stone and Stephen Mennell, eds., *Alexis de Tocqueville: On Democracy, Revolution and Society* (Chicago: University of Chicago Press, 1980), 328–30.

44. Paul Ramsey, *Ethics on the Edge of Life* (New Haven, CT: Yale University Press, 1978), 9.

45. Stanley Hauerwas, *A Community of Character: Toward a Constructive Christian Social Ethic* (Notre Dame, IN: University of Notre Dame, 1981), 160.

46. Ibid., 172.

47. Quoted in Hauerwas, *A Community of Character*, 169.

Chapter 7 Preparing to Hear God's Case for Marriage

1. Polygamy may have been practiced in other households, but the story of Lamech (Gen. 4:19) contains the first specific mention of polygamy in the Bible. There was no written scriptural injunction forbidding polygamy at the time of Lamech's story. The practice embodies, however, the rapid drift away from the one-man, one-woman ideal of the Genesis creation story.

2. The prophet Habakkuk stated, "Woe to him who gives drink to his neighbor, pressing him to your bottle, even to make him drunk, that you may look on his nakedness!" (2:15).

3. In 1 Corinthians 9:5 Paul notes that, after Jesus' ascension to God, Peter took his wife with him as he traveled sharing the gospel. It appears that a strong bond existed between them.

4. Douglas J. Brouwer, *Beyond "I Do": What Christians Believe about Marriage* (Grand Rapids, MI: Eerdmans, 2001), 11–12, italics in original.

5. David Instone-Brewer, *Divorce and Remarriage in the Bible: The Social and Literary Context* (Grand Rapids, MI: Eerdmans, 2002), describes in careful detail the requirements of Old Testament marriage, which included emotional support; emotional neglect was considered grounds for divorce (see 106–10). Romance, however, makes no appearance.

6. Max L. Stackhouse, *Covenant and Commitments: Faith, Family, and Economic Life*, eds. Don S. Browning and Ian S. Evison, The Family, Religion, and Culture Series, (Louisville, KY: Westminster John Knox Press, 1997), 140–42, 146–47; see also Tikva Frymer-Kensky, "The Family in the Hebrew Bible" in *Religion, Feminism, and the Family*, eds. Anne Carr and Mary Stewart Van Leeuwen, The Family, Religion, and Culture Series (Louisville, KY: Westminster John Knox Press, 1996), 55–73; and Allan Kensky, "The Family in Rabbinic Judaism," in *Religion, Feminism, and the Family*, 74–94.

7. Grenz, *Sexual Ethics*, 58, 61–65.

8. Lesslie Newbigin, *The Gospel in a Pluralist Society* (Grand Rapids, MI: Eerdmans, 1989).

9. Marvin Olasky, *Standing for Christ in a Modern Babylon* (Wheaton, IL: Crossway, 2003). Jeremiah instructed God's people in exile in ancient Babylon to settle down, raise gardens and grandchildren, and seek the prosperity of the city in which they were forced to live in exile. They were to live faithfully as God's distinctive people with the hopeful assurance that God would bring them home again to Jerusalem in his time (Jer. 29:4–14).

Chapter 8 Marriage on God's Terms

1. Jurgen Moltmann wrote, "[*Perichoresis*] denotes the Trinitarian unity which goes out beyond the doctrine of persons and their relations: by virtue of their eternal love, the divine persons exist so intimately with one another, for one another and in one another that they constitute themselves in their unique incomparable and complete unity," quoted in Grenz, *The Social God and the Relational Self*, 44.

2. Nancy Tischler comments wryly that the phrase "created in God's image" is "rich in meaning though stingy with specific detail" (*Legacy of Eve*, [Louisville, KY: Westminster John Knox, 1977],12). This may explain why theologians give a wide variety of definitions for the image of God in humanity—the *imago dei*. Older theologians usually listed the attributes of God that are seen in humanity—attributes like spirituality, personality, holiness, love, and dominion. Others list the power of rational thought, an aesthetic structure within, so that we appreciate beauty, the ability to have moral experiences and choice, and a sense of the transcendent. Mary Stewart Van Leeuwen argues that, in addition to these, we are inescapably social, mirroring our intrinsically social three-in-one God, and we have been given accountable dominion (*Gender and Grace: Love, Work, and Parenting in a Changing World* [Downers Grove, IL: InterVarsity Press, 1990], 38–42).

3. Anne Atkins, *Split Image: Male and Female after God's Image* (Grand Rapids, MI: Eerdmans, 1987), 24–70.

4. Ibid., 29.

5. Gilbert Bilezikian, *Beyond Sex Roles: A Guide for the Study of Female Roles in the Bible* (Grand Rapids, MI: Baker, 1985), 217, note 9.

6. The apostle Paul reinforces this in 1 Corinthians 11:11–12: "Nevertheless, in the Lord woman is not independent of man, nor is man independent of woman. For as woman came from man, so also man is born of woman. But everything comes from God."

7. Walter Trobisch, *I Married You*, in *The Complete Works of Walter Trobisch* (Downers Grove, IL: InterVarsity Press, 1987), 377. See chapter 2 for an extended discussion of Genesis 2:24, from which several ideas in this chapter are drawn.

8. The term *sexual* here certainly includes more than coitus. It is "making love" in the widest terms, including the respect and affection for one another that makes satisfying sex possible for both husband and wife.

9. Joy Elasky Fleming, *Book 1: Think Again about Eve: God's Words to the Woman in the Garden of Eden* at www.ThinkAgain.tv; see also Joy Elasky Fleming, *Book 2: Think Again about Adam: God's Words to the Man in the Garden of Eden* at www.ThinkAgain.tv. Available also as printed copies through Christians for Biblical Equality, 122 W. Franklin Ave., Ste. 218, Minneapolis, MN 55404-2451.

10. Note that, contrary to popular opinion, God did not curse Adam and Eve. He merely stated the consequences of their deed, not as punishment but as the natural outworking of their fallenness. A curse cannot be overturned, but it is legitimate to mitigate the effects of sin in the world.

11. Genesis 3:15 is called the *protoevangelium*, the first promise of the Savior to come.

12. God's word to both the man and the woman in Genesis 3 was that each would now be subject to his or her source. The man had been created from "dust," so God said, "dust you are and to dust you will return" (Gen. 3:19). Meanwhile, he would till the soil by the sweat of his brow, subject to that dust, that soil every day of his life. His source would rule him. To the woman who had been created from the man's side, God said, "Your desire will be for your husband, and he will rule over you" (v. 16). Her source would rule her.

13. The authors are indebted for the ideas in this section to Francis A. Schaeffer, *Genesis in Space and Time* (Downers Grove, IL: InterVarsity Press, 1972), chapter 4, "The Point of Decision."

14. Ibid., 71.

15. Schaeffer acknowledges that "It is perfectly true that in making man as he did God made the possibility of evil. But the bare possibility of evil is not the actualizing of it. And in making that possibility, God validated choice and validated man as man. . . . If he had left him without choice, you could speak forever of man being man, man being significant, but it would be only meaningless words," (*Genesis in Space and Time*, 72).

16. See Van Leeuwen, *Gender and Grace,* chapter 2, "Male and Female in the Biblical Drama," 33–51.

17. We know this from Jesus himself in his conversation with the Pharisees in Matthew 19:1–11.

18. Brouwer, *Beyond "I Do,"* 11–12.

Chapter 9 Marriage in the Already-But-Not-Yet

1. *Patriarchy* simply means that the father rules the clan; in a *matriarchy* the mother would have the final word in any matter. Some scholars think that the early Hebrew family was matriarchal because mothers named their children (see, for example, Genesis 29: 31–30:24, which says that Leah and Rachel named their children). But as we move through Old Testament history, this practice slowly declined, and increasingly fathers named their children.

Polygamy (more correctly, polygyny) is the marriage of one man to more than one wife at the same time. God's law explicitly forbade kings from taking many wives (Deut. 17:15–17), but much of the history of the Jews through the centuries records the disregard for this law. David over time had at least seven wives, and his son Solomon is reported to have had seven hundred wives and three hundred concubines (1 Kings 11:3), who turned his heart away from God to worship false gods.

2. Talmudic law set twelve as the legal age for marriage for girls and thirteen for boys. A father might betroth his daughter before puberty, but at the age of twelve she could refuse to go through with the contract, making it null and void.

3. Scholars tell us about a group of Pharisees called "the bruised and bleeding ones." As these men walked along a street, if they saw a woman in the distance, they would close their eyes but continue walking. Often they bumped into walls, causing scratches and bruises to their faces. This became a visible mark of superior spirituality.

4. M. Sota. 3:4, quoted in Aida Spencer, *Beyond the Curse* (Peabody, MA: Hendrickson, 1985), 51.

5. M. Abot. 1:5, quoted in Spencer, *Beyond the Curse,* 55.

6. Note in Mark 3:35 that Jesus did not use the word *brothers* generically but included *sisters.* It is unlikely that Mark would have referred to women (sisters) among the disciples unless it was strongly rooted in the minds of the early Christians when this Gospel was written.

7. Gordon D. Fee, *Paul, the Spirit, and the People of God* (Peabody, MA: Hendrickson, 1996), 52.

8. Hauerwas and Willimon, *Resident Aliens,* 71, italics in original.

9. Ibid., 71.

10. Ibid., 71–72.

11. Ibid., 65–66.

Chapter 10 Missional Marriage

1. "Self-Exercise: The Temporary Gospel?" *The Other Side* (Nov.–Dec., 1975), 36–37.

2. The full text of all six household codes can be found in appendix B.

3. Biblical scholars approach the household codes in different ways. The following are six ways various scholars interpret the codes, from notes taken on a lecture by Liam Atchison, Colorado Christian University, 1992.

- The traditional view states that the six codes are timeless and universal without any particular cultural relevance to the first century.

- The form-critical view states that the apostle Paul took the old Greek Stoic codes and made them universal, bringing Christian families into conformity with the rest of society.
- Others suggest that Galatians 3:28 created so much unrest in the churches that Paul borrowed the household codes from the culture to deal with division in the body.
- Still others believe that because evangelism is the most important task of the church, anything that interferes with its success should be curbed. The household codes advanced Christ's cause in a culture that could not accept Christian egalitarianism.
- Other scholars believe the codes were given for an interim period until the culture could understand and accept the ramifications of a Galatians 3:28 freedom in Christ.
- Still others see the codes functioning to resolve conflict between our spiritual family and our biological pagan family, caused when we practice the equality of the kingdom.

4. Quoted in David Balch, *Let Wives Be Submissive: The Domestic Code in 1 Peter*, Monograph series 26 (Chico, CA: Scholars Press, 1981), 35.

5. Children, especially girls, could be considered a burden on the house, and if so, they were "exposed," that is, they were put on the street to be picked up by temple priests for use as temple prostitutes or by others who wanted them as slaves, or to die. We live in a society with an ethic of loving care for children, and we find it hard to imagine the harshness with which children were treated in earlier times. When we understand attitudes toward children in the Roman Empire, we see how iconoclastic the apostle Paul was in insisting that fathers not treat their children harshly or exasperate them.

6. Because this code does not specifically address husbands and wives, it was not included above in the codes under discussion in this chapter.

7. Balch, *Let Wives Be Submissive*, 119.

8. According to J. B. Lightfoot, Sir William Ramsey, and others, the province of Galatia had been settled three centuries earlier by Celts from Gaul (modern-day France), and in the apostle Paul's time and for several centuries thereafter, people there retained their Celtic speech and Celtic institutions.

9. Bithynia was governed by the Roman Pliny, whose letter to the Emperor Trajan, written around 112 C.E., stated that the whole province was overrun with the contagion of Christianity. The temples were abandoned, the meat of pagan sacrifices was not being purchased, and persons of every age, rank, and condition were joining the new religion.

10. Readers interested in pursuing this subject further can benefit from Joseph Hellerman, *The Ancient Church as Family* (Minneapolis: Fortress Press, 2001).

11. Atkins, *Split Image*, 153.

12. Ibid., 155.

13. Sarah Sumner, *Men and Women in the Church: Building Consensus on Christian Leadership* (Downers Grove, IL: InterVarsity Press, 2003), 143.

14. Those who insist on interpreting *head* to mean "leader" or "ruler" or "authority over" trip up on 1 Corinthians 11:3, which states that "the head of Christ is God." While there are other dangers in a doctrine of subordination in the Trinity, in its simplest form it ignores the three-in-oneness of the Godhead. In Sumner's words, "The relationship of God and Christ cannot be reduced to a picture of a leader and a helper. God and Christ are truly one (John 10:30)," (Sumner, *Men and Women in the Church*, 167).

15. Ibid.

16. Bilezikian, *Beyond Sex Roles*, 169.

17. William Webb, *Slaves, Women, and Homosexuals: Exploring the Hermeneutics of Cultural Analysis* (Downers Grove, IL: InterVarsity Press, 2001), 160.

18. Bilezikian, *Beyond Sex Roles*, 190.

19. Note that both Paul and Peter restrict this submission to a woman's "own husband." Some people teach that women are to submit to all men, but this is not borne out in the biblical texts.

20. "At least one woman in six in the United States and Canada has experienced a violent episode at the hands of her husband within the last year. Furthermore, more than one woman in every four has at some time in her adult life experienced a violent outburst from her partner. Every day scores of children witness their father strike their mother or are victims of parental rage themselves. This violence affects church families, too. Each year, pastors report an increasing number of victims of family violence who seek their counsel. . . . No community or church is immune to the problem of violence in the home" (Nancy Nason-Clark, *The Battered Wife: How Christians Confront Family Violence* [Louisville, KY: Westminster John Knox Press, 1997], 1).

21. Atkins, *Split Image*, 167–68.

22. Mary Stewart Van Leeuwen, *Gender and Grace: Love, Work, and Parenting in a Changing World* (Downers Grove, IL: InterVarsity Press, 1990), 176.

23. The last twenty-two verses of Proverbs 31 form an acrostic poem that men and women were to memorize as a guide to the wisdom of the book, which was exemplified in the wise woman they depict.

24. A number of studies have uncovered women's need to be productive in bringing in some income. R. Helson and J. Picano found that women at midlife who had followed a traditional life plan exclusively as full-time homemakers tended to have more chronic physical problems and less energy than their female peers who had a mix of homemaking and a career ("Is the Traditional Role Bad for Women?" *Journal of Personality and Social Psychology* 59 [1990] 311–20). Francis Purifoy and Lambert Koopman found that working married women had fewer symptoms of stress than did full-time housewives ("Androstenedione, Testosterone, and Free Testosterone Concentration in Women of Various Occupations," *Social Biology* 26 [1980], 179–80).

Chapter 11 A Map for Our Postmodern, Post-Christian World

1. Coontz, *The Way We Never Were*, see chapter 2, "'Leave It to Beaver' and 'Ozzie and Harriet': American Families in the 1950s," 23–41.

2. See Hauerwas and Willimon, *Resident Aliens*.

3. Robert Hicks, *The Christian Family in Changing Times* (Grand Rapids, MI: Baker, 2002), 65. Hicks describes the phenomenon that we have all observed: A couple who appear publicly to be a happy, productive, "Christian" couple but who divorce quietly and slip out of the life of the Christian community before many realize they are gone. Their tragedy, when known, is often greeted with the comment, "Who would have guessed that about *them?*"

4. The authors of this book have collectively more than ninety years in ministry as teachers and counselors. We know that the hard work of speaking in a conference lies in the hours of personal interaction with people who individually and privately "just want a moment of time" before or after our speaking sessions. These people want to share with the "expert stranger" the brutal pain of their lives and often of their marriages. When encouraged to go home and get help from clergy or professional counselors, the great majority of these people (many of whom are women) say, "I can't do that. I can't let anyone know how bad it is." Christians, of all people, must be able to say, "My life is full of pain. I have failed." Christians know that pain and failure are doors through which God calls us to enter into his forgiveness and his limitless grace.

5. According to historian Edmund Morgan, "The Puritans have gained . . . a reputation for asceticism that is not easily dispelled." But they were much earthier than their modern critics imagine. Family life was public, and a man could be put in the public stocks for acts done behind the family door. See Morgan, *The Puritan Family*, 62.

6. The "not yet" will vanish completely, of course, in the new heaven and new earth, where we shall see him as he is and at last be like him.

7. The text of the ad reads: "Spiritual compatibility is vital to a great marriage. But unfortunately, as many Christians get divorced as atheists and agnostics. That's because spirituality is only one of twenty-nine critical matching qualities, and Christians who want to marry their soul mate need to try to match on all twenty-nine. Eharmony.com is the only way to make this kind of matching depth possible. Our software is based on over thirty years of research in the science of compatibility. The results are happier relationships based on harmony in the most important areas of life—starting, but not ending, with spiritual compatibility" (*Christianity Today* 47, no. 8 [2003], 16).

8. A potentially more helpful approach is embedded in the New Century Marriage Initiative, sponsored by the American Association of Christian Counselors in association with the Smalley Relationship Center. The goal of this program is to train one hundred thousand married couples as marriage mentors to new or stressed marriages. The picture of marriage that emerges through the pages of the brochure, however, is one in which there will be almost all "already" and very little "not yet" in their marriages, if only couples take the right courses and have a properly prepared mentoring couple to assist them. Preparation and mentoring are indeed important and helpful. The point here, however, stands. We have a widespread belief as Christians that the struggle of life can be (almost) eliminated if only we learn the "right stuff" and do the "right stuff." "Marriage Works: New Century Marriage Initiative" (Sept. 2002), Center for Biblical Counseling, P. O. Box 739, Forest, VA 24551.

9. G. K. Chesterton, quoted in Stratford Caldecott, "The Drama of the Home: Marriage, the Common Good and Public Policy," *Marriage and the Common Good*, ed., Kenneth D. Whitehead, proceedings from the twenty-second annual convention of the Fellowship of Catholic Scholars (South Bend, IN: St. Augustine's Press, 2001), 1.

10. From years of work with troubled Christians, both authors know well that physical, sexual, and emotional violence can create conditions in which separation becomes necessary to protect the lives and well-being of one or both of the marital partners and of the children present in the household. It is the position of the authors that when one or both of the marital partners are at risk, separation is necessary not only for safety but for the opportunity to develop and implement workable options for change. In the authors' opinion, children's lives must never be placed in jeopardy. Action must be taken at once to place them out of harm's way.

11. Richard J. Foster, *Celebration of Discipline: The Path to Spiritual Growth* (San Francisco: HarperSanFrancisco, 2003); see also Dallas Willard, *Renovation of the Heart: Putting on the Character of Christ* (Colorado Springs, CO: NavPress, 2002), and Dallas Willard, *The Divine Conspiracy: Our Hidden Life in God* (San Francisco: HarperSanFrancisco, 1998).

12. See Robert D. Enright and Joanna North, eds., *Exploring Forgiveness* (Madison, WI: University of Wisconsin Press, 1998), 75–94; also Robert D. Enright and Richard P. Fitzgibbons, *Helping Clients Forgive: An Empirical Guide for Resolving Anger and Restoring Hope* (Washington, DC: American Psychological Association, 2000).

13. Desmond Tutu, "Without Forgiveness There Is No Future," foreword in Enright and North, *Exploring Forgiveness*, xii–xiv.

14. See Marietta Jaeger, "The Power and Reality of Forgiveness: Forgiving the Murderer of One's Child," in Enright and North, *Exploring Forgiveness*, 9–14. See Paul W. Coleman, "The Process of Forgiveness in Marriage and the Family," in Enright and North, *Exploring Forgiveness*,

75–94, for helpful assistance in understanding the steps of the forgiveness process within the context of marriage and family life.

15. Coleman, "The Process of Forgiveness in Marriage," 94.

16. Clapp, *Families at the Crossroads,* see particularly chapter 4, "Church as First Family," 67–88; see also Hauerwas, *A Community of Character,* 155–74.

17. Hauerwas in *A Community of Character,* 168, notes, "Our identification with our family stands as much chance of destroying us as sustaining our lives. When the family is all you have left, then it begins to take on the characteristics of a church. . . . Ironically, therefore, the family is threatened today partly because it has no institutions that have the moral status to stand over against it to call into question its demonic tendencies. The first function of the church in relation to the family must, therefore, be to stand as an institution that claims loyalty and significance beyond that of the family. Only when such an institution exists can we have the freedom to take the risk to form and live in families."

18. Grenz, *Sexual Ethics,* 181–96.

19. Hauerwas and Willimon, *A Community of Character,* 133–36, used with permission.

Chapter 12 There Be Dragons Here

1. Kevin Giles, *The Trinity and Subordinationism: The Doctrine of God and the Contemporary Gender Debate* (Downers Grove, IL: InterVarsity Press, 2002), 260. Giles points out that certain social structures are God-given and sanctioned (e.g., the state, marriage, and the polarity of the sexes). "What is theologically incorrect is to think that one particular historical expression of how these givens are ordered is God-given and permanent" (260). He notes further in a comment particularly relevant to the point here: "It is possible for evangelicals with the Bible in their hand to get the wrong answer from the Scriptures to the questions facing them in their age. Appealing to texts and giving one's interpretation of them does not guarantee either that the scope of Scripture has been correctly grasped or that its teaching is being applied correctly in a cultural setting very different from that of the biblical writers" (261).

2. Hauerwas, *A Community of Character,* 198–229.

3. The work of Stanley Grenz, *Sexual Ethics,* is an example of the kind of work needed from an evangelical perspective. Stanley Hauerwas, a theological ethicist, has done helpful work in developing an understanding of the family within the context of the church; see, for example, Hauerwas's extended essay, "The Church and Social Policy: The Family, Sex, and Abortion" in *A Community of Character,* 155–230. Rodney Clapp has written helpfully around this issue at an easily readable informal level; see *Families at the Crossroads.* Diana Garland has given us a carefully considered study of the family (the way we really are) from the specific context of ministry, *Family Ministry.* Garland's discussion of "family values" (525–30) merits reading and rereading. John P. Bartkowski has helped us think about the families we are becoming in his study of gender negotiation in evangelical families; see *Remaking the Godly Family.* Space prevents listing other helpful contributions. The point, however, holds. Arguably the five best books on a "theology of marriage" from an evangelical perspective have yet to be written.

4. The work of Grenz (*Sexual Ethics,* 146–69) was helpful to counselor and client in this particular case, and in others as well.

5. Hauerwas and Willimon, *Resident Aliens,* 27.

6. Craig Van Gelder, "Missional Challenge: Understanding the Church in North America," in *Missional Church: A Vision for the Sending of the Church in North America,* ed. Darrel L. Guder, with Lois Barrett, Inagrace T. Dietterich, George R. Hunsberger, Alan J. Roxburgh, and Craig Van Gelder (Grand Rapids, MI: Eerdmans, 1998), 16–76.

7. "Missional Church: From Sending to Being Sent," in *Missional Church,* 1–17.

8. Lois Barrett, "The Church as Apostle to the World," in *Missional Church,* 112.

9. Stanley J. Grenz and John R. Franke, *Beyond Foundationalism: Shaping Theology in a Postmodern Context* (Louisville, KY: Westminster John Knox Press, 2001). Grenz and Franke view the current ferment and change in theology—new ideas and shifts in paradigms—as the result in part of the necessity to shift from paradigms with theological presuppositions that have been unknowingly shaped by the modern world and are now seen, in light of postmodern criticism, as irretrievably flawed.

10. Giles, *The Trinity and Subordinationism*, 262.

11. Barrett, "The Church as Apostle to the World," 130.

12. Ibid., 129.

13. Hauerwas and Willimon, *Resident Aliens*, 27.

14. One of the authors remembers as an impressionable teenager such a "sending." Will, the farmer who was lay leader in the congregation, stood, Bible in hand, and read, "I heard the voice of the Lord, saying: 'Whom shall I send, and who will go for Us?'" (Isa. 6:8). He looked out over the congregation, expectantly. There was a pause, then the young designated couple stood, moved forward out of the congregation to the front of the church, and said together, "We will go." There was another pause. Then Will said, "And who will stand by the stuff? Who will uphold them in the battle?" And without a moment's hesitation, the entire congregation rose to their feet and said together, "*We* will stand by the stuff. *We* will uphold them in the battle." We did too. We prayed regularly and sent what we could in a depression dust-bowl economy. We were a small congregation, so other congregations helped as well. God met this couple's needs and gave them more than thirty years in active ministry.

15. Phillips, "The Case against Matrimony," at salon.com/mwt/feature/1999/11/18/unmarried/print.html, 3.

Alice Palmer Mathews earned her bachelor's degree from Bob Jones University and her Ph.D. in Biblical and Theological Studies from the University of Denver and the Iliff School of Theology. She and her husband, Randall, spent seventeen years of ministry in France, and it was during this period that Alice became extensively involved in ministries to women.

Alice has taught, done extensive writing, and is a popular speaker. Currently she is the Lois W. Bennett Distinguished Associate Professor of Educational Ministries and Women's Ministries at Gordon-Conwell Theological Seminary in South Hamilton, Massachusetts. Since 1990 she has served as a producer of the RBC Ministries' daily radio program *Discover the Word*, on which she appears with Haddon Robinson and Mart DeHaan.

Her books include *A Woman God Can Lead* and *Preaching That Speaks to Women*. She has also written chapters for several books dealing with women's issues and theology.

M. Gay Hubbard, a graduate of Moody Bible Institute, earned her B.A. and M.A. degrees from Fort Hays Kansas University and her Ph.D. from the University of Pittsburgh.

Her professional life spans more than thirty years as a Christian counselor, professor, and writer. In addition to being in private practice with Christian Counseling Associates, Gay serves as visiting lecturer in Women's Studies at Gordon-Conwell Theological Seminary and writes from her home in Osborne, Kansas, where she lives with her husband, Joseph.

The author of *Women: The Misunderstood Majority*, Gay has presented papers at conferences and written many articles on women, relationships, and justice. She is committed to speaking and teaching in a wide variety of programs designed to encourage women to greater self-understanding and a deeper journey of faith.